Gender and Digital Economy

Perspectives from Developing World

Gender and Digital Economy

Perspectives from Developing World

A K Singh

MD Publications Pvt Ltd
New Delhi
www.mdppl.com

Published by :

MD Publications Pvt Ltd
"MD House", 11, Darya Ganj,
New Delhi - 110 002
Phone : +91-11- 45355555
E-mail : contact@mdppl.com
Website: www.mdppl.com

ISBN : 978-81-7533-345-1

Published and Printed by Mr. Pranav Gupta on behalf of **MD Publications Pvt Ltd** at Repro India Limited.

PREFACE

Today there is an agreement that our world and our lives are being shaped by the conflicting trends of globalization and identity. The rise of an Information Knowledge society of which the digital economy is a key component is significantly changing our lives today. There are a number of Projects that aim at bringing information and communication technologies to the developing world because of the belief in the transforming potential of these technologies. However there is a divergence of opinion with regards to the impact of this with scholars arguing about the world being homogenized of being divergent.

Ever since the introduction of digital technologies, conventional wisdom imagined that the combined costs of acquiring, storing, retrieving and disseminating R&D documents would decline when compared with costs associated with delivering conventional print products. The theory held that since a large part of the costs of creating and shipping print on paper-printing, paper, binding, postage-would disappear; organizations would achieve great savings soon after their files were converted.

While the digital age promised to deliver information to end-users in better and faster ways, today managers have discovered that while costs per end-user served appear to have declined and while access has also improved markedly, investments in developing, installing, and maintaining technological infrastructure have escalated. The "cheaper" goal of "better, cheaper, faster" may yet be realized, but only after further investments in technology and human resources are made. If measured in terms of increases in productivity, decision quality and mission effectiveness, however, the return has already been-and will continue to be-enormous.

In the global discourse on ICTs [information and communication technologies], the concern so far has primarily been outsourcing and the loss of service sector jobs from the developed world. This book focuses, instead, on the positive aspects of the digital economy as they relate to women in the developing world. It illustrates - with case studies from Argentina, Morocco, India, Malaysia and the Philippines - how economic empowerment through the medium of ICTs can change the position of women within their families and the workplace, even in the face of uneven development processes. This timely volume, which is rooted in primary and original research, illuminates the gender-related facets of the emergent information society while raising key questions about the implications of the digital economy on women's work and lives.

I am very grateful to Mr. Pranav Gupta, Director of MD Publications Pvt Ltd, New Delhi, for his kind cooperation and support for this book.

A K Singh

Contents

1

Understanding the Rural-urban Interface

The rapid population growth of Third World cities gives rise to concerns about the changing nature of the relationship between urban and rural. The evidence for this is in a growing number of recent publications, research reports and policy documents of international organisations, which emphasise key development concepts such as decentralisation. The UNCHS (1999) estimated that the world's urban population would be 2.9 billion in 2000, accounting for 47 per cent of the global total. This is an increase on the 30 per cent in 1950; the urban population is likely to go over 50 per cent in 2007.

Until relatively recently much rural-urban research has focused on a single city and its hinterland. However, the increasing importance of international links and the process of globalisation have an impact on rural-urban relations. In addition, cities throughout the world are often caught between the pressure to be included in the world economy, on the one hand, and on the other the need for links with their rural hinterlands. Such tensions raise issues that have not been considered until recently. This tension is paralleled in the competing processes of globalisation and decentralisation.

A further reason for writing a book that focuses on the relations between urban and rural areas relates to the fact that these relations have been important throughout history. Many major world developments have been linked to the relations between urban and rural realms. For example, on coming to power in 1949, the revolutionary Chinese government was faced with one of the world's greatest urban-rural dilemmas. It was made up of politicians largely from peasant backgrounds and with peasant support, but it took control of a country already struggling to cope with the demands of its many large cities. By 1950 Shanghai was already estimated to number 5.3 million people, Beijing 3.9 million, and Tianjin 2.4 million.

Some of the earliest government actions were designed to impose state-controlled marketing of agricultural goods and rationing of urban food consumption, and to control the movement of people - especially rural-urban migration. In addition, the level of land scarcity experienced by rural dwellers convinced the Chinese government that urban-based heavy industrialisation was the only way the country would be able to support its population which was 541 million in 1952, of whom 57.7 million, or 10.6 per cent, were urban.

One of the issues that worried the Chinese government was that in 1964, the second census under communist rule found that the urban population had grown to 129.3 million, or 18.4 per cent. Such rapid growth, both nationally and in the cities, alarmed the government, which decided that there was a need to control population growth and to create employment for the urban population.

The hostility of external global powers meant that foreign investment was unlikely. Therefore the only possibility of producing savings to invest in industrialisation was to extract surplus from rural agricultural production, resulting in a bias of policy towards the urban rather than the rural areas. The result was that the State Purchase and Marketing Cooperative's main function was to 'extract as much of the harvest as possible from the peasants'. The Cooperative also supplied agricultural inputs and the state controlled the banking. The state therefore mediated all rural-urban flows of goods and capital other than household remittances.

The pro-urban bias was compounded by the agricultural tax which amounted to approximately 30 per cent of farm proceeds. The Chinese government therefore funded its industrialisation by mobilising the rural areas to produce and save more in order to provide the capital and the tax revenue for investment. Common ground is emerging here. There is a consensus that more flexible approaches are required, that flows may wax and wane over time, that the role of small towns in rural-urban interactions must be considered and that interventions in either rural or urban areas have implications beyond their locality.

One of the challenges appears to be that it is not always clear which department or division should be responsible for the agency approach, with some agencies considering an issue from a rural-focused division andothers from an urban-focused division.In a recent report Mutizwa-Mangiza (1999), Planning and Coordination Officer for UNCHS, highlights past views on the rural-urban divide as either pro-urban or anti-urban.

According to Mutizwa-Mangiza, these biases have underpinned much development policy and intervention affecting both urban and rural areas. However, he argues that promoting rural-urban linkages offers considerable potential for developing the entire rural-urban continuum. He highlights the importance of this balanced approach, referring to its place in the Habitat Agenda agreed at the Habitat II Conference organised by UNCHS in Istanbul in 1996.

- 'To promote the sustainable development of rural settlements and to reduce rural-to-urban migration...' (para.165);
- 'To promote the utilization of new and improved technologies and appropriate traditional practices in rural settlements development...' (para.166);
- To establish '...policies for sustainable regional development and management...' (para. 167);
- 'To strengthen sustainable development and employment opportunities in impoverished rural areas...' (para.168); and
- To adopt 'an integrated approach to promote balanced and mutually supportive urban-rural development...' (para.169).

According to Mutizwa-Mangiza, achieving these objectives will require:

i. Strengthening of rural-urban linkages mainly through the improvement of marketing, transportation and communication facilities;
ii. Improvement of a number of infrastructure components which, while enhancing rural-urban linkages, are also essential for economic growth and employment creation (both farm and non-farm) within small urban settlements and rural areas themselves, especially roads, electricity and water;
iii. Bringing private and public services normally associated with cities to the rural population; and
iv. Strengthening of sub-national governance at the regional, rural-local, and city-region levels.

While the Chinese example illustrates a deliberate policy of exploiting rural areas, Hodder (2000) argues that inevitably rural agricultural sectors and urban industrial sectors play strategic roles in each other's development. He identifies six key reasons for these close links between the two sectors (2000:80-82):

i. Agriculture depends on manufactured goods both for the transformation of produce (for example, farm tools, machinery, inputs) and for the consumer goods which are in demand as agricultural incomes rise (such as radios and bicycles).
ii. As agriculture incorporates more technology in its activities, labour becomes a less significant factor. More technologically advanced agriculture releases capital and labour which move into the urban industrial sector.
iii. Agriculture provides raw materials for some industries, such as tobacco, cotton and sisal.
iv. Agriculture for export can earn foreign exchange which is important for purchasing items which are vital to industrial processes. These include commodities such as petroleum, chemicals and technology which is not produced locally.

v. There is an important balance to be struck in incomes, prices and taxation between the urban and the rural areas. For example, high food prices provide rewards to farmers and incentives to increase production, but may mean high prices in urban areas which can lead to poverty and unrest. Taxation in the agricultural sector may be necessary to raise revenues to finance public expenditure, but may act as a disincentive to farmers, particularly if much of the expenditure is urban or industrial focused.

vi. In rapidly urbanising countries agriculture produces strategically important food for the growing number of urban residents, thus ensuring food security at prices that are affordable.

International and national agencies are beginning to realise that their programmes of urban and rural development intervention have impacts on each other and that there is a need to integrate some of the thinking behind them. The six reasons listed above explain the key interdependencies between rural and urban areas. While the discussion has so far concentrated on the flows between the urban and the rural, one of the main reasons for the separate approaches is the attempt frequently made to identify the defining characteristics of what is 'urban' and what is 'rural'. However, Rigg (1998a) cautions against 'pigeonholing' when it comes to such definitions.

For example, he argues that to separate people into urban or rural categories is problematic. He outlines three main difficulties associated with such categorisation.

i. Registration records often do not detect changes in residence. For various reasons it may be undesirable for recent in-migrants to be registered as urban dwellers. Rigg gives examples of under-reporting of urban residence, particularly in relation to the controversies this can pose during elections when how an area is defined can have implications for the number of political representatives or the authority into which they are elected.

ii. Allocating people to discrete categories such as 'urban' or 'rural' assumes that these categories accurately reflect their realities. Rigg's own empirical research in Thailand (1998b), among others, has demonstrated the significance of fluid, fragmented and multi-location households to survival strategies. This results in households straddling and moving across the rural-urban interface. Thus categorising them as one or the other makes no sense. In addition, there is the problem of defining the boundaries of urban places which is usually done on some arbitrary basis.

iii. Rigg argues that many Asian urban residents do not consider the cities and towns they live in as 'home'. This is because they ultimately intend to return to their rural origins. This, he argues, brings the issue of the identities of individuals into focus and ' "home" and "place" are ambiguous and shifting notions, where multiple identities - both - can be simultaneously embodied'.

A final concern that could be added to Rigg's three points above relates to the blurring of the actual geographical definition of the rural-urban divide. This is particularly the case where cities are expanding rapidly and extending their physical limits and influence outwards into the rural areas. To add to the difficulty of definition, we find that different sizes of settlement are defined as 'urban' by different countries. For example, in China, relatively small settlements are not counted as urban.

However, a city, or city-region, may include a conglomeration of areas extending beyond the city proper. While such data make it possible to monitor demographic changes in countries across time - for example, comparing rates of urban growth from one census to the next - this problem of differences of definition suggests that comparisons between countries are problematic to say the least. For example, Afsar (1999) reports that Bangladesh, the world's ninth largest country by population, experienced urban population growth of 6 per cent per annum between 1970 and 1996 and the proportion of the population living in urban areas grew from 7.4 per cent to 20 per cent of the total.

However, she points out that the designation of new urban areas accounted for 8 per cent of urban growth from 1961 to 1974 and this increased to about one-third between 1974 and 1981. The result is that the progression from rural to urban or vice versa is very unclear and varies from one country to another. The fact that such enormous populations as the Chinese and Bangladeshi are reallocated arbitrarily from rural to urban areas raises questions about the validity of globally aggregated data on urban growth rates and urbanisation.

Hardoy et al. suggest that it is best to consider the proportion of urban and rural populations not in terms of precise percentages because of the difficulty of enumeration, but rather in terms of a range. This concern over the headline figures is reinforced when two more issues are considered. First, static definitions of 'urban' and 'rural' fail to take account of how the seasonally migrant populations, who move between urban and rural in some countries, are classified. Second, it is important to consider the definition of the physical boundaries between the urban and rural areas and the problem which prompted the development of the concept of the 'urban fringe' and the 'peri-urban interface'. Should these be classified as urban or rural?

These issues are not consistently defined around the world and so it is in fact problematic to consider such data as comparative. There is a range of approaches to defining them. Beyond the issue of numbers is the fact that assumptions are made about people's livelihoods and activities in terms of whether they are 'urban' or 'rural', when in reality the key issue for the people concerned is the opportunity for livelihoods. These ambiguities are to an extent accepted by major international donor agencies, as illustrated in recent documents and discussions.

It is therefore vital to consider the following discussions in the light of these four concerns. One approach that is put forward by this is to focus not so much on the boundaries between rural and urban areas as on the links between them. This serves to emphasise the interdependence of town and country. It will allow for the assessment.

URBAN DEFINITIONS IN CHINA

Most authors writing about either population or urban issues in developing countries draw attention to the problems of population data, which in many cases are a result of the general problems of data collection. However, one challenge that is often overlooked, especially when considering aggregate population data at a world or regional level, is the variation in definitions of urban and rural areas, a variation not only between countries but over time. In China, a number of changes in the definition of urban areas have taken place through time which affects the available data. This is particularly important when considering the global situation because China accounts for more than one-sixth of the world's population. Changes to the definition of what areas are rural and what are urban can have an effect on the headline categorisations of the urban and rural populations of the country.

The result is that the urban population growth as a result of definition change is considerable. Rakodi (2002) estimated that 40 per cent of China's urban population growth was due to changes in the urban administrative system. For example, the 1982 definition resulted in a drop in the rural population from 932 million to 535 million. This raises questions about changes in other aspects of the development process in China, for example the country's much-discussed 'rural' industrialisation initiatives and of relations that may favour one realm or the other.

It will also allow for some ambiguity about the boundaries between the realms and about the identities of those who live in, between or across the so-called rural-urban 'divide' or 'gap'. This approach will provide more powerful and more flexible understandings of the geographies of the relations between the urban and the rural, as it focuses more on the relations and overlaps than on the divides. Indeed, the growing interest in the fringe between the urban and the rural suggests there is no divide, but an overlap which provides both positive and negative flows in either direction, sometimes referred to as 'peri-urban'.

Researchers have also presented arguments for the separate definition of high-density rural areas that can occur under a particular set of characteristics. For example McGee describes a kind of high-density rural area which he calls desakota, arguing that it is peculiar to Asia and suggesting that it forms as a result of the metropolitan urban area extending its economy and influence into the surrounding rural areas and creating an intense mixture of agricultural and non-agricultural activities. Examples include areas around Jakarta, Manila and Bangkok.

Mortimore carried out research on the environmental implications of what he called the 'close settled zone' around Kano in northern Nigeria, a densely settled area that is extensive but has maintained its rural nature. Qadeer (2000) argues that it is important to consider such areas because some countries have rural population densities which are higher than 400 persons per square kilometre, a threshold used by some countries as a minimum for defining an area as urban.

Qadeer (2000) examines examples of 'ruralopolises' comprising most of Bangladesh, from West Bengal to Uttar Pradesh and Kerala provinces in India, and the Punjab and Peshawar provinces of Pakistan; other examples he mentions include the South Yangtze Valley in China, the Mekong Delta in Vietnam, and the lower Nile Valley in Egypt. He concludes that a ruralopolis is an alternative route to urbanisation, bringing about similar social transformations and spatial reorganisation in a rural setting, and 'the future form of human habitat in large parts of Asia and Africa in the 21st Century'.

There is evidence that suggests that cities in the developing world rely more heavily on their own hinterlands than do cities in the developed world, particularly as the majority of the national population is still rural, so their relationship with their hinterland is very important. This link is reciprocal, since the rural primary production that makes up much of the export production of most developing countries usually has to be distributed through the cities. Meanwhile, the cities represent important sources of processed food, finance, services, information and imported products such as manufactured goods and some agricultural inputs. Cities therefore represent the links between rural areas and world markets. These interdependent links can form the basis of positive cycles of interaction.

A recent development brought about by colonialism which has added a further layer of complexity to rural-urban linkages is that cities in the developing world often form the interface between the rest of the country and international markets. This confuses the relationship between the city and the country. For example, Potter et al. (2004) discuss models of colonial space economies which illustrate how the territory is organised to suit the export of raw materials to the colonial power. Much national infrastructure was developed to support these rural-urban linkages, making many of the cities a focal point for export production.

The legacy of this is that many developing countries are left with a structure that places one city, or a small number of cities, at the heart of the nation's activities. Overlapping relationships between city and countryside are therefore a legacy of an exploitative pattern which, some have suggested, has reproduced a neo-colonial relationship between town and country. Changes brought about during the colonial period, when many towns and cities were essentially internally focused, meant that external concerns were forced upon them as the colonies' economies were adapted to suit the needs of the metropolitan cores. This changed during the middle of the last century when 'import substitution' and later 'export production' policies were introduced by newly independent countries in order to develop their own industrial base.

Examples of countries pursuing such policies of import substitution include Brazil, whose importation of capital goods fell from 65 per cent in 1949 to 10 per cent by 1964, while its importation of consumer durables declined from 65 per cent in 1949 to 2 per cent in 1964. Then during the 1970s the Brazilian government pursued a policy of export production raising its manufactured exports from 3 per cent in 1960 to 26 per cent in 1977 and 56 per cent by 1991. In the case of China, discussed earlier, during the Great Leap Forward the communist government promoted industrialisation of both the cities and the countryside, raising the industrialisation and industrial employment of China as a whole.

However, the massive government investment amounted to a subsidy and most industries were running at a loss by the time of Mao Zedong's death in 1976. Since then Communist Party leaders have opened China to inward investment and the industrial sector has grown very rapidly, at an average of 14.4 per cent, with exports growing at 11 per cent during the 1980s. In both Brazil and China, during the period of import substitution an industrial base was developed which later turned into an export-producing sector. Such policies, though intended to engender national development, focused again on the city. Whereas China's industrialisation had been focused on maintaining people on the land, the later export production policy has focused far more on the cities. By 2000 Shanghai had grown to 12.9 million, Beijing to 10.8 million and Tianjin to 9.2 million.

To some extent this focus on the dominant urban core - often a primate city - resulted in the neglect of the smaller towns and prompted responses which attempted to move the focus from the dominant urban areas. In the case of Brazil this has resulted in a strongly regional concentration of growth in the south-east around the huge cities of Rio de Janeiro and São Paolo, leaving much of the rest of the country experiencing such poverty that Brazil is often counted as one of the most unequal economies in the world.

The case of Brazil formed the basis for much of Frank's (1967) underdevelopment theory which argues that the development of the core areas in the south-east led to the active underdevelopment of the rest of the country. However, such industry-focused policy responses were based on research that saw an urban focus as ultimately counter-productive, apart from the fact that it favours city dwellers over rural inhabitants. Hinderdink and Titus (1998) argue that whether your perspective is pro- or anti-urban, the role of small towns is a very important and much neglected element in rural-urban interactions. In particular Rondinelli (1983) emphasised the developmental role of secondary cities in providing a range of services for their hinterlands.

This prompted the so-called 'growth-poles' policies which developed intermediate settlements as poles around which growth would be encouraged to balance the dominance of the urban core. Such an argument suggests that interactions can focus on small and intermediate towns in order to encourage more beneficial relations between core and periphery. This kind of approach, focusing on the potentially positive interactions between cities and countryside, is presented by the Club du Sahel as absolutely essential to the future of West Africa because of its rapidly growing urban population.

One factor that is particularly important for an understanding of developing areas is that urban and rural dwellers have very different ways of life. This makes comparative analysis very difficult. Urban dwellers tend to have a more monetary-based existence in which consumption practices are limited by income and decisions are defined more comprehensively by income in relation to the cost of living. In rural areas, by contrast, there is evidence that while income is important, rural dwellers are able to juggle a range of livelihood strategies based on their economic, social, cultural and ecological capital. This situation is further complicated by the growth in non-farm income in rural areas and the 'peasantisation' of urban life.

For example, the practice of urban agriculture is reportedly widespread, the growth in informal-sector activities is a major part of urban economies and the number of households which deliberately aim to straddle the rural-urban divide in an attempt to diversify and maximise their opportunities for sustaining their livelihoods appears to have increased. In part this may be explained by the fact that rapid urbanisation processes in developing countries mean that within the last 30 years up to half the urban population may be rural in-migrants.

UNDERSTANDING DEVELOPMENT

Potter et al. (2004) argue that geographies of development are about relationships between people, environment and places in different locations and at a variety of scales. The nature of the interaction between city and countryside is at the heart of this focus. The relationships, by implication, involve geographies of groups and individuals. The location of a household, whether city or countryside, of the region, the total population of which grew from 85 million to 193 million between 1960 and 1990, with the number of settlements of more than 100,000 inhabitants rising from 17 in 1960 to 90 by 1990.

The report projected that at current and predicted rates there will be 300 cities of over 100,000 in the region by 2020, resulting in the merger and overlap of city hinterlands. There are two shaded areas represented in the maps. The darker area is what the Club du Sahel researchers describe as 'market attractiveness', or an indicator of market density, and is based on comparisons of price data. The lighter shaded area indicates a rural population density of 50 persons per square kilometre or more. Their conclusions were that the positive impact of market density as a result of proximity to urban areas is greater than the negative impact of the increased rural population density.

The implications of this for the rural areas are important. First, the report argues that as the cities expand, so the rural areas close to them begin to find that they benefit from better market information and lower transaction costs, but are affected by higher labour costs because of non-farm alternatives and greater pressure for land because of higher population density. The report argues that the balance of evidence suggests that the benefits outweigh the disadvantages.

The report goes on to state that there is evidence that some of the negative impacts are the result of time-lags in responding to the growing and changing market situation. However, this time-lag peaked during the 1980s with bad weather, high commodity export prices and ineffective national food policies. This pattern is matched by food imports as a percentage of the total food availability which has shrunk considerably since the 1980s; never havng reached more than 15 per cent. As a consequence, the report concludes that: 'it is only when they have reliable access to food markets, where outlets are sufficiently regular and profitable, that rural dwellers develop real strategies of commercial farming of food surpluses'.

This study therefore provides evidence of the importance of the interdependence of urban and rural areas. Their prognosis for the region is that there can be a positive outcome for the rapid population growth and urbanisation. This is mainly a function of the evolution of large urban markets that will result in dynamic rural agricultural production areas. However, plans have to be put in place to ensure that the rural areas are prepared to take advantage of these opportunities. They should include the dissemination of strategies for the management of soil fertility, the intensification of agricultural production, and the organisation of farm labour; finally, the requirements for each region will be different, so these strategies must be flexible.

The limitations of large parts of the region for agricultural production should not be ignored. However, they have resulted in a relatively mobile population seeking out areas of relatively high agricultural potential. Areas of population density of more than 50 inhabitants per square kilometre account for only 7 per cent of the region's territory, but almost 40 per cent of the population. In other words, according to this work, the key to the region's future is a dynamic and flexible set of positive interactions between the urban and rural areas has a bearing on its livelihood assets and opportunities. This is discussed in more detail later.

The interaction between urban and rural is initiated in an attempt to take advantage of the differentials or complementarities between the two areas. The differentials may be in the form of income and cost of living, supply and demand or security and hazard. Potter et al. (2004) go on to argue that the 'nature and relative significance of these relationships are changing constantly, both through time and space, and are themselves determined to a large extent by complex movements and flows of people, commodities, finance, ideas and information'. This sets out to examine such complex flows and relations, focusing on the links involving urban and rural areas.

The relationship between rural and urban areas has been an important part of underlying assumptions of development theory and practice. The nature of the relationship is interpreted differently according to different theoretical perspectives. This can be illustrated by contrasting two frameworks used for analysing colonial and post-colonial development. The first is put forward by Gould (1969) who saw development as a process of modernisation.

At the time, he was writing on applied quantitative methods which were the focus of an emergent approach in geographical research. Gould, being in the vanguard of this approach, applied these methods to the analysis of modernisation diffusion in Tanzania. He divided the country into a series of cells of equal area and recorded indicators of modernisation, such as miles of metalled road, number of government offices, and number of hospital beds. He did this for a selection of time periods throughout the first half of the twentieth century and mapped the changes through time and space. Not surprisingly, he found a strong bias towards the cities, in particular Dar es Salaam, then the capital.

As the century progressed only the most remote areas beyond the main feeder roads remained untouched by modernisation. There was evidence, according to Gould, of a diffusion of modernisation from the urban core of Dar es Salaam down the urban hierarchy and then out into the rural areas. Arguably this is evidence of what has been described elsewhere as the 'trickle-down' effect.

However, Slater approaches the same period and the same colony and then country in a more radical way. He argues that rather than the country experiencing modernisation, what is in fact occurring is a far more sinister process that suits not the Tanzanians in the rural areas, but those in the metropolitan core, in this case the elites in Dar es Salaam and the colonial power, Britain. According to Slater, therefore, three key processes occur during the period of colonisation.

First, the colonialists engage in a process of penetration, as they penetrate the territory and adapt it to suit their home markets. As the colony develops, so the need for labour and resources becomes greater and there is a realisation that more labour and resources are available beyond the immediate core of the colony. There is then a process of integration of the territory and its people and resources. Labour is persuaded, drafted and encouraged into the cash economy through a range of policies designed to make people need cash and begin to sell their labour.

This requires migration to the main sources of employment, the cities and the plantations. The final transition sees the process of disintegration affect the colony and later the independent nation as families in remote rural areas send members in search of employment in order to pay hut taxes and school fees. This maps out on the territory of Tanzania as three distinct zones. The first is the zone of the export production economy, dominated by the production of goods for export. It includes the urban areas that act as trading, transport and administration hubs for these extractive activities.

The second is just beyond the export production zone and is the zone of support, engaged in the provision of resources such as food, energy and water to the export production zone. Last comes the periphery which benefits very little from the core activities, but supplies seasonal or periodic labour. This maps a political economy on to the territory that suggests, rather than a process of modernisation diffusion, exploitation of Tanzania's people, resources and space by both Tanzanian elites based in the core and the colonisers and later the international markets.

Although these two contrasting approaches focus on Tanzania, they have been applied to other countries and to models of development throughout the world that saw contrasting roles for urban and rural areas. The Club du Sahel's recent research on urbanisation in West Africa points out that population growth in the region will increase the size of the cities and therefore the urban food markets. It is therefore necessary to adopt a positive approach to rural-urban interaction in order to ensure that this urban growth is sustainable. Earlier, the theories of W. W. Rostow identified three major roles for agriculture in the transition between traditional society and the successful take-off of development. These are:

- Agriculture must supply food. This is particularly important for urban-based industrial workers who have no access to the resources needed for food production, such as land and labour.
- The extent to which agriculture can develop and earn foreign exchange may set the limit within which the transition to modernisation can take place. The development of agriculture provides both a supply for a modernising economy, for example in terms of food and industrial raw materials, and a demand for industrial outputs, for example for machinery and chemical inputs, which can further stimulate the process of industrialisation.
- Agriculture must provide its surplus income to the modern sector. Rostow points out the importance of landowners to investment in the industrial revolution. Key to the land reforms of countries like Russia and Japan was the ability of the economy to raise investment, whether public or private, for the economic and social needs of the modernisation process.

Rostow's original account, published in 1960, suggests that economic growth progresses through a number of stages. This idea is centred largely on industrialisation and modernisation as the ultimate aims of development. Some researchers have criticised his work for being Eurocentric, because he appeared to assume that all development takes a similar pattern, each economy following a parallel path of modernisation towards a west European and North American model.

However, Rostow illustrates the intimate links between the rural-agricultural and the urban-industrial in very clear terms. In the third edition of his book published in 1990, he suggests that the extent to which agriculture develops may limit industrialisation and ultimately modernisation. In addition, he suggests that the relationship between the two sectors may be interdependent. Therefore, in addition to the three roles for agriculture listed above, Rostow also argued that the income earned in developing agriculture may also be important to the transition to modernisation. 'For it is from rising rural incomes that increased taxes of one sort or another can be drawn necessary to finance the government's functions in transition without imposing starvation on the peasants or inflation on the urban population'.

The exploitation of the countryside by the city in the development process is very much the kind of extractive relationship between city and countryside developed by China. It is ironic that Rostow was explicitly anti-communist while China's analysis and development took place under a communist regime. This is also a key part of Myint's (1964) theory of dual economies. This idea identifies two techniques of production, one traditional and one modern. Myint's dual economies comprise basically Western capital-intensive production and 'backward' rural-based labour-intensive sectors. This is not far from Slater's (1974) account of the three zones of the colony, though he interprets the spatial patterns quite differently.

Followers of the dual economy analysis were often explicitly procapital, and by implication pro-metropolis, and anti-rural. According to Mehmet (1995), they often characterised the rural areas as having a high labour surplus, and the modern urban sector as the engine of the economy. A consequence of this kind of analysis was the belief that the rural areas were the source of underdevelopment in the developing world, implying that investment for development should be targeted at the productive sectors where the greatest return was possible, the urban and industrial sectors. For Mehmet (1995) one of the main objections to this idea was the underlying assumption that the rural producers were 'irrational' because they were unproductive.

These aspects of the links between the rural and agricultural sectors of the economy suggest that it is important to study them so as to understand the process of development itself. Development theory, and research on the process of urbanisation, highlight polarisation of societies in relation to urban and rural, traditional and modern, industrial and agricultural. Some theorists argue that development is about progression from one state to another. In the past this has been tied in with the urbanisation of rural areas. Rostow was one of the most influential of these modernisation theorists, suggesting that, based on research on the modernisation of European markets, all economies aspired to the condition of 'high mass consumption'.

Rostow argued that all economies began from a stage of low productivity, which he described as the 'traditional society'. He suggested that societies progressed through a number of stages at various speeds to a final stage of 'high mass consumption'. He conceptualised traditional society as one with rudimentary production functions, 'based on pre-Newtonian science and technology and on pre-Newtonian attitudes towards the physical world'. Such societies are highly agricultural, largely dependent on agriculture and with social structures that are essentially agrarian.

One of the crucial stages, according to Rostow, is the third stage of growth which he described as the 'take-off ' stage, using the analogy of an aeroplane beginning at a slow speed and having to achieve a take-off speed before its final ascent to cruising altitude. Before achieving take-off, Rostow argued, it was necessary to have in place the 'preconditions for take-off '. These preconditions include changes in attitude and political and economic structure which prepare the economy for investment in infrastructure and a widening of economic activity within the nation and beyond, in industry and in agriculture.

This implies both the demise of the power of the traditional landed elite, which Rostow sees as blocking development, and the emergence of a modern nation state which is intent upon progressing to modernisation. It also implies a shift in power base from rural-based elite interests to an urban-based political elite, increased rural-urban trade and increased migration. These changes first occurred in western Europe, as developments in modern science began to be translated into improved restructuring and efficiencies in production in both agriculture and industry, periods of change referred to as the agricultural and industrial revolutions.

Rostow seems to suggest that Britain first achieved the preconditions for take-off by accident of history and geography. The more common pattern is for a society's transition to take-off to begin as a result of external initiatives, such as colonisation, the implication being that modernisation was a process of diffusion triggered first by colonisation and later by international trade, aid and investment links.

Rostow describes the crucial 'take-off' phase as 'the great watershed in the life of modern societies'. During this phase the old blocks to progress such as low levels of savings and investment, high levels of agricultural dependence and slow industrialisation are overcome and the forces for economic progress come to the fore. New industries expand rapidly, generating other industries which supply and service them and their labour force directly. New methods of production become more widespread in both agriculture and industry.

Agriculture becomes more market oriented, making its contribution to the development of industry and the economy through the three links described earlier in the chapter, first supplying food, second generating food, raw materials and demand for manufactured goods for inputs and, finally, supplying surplus to the modern sector in the form of goods, labour and investment. Once take-off has begun, the next in Rostow's stages of economic growth is a long, sustained 'drive to maturity', as the developments in industry and technology are diffused throughout the society, integrating all parts of the economy to contribute to and benefit from the economic growth that has occurred.

In relation to urbanisation, Rostow argued that the 'take-off' stage 'sets up a requirement for urban areas, whose capital costs may be high, but whose population and market organisation help to make industrialisation an on-going process' (1990:58). Rostow implied a change in the nature and role of cities since clearly urban areas pre-date the 'take-off' stage. So the development of settlements is seen by Rostow as a necessity for economic growth, implying that modernisation will diffuse outwards from the core city into the rural hinterland and beyond.

Once this phase is complete, incomes rise to a level where the majority earn enough to go beyond basic needs into a phase of 'high mass consumption'. Economies begin to focus on consumer durables, such as bicycles, sewing machines, various household electrical goods and, perhaps most important, cars. Societies begin to consider issues of social welfare and security. In the third edition of his thesis, Rostow speculates on what comes beyond this stage. This resulted in the addition of a fifth stage, in the row titled 'Beyond mass consumption'.

In this stage Rostow suggests that there will be an increase in the flexible working arrangements facilitated by improvements in communications technology.In Rostow's model transition from a traditional to a modernised society there will inevitably be a change in the relationship between the rural-agricultural sector that dominates the traditional society and the urban-industrial sector that dominates the high mass-consumption society. Some of Rostow's critics suggest that he is not only proindustrialisation but also biased against rural-agricultural sectors (Harvey, 1989). It is hard not to arrive at this conclusion in light of his suggestions that the urban-rural links will increasingly favour the urban-industrial sector and that this is an important precondition for the 'take-off ' stage.

According to the model, agriculture is exploited to provide for the needs of an industrialising and urbanising society. Under such a transition, then, not only are the rural-urban interactions in the developing world increasingly exploitative of the rural-agricultural sector but this are a necessary precondition for economic growth. According to Rostow's analysis, this is a positive development for society in general.A more recent approach to this question, focusing in particular on the agricultural-to-industrial employment transition, is that put forward by Tiffen. The model is based on 'some of the most basic and durable concepts in economics', including:

- The division of labour by specialisation, leading to improved productivity and technological improvements;
- The accumulation of population, facilitating the exchange of services, goods and information;
- The division of labour being constrained by market costs in relation to market values;
- Productivity improvements requiring investment of either labour or capital and diminishing returns on this investment until a change in technology or in product take place.

The result is a process of change in the employment structures of an economy over time. Tiffen suggests that the periods of change can be divided into three. In phase A almost all labour is applied to subsistence food production. The population is sparse and scattered and so surplus is rarely sold on. In phase B, or the transition phase, access to external capital facilitates the expansion of the nonagricultural sector and the transport infrastructure. 'Change accelerates as productive technologies and technologies for the exchange of goods and information improve. Concentrations of people facilitate the exchange and development of ideas'.

This change and the increasing contact with cities and international markets give farmers opportunities to benefit by producing surplus. This surplus in turn promotes the development of the consumer goods and services sectors of the economy that are largely located in cities. The introduction of improved technology and methods of farming releases labour to work in the urban industrial and services sectors which in turn stimulate greater markets for agricultural goods. Some regions have never benefited from the appropriate conditions.

For example, in many Latin American countries the structure of land holding meant that the benefits of export agriculture accrued to a small elite, creating insufficient stimulus to the services and consumer goods sectors. In Africa, major transport infrastructure investment was patchy until the late twentieth century. In phase C the internal market becomes very large, supporting a manufacturing and services sector that is no longer dependent on links with agriculture. As this sector grows and incomes increase, the range and diversity demanded in agricultural produce also increase. The phases have no fixed time period and Tiffen suggests that phase B could take between 50 and 500 years, with the possibility of moving both up and down the gradient.

A similar model of agricultural transition is presented by Hill for South-East Asia. In this, Hill suggests that there is a productivity gap which occurs during the transition as the number of farmers increases, but the proportion begins to decline, resulting in periods of shortage in agricultural labour (even in densely populated regions) before the introduction of improved techniques and mechanisation. An alternative analysis of the relations between rural and urban realms focuses on the way that 'rural' and 'urban' are interpreted themselves. For example, some radical theorists (such as Slater, 1974) have argued that cities are the gateways through which the developing countries have been and are being exploited. The counter-argument to this, of course, is that cities are the gateways through which the rural areas access international markets and international investment and aid.

Since the end of the Second World War a number of national-level initiatives have been rolled out by urban-based governments in an attempt to achieve rural development. These have incorporated rural dwellers' needs and priorities to varying degrees. For example, early initiatives focused on the restructuring of the organisation of the main means of production, labour, land and capital, to take advantage of the 'trickle-down effect' from industrialising urban core areas. Examples of these approaches include rural production sector reform, land reform and village resettlement.

As these policies were found wanting and the expected benefits of urban-based development did not find their way to the rural peripheries, there was a shift towards integrated rural development approaches which emphasised the requirement to meet the needs of the rural dwellers, such as nutrition, water, health care and transport. However, as large amounts of money were invested in this approach with limited results, the focus shifted to reducing state involvement in development initiatives and attempting to encourage the private sector. During the 1980s there was a shift in interventions and government policy back towards more market-based approaches. These emphasised the need for smaller, locally oriented approaches.

Evidence suggests that the sustainability of urban and rural areas appears to be intimately linked. Whether considering the environmental or economic sustainability of the rural population, or the food security and energy needs of the urban population, most research finds links across the urban-rural divide. Despite this, there is little evidence of policy makers appreciating the importance of these links. Only recently are international and other aid agencies developing interventions which show an acceptance of the importance of these links.

Discussion later in this includes examples of rural and urban dwellers developing survival strategies that bridge the urban and the rural realms. Indeed, the different benefits and costs of urban and rural areas provide precisely the opportunities that multi-locational and migrant households are seeking. The next section briefly discusses the theory on the role of cities and the relation between cities and the rural areas. As a result of this discussion it can be seen that the relationship between city and countryside in developing countries is qualitatively different from that between city and countryside in the developed world.

In the world's poorer countries there is a higher dependence on rural activities for wealth and employment, for example in agriculture, mining and fisheries. By contrast, in the developed world most wealth is created in the urban areas. This has implications for the power relations between the city and countryside and results in overlapping and conflicting concerns.

THE SHIFT IN EMPHASIS BETWEEN URBAN AND RURAL

While rural and urban dwellers exploit urban-rural differentials as a strategy for enhancing their livelihood options, a longer-term process is under way in developing countries which creates additional opportunities and threats to households which are urban, rural or straddling the continuum. This process is urbanisation. Urbanisation is often conceptualised in terms of shifting demographic structures, through migration, rapid natural urban growth, or physical city expansion.

However, urbanisation is also conceptualised as the spreading influence of the city on rural areas. This takes the form not only of making bits of the country into cities through building, but also of extending the activities and influences of the city into the countryside and making what happens in the countryside increasingly influenced by the needs of the city. The main consequence of extending urban influence into rural areas is that relations are altered over time and under different influences. For example Potts and Jamal and Weeks (1988) illustrate the different influences of structural adjustment policies on migration and urban bias in rural and urban areas.

PREVIOUS WORK ON RURAL-URBAN INTERACTIONS

McGee describes an Asian version of an urban conurbation which he calls a desakota, derived from Indonesian (desa - village; Kota - city). This combination of city and village describes a complex area of urban and densely settled urban-influenced rural hinterland. This hinterland shows signs of close interrelationships with the urban economy. McGee also describes a process of desakotasi, or the dynamics of the development of the desakota. The interesting element in this theory is the idea that the distinction between urban and rural is without purpose since the interconnections between their populations are more important than the differences between them. The process of desakotasi has only been identified to a limited extent outside Asia.

This idea of the continuum between what is urban and what is rural is suggested in an earlier model provided by McGee. In this he suggests that it is possible to conceptualise the urban and rural as being on a continuum. The development of urban areas is seen as inevitable. What varies is the speed of the development process. This creates urban and rural differences. However, the model suggests that these will ultimately even out. The means by which this will occur are the links between the two realms. For example, as economic development takes place and urban areas develop ahead of rural areas they will attract the unemployed through rural-urban migration.

This will eventually free the rural sector from the burden of surplus labour. This does not, however, take account of the economic crises of the 1970s and 1980s when, some researchers suggest, certain urban and rural areas actually reversed their development relationship. This chapter has set out the broader context in which the research on rural-urban interaction has taken place. This has involved discussion of a number of key themes relating to the causes and consequences of this interaction. One key debate in the literature focuses on whether the relationship between the city and the countryside is a benign or exploitative one. This debate links this area of research into the heart of development theory where there has long been a focus on whether core-periphery relations are positive or negative.

The debate usually focuses on the consequences of the very rapid urbanisation and urban growth experienced by the countries of the developing world. A second key issue is the problem of defining the territories under study as 'town', 'city' and 'countryside' and the divide between - especially in countries where cities are growing outwards very quickly. A third issue is that cities in the developing world often form the gateway between the rest of the country and the international markets. The evidence suggests that they rely more heavily on their own hinterlands than do cities in the developed world, so their relationship with their hinterland is very important. This link is reciprocal, as the cities of the developing countries provide the rural areas with their links to world markets.

One of the key roles that rural-urban links play in the development process is in the exchange of finance. This can take a number of forms. Finance can be passed to rural areas from urban-based banking and finance institutions in the form of credit provided to farmers and rural businesses. It can also take the form of investment in rural industries from either private sources or government or donor projects. Informal flows of finance may take the form of remittances sent by urban dwellers to their rural-based relatives.

One of the themes of this is that the increased flows between rural and urban areas in the developing world appear to facilitate economic and social activity and can help to build economic and social capital. This chapter focuses on flows of finance and sets out to examine the evidence for their existence, their patterns and the extent to which they can contribute to development in both urban and rural areas.

ECONOMIC THEORIES RELATED TO RURAL-URBAN LINKS

Knight and Song (2000) argue that there are three basic economic theories that apply to economic relationships between rural and urban areas. The first is the Lewis model of economic growth with surplus rural labour. The 'coercive' or 'price-scissors' approach suggests that urban industrialisation draws on abundant rural labour. Capital mobilised from rural productivity gains is invested in industrial development which creates increasing demand for agricultural goods and promotes further improvements in the efficiency of agricultural production.

The result, according to the model, is improving dynamic equilibrium in rural-urban terms of trade. This has some resonances with Tiffen's (2003) model discussed. The second model is of economic growth financed by extracting rural surplus. This is related to the Rostow stages of economic growth model. Thus the growth of the industrial sector is funded by reducing agricultural producer prices, consequently depressing rural income and therefore consumption, and promoting urban industrial capital accumulation. The final model of rural-urban economic exchange is based on the notion that economic policy favours the urban over the rural sector - Lipton's (1977) 'urban bias' thesis.

The argument is that urban dwellers exert a considerable influence on government because they are politically aware, more vocal and better organised, and include elites such as bureaucrats. The result is improved urban living conditions, promoting rural-urban migration. The Todaro model of rural-urban migration is based on the idea that migration will take place if there is a perceived differential between urban and rural incomes. These three theories all suggest capital, or wealth, flows from the countryside to the city as a nation develops. However, some researchers are beginning to find evidence of wealth flows in the opposite direction, suggesting that circumstances may influence the direction of wealth flows between urban and rural areas.

An element of dependency theory suggests that wealth flows are rural to urban; while classical economic theory suggests that there is the potential for a 'trickle-down effect' from urban to rural. This was an early focus of the research on interactions between urban and rural areas. The reality is more complex and fluid and depends on local circumstances and changing situations. This is reflected in more recent research, which suggests that some households have adopted a strategy of obtaining access to both the income-earning opportunities of urban areas and the productive resources in the rural areas.

However, the impacts are seen in families which have fragmented as a survival strategy, resulting in break-up of the structure of their society due to economic pressures. The so-called 'multi-locational household' represents an attempt to overcome the difficulties of each location while at the same time retaining its benefits for the whole household. This is similar to Epstein's (1973) concept of 'share families' resulting from his research in South India, where family units lived separately, but agreed to pool resources and expenditure. This suggests that migration in various forms is one of a range of strategies adopted by rural dwellers that may lead to some period of time spent in cities.

[L]abour migration is indeed a forced livelihood response, although it arises from a complex set of social relations (including relations of debt and dependency) rather than simply ecological crisis and subsistence failure. For others, however, migration proves a positive opportunity to save, accumulate capital or invest in assets.

De Haan (1999) regards remittances as one of the most important aspects of migration and one likely to provide a 'trickle-down' effect. Which way do wealth flows go?

In Zimbabwe during the 1990s, the government enacted an economic structural adjustment policy (ESAP) which was intended to reduce the economic burden of the state and ensure that the economy was able to function efficiently. It is debatable whether Zimbabwe needed such an urgent and draconian approach, as its economic indicators were stronger than those of other sub-Saharan African countries, but there is some suggestion that they were under pressure from the International Monetary Fund. Potts and Mutambirwa (1998) carried out a survey of the impacts of ESAP among recent in-migrants in a high-density residential area of Harare, Zimbabwe's capital.

This survey found that the majority of respondents perceived that ESAP had made things worse in both the Communal Areas and the cities. Most respondents (72 per cent) also felt that the worst effects of ESAP were felt in the urban areas rather than in the Communal Areas (CAs) where the majority black rural population live. Potts and Mutambirwa hinge their explanation on the increase in prices for all goods; urban residents had to buy much more, since rural residents can grow their own food and so avoid grocery bills. The following quote, in response to a question about the biggest problem about living in town, illustrates this:

Eating bought food. At home we eat what is grown...you know a cucumber? [In town] I buy a cucumber for a shilling. A cucumber which is eaten by a baboon at home! Ah no...[But here in town] you put a bought thing in your mouth! A chicken's egg is bought for twenty cents! Two bob! An egg!

So that's a hard life. You buy firewood. Are trees bought? No. You go and break it in the bush. No...they are selling my tree to me. That is what is hard about living in town.

However, perhaps one of the more interesting results of the survey was that the links between urban and rural areas were highlighted by the respondents, as shown by the following quotes. Retrenched people went to the Communal Areas and increased the burden there. Rural people depend on those working in town. Retrenchments in town equal retrenchments in the Communal Areas. Urban workers support the rural poor.

These quotes reveal how urban and rural people are affected by rural-urban linkages when the economy is under pressure, in particular when urban residents are retrenched, 161 or made redundant. The results of the research suggest that the rural dwellers were no longer receiving the same level of remittances as previously and had to absorb extra family members who had been retrenched and would otherwise be living in town. The link to the rural area is characterised by Potts and Mutambirwa as a 'safety net'.

Urban destitution is becoming more evident in Harare in the 1990s, particularly for those who have no rural alternative such as the landless, widows and orphans. The safety net of the CAs has always been vital for the urban households and the ESAP era is proving yet again the significance of that safety net.The research which illustrates the positive benefits of remittances argues that they can fulfil insurance and an investment role. There is debate about the relative significance of the roles in rural society.

One of the difficulties of assessing the relative value of remittances is that small amounts sent from an urban cash-based economy can represent substantial amounts in a cash-starved rural economy. One of the problems in assessing the economic and financial linkages between urban and rural areas is that the role of the cash economy differs between the two. This is illustrated, which discusses the rural-urban wealth flows in Zimbabwe during the introduction of economic structural adjustment policies in the 1990s. Satterthwaite (2000) highlights the greater need for cash in the urban economy, identifying some of its main uses:

- For public transport to commute and access essential services. This can be a higher proportion of low-income households' expenditure, especially those located in peripheral settlements;
- For school fees and associated costs such as getting to and from school, buying uniforms, and paying exam fees which tend to be higher in urban areas;
- For housing and associated costs, such as water and other services;
- For access to water - and in some instances to sanitation and garbage collection; these can represent a higher proportion of expenditure among low-income households;
- For food, which is more expensive for urban households, most of which have to purchase their food needs, in contrast to rural areas where most produce their own;

One of the reasons for this is the increasing tax burden imposed on rural dwellers because the more remote village and town governments have fallen deeper into debt following the failure of their enterprises. Town and village enterprises (TVEs) were encouraged as a means of local development and grew rapidly during the 1980s, but during the 1990s they failed to compete with the dynamic new industries establishing themselves on the coast. Many of these coastal enterprises were able to attract inward investment and developed by selling to large markets nearby.

They quickly set up distribution networks in the rural areas where they were able to outperform the smaller TVEs, many of which failed as a result. These failures have adversely affected many of the 40,000 rural credit cooperatives that provide 70 per cent of TVE credit and 80 per cent of peasant loans. Approximately half of the loans are non-performing. Local rural government debt has recently been estimated at Rmb 600 billion, a burden that the rural dwellers have to bear. According to the article, local government officials are sometimes over-optimistic in their estimates of agricultural productivity, resulting in promotion for them and an increased tax burden for the farmers. This problem has led to conflict, even rioting in some areas.

The article concludes that the implications of this 'rural malaise' are potentially very serious indeed. If it continues, then it is likely that more people will attempt to move to the cities in search of employment. The government is not in a strong position to rectify the situation. It is reluctant to take steps which might adversely affect the rapid growth of the coastal cities; it has very little income to invest in the rural areas due to other - mainly urban-based - fiscal difficulties, such as pensions and state banking liabilities, which the article estimates are equivalent to 100 per cent of the country's GDP. Ironically, this is the latest generation of a regime that came to power on the back of a peasant revolt.Adapted from James Kynge:

- Perhaps for health care which may be more expensive in urban areas; if no public or NGO provision is available, private services have to be purchased. This can be exacerbated by the higher incidence of contagious disease and environmental health problems in urban living conditions;
- For child-care, which may have to be paid for if older members of the household need to earn;
- For payments to community-based organisations, bribes to police, fines when arrested for illegal street vending.

In contrast to its role in urban living, cash tends to be a relatively scarce rural commodity throughout much of the developing world. This is illustrated which shows that circumstances in rural China contrast starkly with the rapid development taking place in Chinese cities. The example of China illustrates how the state can place a double burden on the rural economy. In general terms, the urban-based members of a household may be able to provide relatively small amounts of cash which can still be beneficial to the rural-based household.

On the other hand, where necessary, rural-based members of a household can provide the urban-based members with rural resources such as food, woodfuel and so on, which may be in abundance in the countryside and can keep down the costs of urban living.The rural economy of most developing countries is dominated by small-scale activities. Where trade or production and processing exist, it is mostly small and often informal. 'Formal financial institutions find offering services to this [small enterprise] economy risky, costly and unprofitable'.

According to Rogerson (2001), in surveys of all sectors of economic enterprise, whether urban or rural, access to finance stands out as a key constraint. In Africa most small enterprises have no access to institutional credit and in rural areas this constraint is far more acute. These circumstances have led to the development of micro-credit schemes rather than non-financial services and support which were criticised as expensive and ineffective.

Social and kin networks have proved very important as sources of informal flexible loans, gifts, savings, and rotating credit and savings associations. Other informal sources of finance that figure prominently are suppliers and merchants, and such informal credit sources are often used for mobilising household savings and financing small businesses. This is where urban-based households can prove extremely useful to rural cash-poor relatives.The rest of this chapter discusses research on the different types of financial flows:

- Formal, institutional;
- Informal, such as migrant remittances;
- Investment by government, aid agencies and private finance.

FORMAL CAPITAL FLOWS

Robinson (2001) highlights a debate within the literature on micro-level finance, focusing on the means by which credit is provided to the lowest-income households. These are:

- The financial systems approach, which focuses on large-scale outreach to poor, economically active households who will be able to contribute to savings and repay small loans out of household and enterprise incomes. The institutional self-sufficiency of the savings and loan provider is a key principle of this approach, the argument being that this is the only way the huge worldwide demand for micro-credit can be met;

- The poverty lending approach, which concentrates on reducing poverty through the provision of credit in combination with a range of additional services, such as education and training, employment, health and nutrition.

Robinson (2001) argues that the huge unmet demand for micro-credit is only likely to be satisfied through the financial systems approach because it does not rely on subsidies. Governments and donors cannot finance the hundreds of millions of people who constitute present unmet demand for microcredit services. In addition, the poverty lending approach, as indicated by its name, does not attempt to meet the vast demand among the poor for voluntary savings services.

It is through the mobilisation of savings that the credit services can become viable. Under the financial systems approach any subsidies provided by government or donors are used to disseminate lessons and to transfer best practices, while the micro-credit approach uses subsidies to finance their lending.

There have been problems with financial institutions that mobilise savings. Hulme et al. (1996) identify co-operative rural banks in Sri Lanka as a conduit through which rural savings are channelled towards the capital. 'In effect, the CRBs mobilise rural savings for transfer to Colombo where they have helped to finance the growing budget deficit. They are a major contributor to making finance scarce in rural areas: in 1992 for every Rs100 they took on deposit, only rupees 14 was lent out' (1996:229).

Alternatives to the CRBs do exist in Sri Lanka, such as the credit and thrift cooperatives (SANASA) which circulate savings in the form of micro-credit within the rural areas and which have a far better record of recovering repayments. The challenge comes in providing affordable micro-finance. This is the case because the cost of providing small-scale credit can be relatively expensive. However, Robinson (2001) provides evidence

Micro-credit programmes Hulme and Mosley (1996a) argue that complex as the process of development is, two ideas about it are broadly accepted:

- Capital investment is an important determinant of raising incomes and of economic growth;
- Capital markets in developing countries rarely work well.

This presents a major challenge to development initiatives: in the absence of effective private finance, how is capital investment raised for poverty alleviation? In both urban and rural areas the answer has been through the introduction of development finance institutions (DFIs). Hulme and Mosley (1996a, 1996b) carried out a detailed study of DFIs in countries across the developing world.

Their findings broadly support their argument. In addition, their work underlines the role of credit for micro-enterprises (including small-scale farming) in raising the incomes of micro-entrepreneurs, reducing poverty and facilitating investment in new technology such as tools or high-yielding seed varieties. For example, the Federation of Thrift and Credit Cooperatives (SANASA) in Sri Lanka is a federation of groups ranging from ten to 700 members who contribute to share capital, attend meetings, save regularly and help to ensure the cooperatives are democratically run.

The savings create the basis for lending. Some cooperatives run basic savings and loans services, while others employ staff and effectively establish a local rural bank. Hulme et al. (1996) found in a survey of SANASA borrowers that their mean monthly income raised over the period of their last loan, supporting the conclusion that credit is important to raising incomes. They also found that this credit is creating an increased demand for labour as the borrowers employ more workers to advance the purpose for which the loan was taken. '

As labour is a key to higher outputs and incomes amongst households in the South Asian context, this is an important finding'. One of the most important findings concerns the wider social and economic benefits of such institutions. This is an important basis on which to argue for some level of continued support for these finance institutions. For example, reliance on mudalali (money lenders) in the nearest towns, who often charge interest rates of 20 to 30 per cent per month, has almost been eradicated. Farmers' reliance on 'in-kind' credit from traders for the purchase of seeds or fertiliser on credit in return for higher prices or lower crop purchase prices has also been reduced.

The alternative is market-based bank lending which stays clear of micro-lending and sets conditions that small-scale borrowers such as farmers are unable to meet. In the main commercial services such as banks are located in large towns and cities. Urban households that are already circulating higher levels of finance because of their higher cash incomes and costs are in a stronger position than small-scale farmers for whom the cash economy is important but who are dealing in relatively small amounts of cash. The rural dweller interested in taking a loan therefore has both an economic and a geographical barrier to overcome.

Robinson (2001) adopts an alternative approach to the analysis of finance for the poor. She argues first that a wide range of financial services are already available in rural areas and low-income urban neighbourhoods through local traders, employers, landlords, commodity wholesalers, pawnbrokers and various types of private money lenders. However, these various informal money lenders typically charge high interest rates. She argues that poverty is the reason for the introduction of development finance institutions. However, a clear distinction should be made between poverty reduction initiatives and micro-finance initiatives.

According to this view, the world is littered with examples of failed DFIs, in large part on account of credit being given to those she calls the 'extremely poor' who are mostly unable to repay it, causing the failure of the credit institutions. Providing subsidised loans (which are usually rationed) to the economically active poor prevents them from having widespread access to commercially available loans and uses scarce government and donor funds that would be better used on other forms of poverty alleviation that poor people are willing to pay relatively high rates for micro-loans, mainly because the alternatives are no access to credit at all or borrowing from informal money lenders at much higher rates of interest or with unacceptable in-kind demands. Successful examples of the micro-finance approach include the Indonesian local banking system, or unit desa, of the state-owned Bank Rakyat Indonesia, discussed by Robinson (2001), and the BancoSol, analysed by Mosley (1996).

INFORMAL MONEY MOVEMENTS

Informal monetary movements across the rural-urban interface may take a range of forms. They can include rural to rural, rural to urban, urban to rural and urban to urban. Montgomery et al. (1996) report that the informal financial markets in Bangladesh were estimated at approximately two-thirds of the total during the 1980s indicating the importance of this source of credit. By contrast, in Kenya, Buckley (1996) found that only one respondent of his study of rural credit reported using an African private money lender, while the few other cases that were disclosed involved Kenyan-Asian money lenders, with one respondent quoted as saying: 'Asians do it because they were not African' (1996:285).

This suggests that access to rural informal credit sources is highly variable.The opportunity of initiating informal flows of money from urban migrant to rural relatives is one of the main motivations behind rural-to-urban migration. In addition, informal migrant remittances are a key impact of migration. Regmi and Tisdell (2002) discuss a number of forms and motivations for sending remittances, arguing that each may have different levels of significance to the rural area:

- Regular transfers - where a migrant sends regular sums - often relatively small for the migrant, but with profound benefits in the rural destination; these may be motivated by obligation, an aspiration to inherit land or altruism;
- Insurance payments - where urban residents send money to help rural relatives in times of difficulty;

- Loan payments - the migrant loans money to the rural relatives, though the expectation of repayment may not be high or may involve not cash but in-kind repayment;
- Education repayments - the migrant repays the family for the education he or she received when younger that made the migration possible.

Regmi and Tisdell (2002) found in their analysis of data from Nepal that an average of 4.07 per cent of income was remitted home. However, the range went from 15.56 per cent among those who earned up to 10,000 Nepalese rupees, to 2.25 per cent for migrants with an income of over 50,000 rupees. The absolute amount remitted increased with the income bracket from an average of 889.56 to 2,775.30 Nepalese rupees. They report very different data for other countries, with remittances of 38 per cent for Pakistan and 10-13 per cent for Kenya.

More comparative work is required in this area to discern general trends. However, remittances are a very difficult subject to research as considerable trust between researchers and researched is required before details of household finances are divulged. Other than the amounts and proportion of remittances, researchers have been concerned to find out their economic and social impact. Regmi and Tisdell's (2002) survey found that 55.1 per cent of the remittances were used to supplement household expenditure; in particular, they suggest that this money accounts for the purchase of necessities such as soap, kerosene, clothes, salt, sugar and clothes.

As a result of consideration of a number of variables they suggest that the hypothesis - in the Nepalese case at least - that the motivation for sending remittances is to secure inheritance of property, in particular land, may be an important explanatory factor. Chaudhuri found evidence that among migrants to Durgapur in India, 86 per cent of remittances sent are to rural areas. Some 44 per cent of the remittances are used for what Chaudhuri describes as consumption spending. This corroborates the findings of Hulme et al., that much of the credit borrowed from informal sources, such as relatives, money lenders and credit cooperatives, was used for consumption spending, such as investment in dwellings, expenditure for special occasions and bridging the gap between agricultural incomes and production costs.

Similarly, Buckley (1996) found that rotating credit schemes in Kenya, or 'merry-go-rounds' as they are known, are typified by consumption investment such as hi-fi equipment. This consumption credit, according to Hulme et al., has the benefit of protecting household assets and future income that might otherwise have been spent on the purchases. Much of this kind of credit is repaid very quickly. SANASA, the federation of credit and thrift cooperatives in Sri Lanka, has a very high level of loan recovery.

In an in-depth analysis of the relationship between the urban and rural areas of the Yogyakarta Special Region (or Daereh Istimewa Yogyakarta, known as DIY) in Indonesia, Rotge (2000) studied the development of local community mutual self-help networks. The emergence of these networks, known as gotong royong, has meant that ways of sharing and distributing wealth have evolved which provide a very strong incentive for the urban residents to remain closely tied to the rural community. Such ties are an example of what Rotge describes as centripetal forces which encourage the rural dweller to stay at home.

They are countered by centrifugal forces encouraging out-migration, such as dissatisfaction with the local means of earning a living, mainly wet rice cultivation. The result in the villages studied was that the people developed a series of variations of commuting, regular migration and circular migration as a compromise between the centripetal and centrifugal forces. In particular Rotge and his co-workers found evidence that these relationships involved mutual responsibility between the wealthy and the poor in the communities. As members of such a community, individuals need not worry about starvation as long as they remain with their kin. Consequently, it would be a high risk to leave the community for long periods, because of the uncertainty of whether paid employment could support them at their destination.

The importance of this strategy became particularly clear when the Indonesian economy collapsed during the 1997 crisis which saw the rupiah fall to 15 per cent of its exchange value against the US dollar, 20 per cent of formal-sector jobs lost and 15 per cent knocked off the value of GDP. Atkinson (2000) reported that official estimates of those living in poverty had declined to 10 per cent by 1996, a year before the crisis. A year after the crisis, the proportion living below the poverty line was estimated at just under 40 per cent and rising.

Rotge's (2000) research into villages close to the DIY considered the role of income from remittances sent by circular migrants. This research carried out in 1986 found approximately one migrant for every five households in one district near Yogyakarta. Research in this region also found that remittances can raise household income by up to 15.6 per cent. The Gini coefficient (a statistic commonly used to calculate the imbalance of distribution of income) among non-migrant households was 0.39, indicating inequalities of income, but much lower at 0.21, among households benefiting from remittances from a circular migrant. Thus, remittances from migrants appear to reduce the income inequalities that are a characteristic of the rest of the population in the areas studied.

In sub-Saharan Africa, research on livelihood strategies of rural dwellers has found evidence of a virtuous cycle of cross-investment between agriculture and non-agriculture. For example, Madulu (1998) demonstrates that the efforts of farmers in Sukumaland, Tanzania, to acquire ox-carts and bicycles have resulted in increased mobility and productivity in agriculture. This has, in turn, provided an important incentive for agricultural work; he finds evidence that 40 per cent of entrepreneurs received their starting capital from agriculture.

A clear pattern of cross-investment between non-agricultural and agricultural activities was identified in many study sites of a multiple country study led by Deborah Bryceson (1999). In Tanzania's Usambara Mountains, 75 per cent of the respondents invested money earned in agriculture in enterprises, whereas the counterflow was even stronger with

84 per cent deriving some of their agricultural capital from non-agricultural sources. Similar cross-investment in both directions was found in Nigeria's cocoa-producing zone.

In north-west Nigeria, Iliya (1999) reports that 85 per cent of household heads derived their start-up capital from agriculture or livestock keeping, but only very large households with high incomes invest part of their non-farm revenue in agriculture. Most use these earnings for the purchase of daily needs. The bifurcation of investment strategies between rich and poor households is also evident in the Nigerian savannah village of Nasarawan Doya where 56 per cent of higher-income households and 16 per cent of middle-income households derived start-up capital for non-farm activities from agriculture.

In Nigeria's Middle Belt there was relatively low cross-investment, as only 10 per cent of the non-farm entrepreneurs reported using their earnings to fund agriculture. The agricultural investment cycle here is therefore largely internal to the farming process. Nonetheless, Yunusa stresses that the rural non-farm sector vitally depends on the purchasing power generated by agricultural proceeds and there was evidence that during periods of economic pressure the rural-based non-farm activities were used by urban-trained non-farm operators as a means to mobilise rural capital, after which they may move the business to the city.

In Latin America, Tacoli (1999) found that Paraguayan farmers on the urban fringe of Asunción were not able to benefit from proximity to the urban financial markets. This was because their plots of land were too small to be used as collateral for a loan to invest in their business and take advantage of the proximity to the urban markets for food. She reports that in many cases they are forced to sell to larger farmers. 'The optimal use of productive and physical capitals is therefore intrinsically linked to access to financial assets'.

However, she goes on to enumerate social resources (networks of friends, relatives and business associates) and cultural capital (perceptions of creditworthiness, reliability and trust) that could be mobilised to secure credit. In Bangladesh, Afsar found that improvements in communications and transport have led to an increased incidence of what she calls 'reverse investment' as urban migrants return to provide capital and take part in decision making about agricultural activities. In Dhaka, more than a third of slum residents had cultivable land and around a quarter derive regular income from it. There has also been an increase in rural manufacturing and other non-farm economic activities, with growth rates of 10 per cent for rural processing and manufacturing and 5.5 per cent for rural services between 1988 and 1996.

This forms one of the strands of Afsar's (1999) argument that contrary to orthodox migration theory, rural-urban migration does not always adversely affect the rural areas. However, she points out that the communications and transport infrastructure is crucial to ensuring that the benefits return to the rural areas.Bryceson's (1999) 'betwixt and between' conceptualisation of the rural household emphasises the fact that no two households earn their livelihood in the same way. Thus policy interventions that emphasise a particular livelihood strategy are unlikely to benefit all.

This can be considered as analogous to the livelihood strategies that straddle the rural-urban interface. The empirical evidence presented by Bryceson (1999) suggests that the mixing of agricultural and non-farm employment can result in flows of investment between these activities. Similar outcomes can result from flows of finance between rural and urban areas. In addition to these arguments, de-peasantisation may also be an explanation for the development of non-agricultural activities in African rural areas that sheds light on the relationship between cities and the countryside at a more general level. This research is mirrored by similar findings in the South-East Asian context and in Latin America. The bulk of the interpretation explains the development of non-farm employment in terms of:

- Declining employment and earning opportunities in cities under structural adjustment programmes;

- The consequent presence of returned migrants in rural areas;
- The low esteem in which younger people in rural areas hold agriculture as a means of income earning;
- The decline of rural services as a result of structural adjustment;
- The low viability of using agricultural inputs to boost productivity;
- Growing population pressure.

COCOA TRADE AND FINANCE FLOWS IN GHANA

Ghana in West Africa is one of the world's leading cocoa producers. It produces over 400,000 tons of high-quality cocoa per year. In 1999 cocoa was estimated to be generating 13 to 14 per cent of the country's GDP, 11 per cent of its tax revenue and 30 to 35 per cent of its foreign exchange earnings. It accounts for approximately half of the economically active population and is grown in six of the country's ten regions. Cocoa is therefore of enormous economic and political significance to the people of Ghana. But how are the contributions and benefits of cocoa production distributed between urban and rural areas?

In Ghana, one of the main reasons why rural employment in the cocoa sector is so extensive is that most producers are small-scale farmers who also sun-dry and ferment their cocoa harvest themselves. This processing gives Ghana's cocoa a better taste and higher butter content than the plantation-produced and mechanically dried cocoa of countries such as neighbouring Côte d'Ivoire. The higher quality can bring Ghana $70 per tonne more than other countries in the region. Thus in Ghana more people are employed in production and they receive a better price than in neighbouring Côte d'Ivoire. The floating of the cocoa price in Côtte d'Ivoire when the world price fell has been linked to the political unrest in that country in recent years.

With a backdrop of an insecure banking market and limited affordable credit available - in some cases more than 40 per cent interest - to Ghanaian small-holding rural dwellers the income from cocoa production provides an important inflow of cash to the country's rural households from the international markets. The high cost of credit hampered modernisation in the agricultural sector and is partly responsible for the low levels of fertiliser and other inputs used.

This is particularly the case since subsidies on inputs were removed under pressure from the World Bank. However, the cost of credit also means that these producers are more dependent on the decisions taken by the government about the prices to be paid to producers. The result is that although the farmers are able to avoid urban-based banks that charge high rates for credit, they are dependent on the decisions made by government in the capital about the prices to be paid. The cities are therefore vital to the livelihood of the farmers.

Ghana came under pressure from the international trade and financial institutions in the late 1990s to reduce the level of state intervention in its cocoa market. Despite the licensing of 18 private traders and the prospect that up to 30 per cent of cocoa would be exported privately, the main issue of concern to the international institutions was that the state cocoa marketing board, Cocobod, was paying farmers more than the planned price, thus a higher price than farmers were being paid in neighbouring countries. The price paid was higher than could be sustained by the higher premium attached to high-quality Ghanaian cocoa. For example, in 1999, despite oversupply and slow demand, Cocobod paid farmers the same price as it had in 1998. The experience of privatisation of cocoa marketing in nearby countries such as Nigeria and Cameroon is instructive in that a drop in production and quality followed.

Farmers' representatives argue that guaranteed prices for this international commodity are vital to ensure that national production increases in line with the target of 500,000 tons by 2004. This policy of supporting national production has also provided an incentive to rehabilitate flagging cocoa production and has attracted farmers back to this activity. In particular, it is vital if younger farmers are to be attracted to the sector - the average age of Ghana's farmers is 55 - and to provide an economic base for Ghana's rural population.

The question is: should governments be involved in supporting the production of an international agricultural commodity like cocoa? The indications are that the country benefits: notably, farmers have some assurances about prices and a market outlet, and this encourages younger farmers to remain in the rural areas and grow cocoa, rather than migrate to the cities in search of employment. It is clear that Ghanaian cocoa farmers rely on access to finances from institutions located in the cities, whether these are government or private. By retaining their role in processing the cocoa themselves, the Ghanaian farmers create greater wealth for themselves, bring employment to the rural areas and earn foreign exchange for their country. This inflow of money is vital at a time when Ghana is still very dependent on the export of this commodity, whose price trend is one of long-term decline.

GOVERNMENT INVESTMENT AND AID

There are numerous examples of ways in which governments have used income from agricultural production to swell the size of their bureaucracies. However, the use of rural surplus to support an urban-based bureaucracy is also illustrated by the example of Ghana. Toye (1991) reported that in 1985 Jerry Rawlings, president of Ghana, condemned the urban exploitation of rural cocoa producers.

This condemnation was followed shortly afterwards by a reduction of 16,000 in the staff of Cocobod, the national cocoa marketing organisation; then 10,000 'ghost workers' were removed from the payroll by early 1987 and a further 14,000 were 'retrenched', that is made redundant, by the end of 1987. While this was part of a wider programme of government retrenchment, the implication in Toye's (1991) report is that it was intended to reduce the urban-based burden placed on rural cocoa producers. Despite these retrenchments, at the time Toye was writing in the early 1990s, some observers still thought that the remaining 50,000 Cocobod employees constituted too heavy a burden for the cocoa-producing sector.

Many studies have demonstrated that research in agriculture can yield economic returns, providing improvements in production, post-harvest handling and other areas of agricultural business. For example, the links between the rural and urban economies are illustrated by the statistic that every $1 of additional investment in African agriculture leads to an extra $1.50 of non-farm output while in Asia the figure is $1.80. Many such studies on the developing world highlight the positive impacts of agricultural research on rural poverty. Moreover, Fang et al. (2003) find that in China there is a positive relationship between government investment in agricultural research and reducing urban poverty. One of the main causal links in this relationship is that Chinese urban dwellers living on less than $2 per day spend 58 per cent of their income on food.

Fang et al. conclude that in 1992, for every 1 per cent decline in the cost of food, urban poverty is reduced by 3.08 per cent. As might be expected, investment in agricultural research results in a reduction in poverty in rural areas, but their data suggest that for every 10,000 yuan of agricultural research investment 10.94 people are raised above the $2 per day poverty line and that by 1998 this amount of investment was raising 6.31 people above the poverty line. This means a total of 4.68 million urban residents were raised above the poverty line in 1992 and 3.16 million in 1998. They argue that the decline in impact on poverty reduction between 1992 and 1998 is mainly due to the declining proportion of income spent on food as it becomes cheaper and more widely available.

However, they argue that continued agricultural investment is required in order to ensure that both urban and rural areas continue to reduce levels of poverty: 'with rapid urbanization, agricultural research will still need to play a key role in supplying adequate food at affordable prices to ensure that urban and rural poverty remain low' (Fang et al.,

2003:740). This begs the question of whether investment in urban and industrial development has the same multiplier effect in rural areas.

As discussed above, Afsar (1999) suggests that at least in the case of Bangladesh the benefits of urban income can be passed on to rural areas where social and familial links are maintained by rural-to-urban migrants and where these links are facilitated by good communications and transport infrastructure. Similar findings are reported by other authors such as Potts in sub-Saharan Africa, Rigg in Thailand and South-East Asia generally, and Rotge (2000) in Indonesia. In the latter case comparative village surveys found that proximity to a main road increased the economic and social benefits of linkages with the urban area.

Rutherford et al. (2002) found in a survey of the use of financial services over a full year by urban residents in Bangladesh that none had used less than five separate types of service during that period. One had used as many as 18 and the average was ten (2002:115). Attwood and Baviskar (2002) have two key concerns about the results of research on the way development finance institutions (DFIs) operate in India. The first is that countries like India have poured considerable amounts of capital into DFIs, whose assets rarely consist of members' savings. The credit is mainly provided to landowners, who are mostly men, and the level of repayment is low. 'Thus, formal "co-operative credit" is neither self-supporting nor beneficial to the poorest villagers, including women'.

The second key concern is that many of the DFIs overlook the need for services other than credit. Services such as micro-savings and insurance are in demand among the poor and represent an important means by which they can reduce their vulnerability to adverse events. Formal financial institutions have a role to play in facilitating the flows of capital between urban and rural areas and between farm and non-farm sectors. However, the literature is replete with examples of them failing to achieve this, on account of corruption, incompetence or poor structure.

Moreover, there are many cases where poor rural savers and producers have their surpluses expropriated for the development of industrial and urban development. Careful empirical studies, however, appear to show notable examples of successful approaches that focus on the needs of the user, on ensuring long-term financial viability and not restricting activities to the provision of credit, but providing savings, insurance and other financial services at an appropriate scale for the rural residents.

Theories of the nature of financial flows between urban and rural areas tend to focus on ideas of urban extraction of rural wealth and economic assets. Past research has provided evidence of exploitation of rural areas by both urban private interests and urban-biased governments. However, governments and aid donors have attempted to balance this bias by providing rural credit.

Although the barriers to obtaining credit in rural areas are considerable, there are some examples of successful rural financial services. Evidence suggests, however, that these are a minority; most rural credit institutions, while providing small but welcome capital to cash-starved rural economies, have a poor track record. There is potential to develop a wider range of financial services including not only credit but also savings and insurance services. However, it is important to the success of such schemes that control remains in the rural area with the clients in order to avoid transfers in favour of the already more solvent urban economies.

2

The Politics of Informalization in Bissau, Guinea-Bissau

Informal activities in African cities have experienced a rapid expansion in recent decades. Policies of structural adjustment and a marginal position in the global economy have changed the conditions under which African urban dwellers make a living. In the face of poor availability of wage jobs and declining real wages, urbanites increasingly rely on informal ways of income earning. Thus, while African cities have long been characterized by the presence of an "informal sector", they are now experiencing new waves of "informalization".

In this context, understanding the dynamics of informal economies seems to be of relevance. This chapter attempts to make a longitudinal analysis of social processes of informalization in Bissau, the capital of Guinea-Bissau. It aims to show that the production of informality is a more complex process than is often assumed, as it may involve a variety of groups and interests. Further, it uncovers how various groups in Bissau are faring differently in the context of the current extensive informalization.

The literature where state-society relations and informal economic activities cross paths is one useful entry point into understanding processes of informalization. One position within this literature has been that much informal activity in Africa can be traced to a societal "disengagement" from the state and formal market channels. Unfavourable state laws and policies, poor performance and declining opportunities for political participation prompt urban residents to develop alternative solutions such as circumventing official channels and regulations and withholding production, in order to reduce dependence on and gain autonomy from those channels.

It is often argued that such rather unorganized popular responses may have far-reaching consequences, in terms of undermining the credibility, the outreach and revenues of the state. In this line of reasoning, economic informalization in a context of structural adjustment is seen as bearing the seeds of the liberation of society, and informal activities are portrayed as in opposition to and autonomous from state power and as inherently democratic. This celebratory view of informal activities has inspired a great number of studies of urban informal economies. These assumptions have been strengthened by other influential texts such as Hyden (1990) and de Soto (1989), and appropriated by the anti-state agenda of donor agencies.

The basic assumptions on which the above understanding is based have however been challenged. Firstly, some have emphasized the inseparability and symbiotic interactions between the informal activities, the state and the formal economy, and how the expansion of informality usually involves a large degree of political networking (for example, Bangura and Gibbon 1992; Roitman 1990; Lemarchand 1991; Macharia 1997). Actors may seek to have one foot in each sphere and may neither need nor wish to disengage from the state.

The implications are that informal actors are not necessarily autonomous from the state and that the growth of informal activities does not necessarily signal their liberation or the increasing irrelevance of the state in the economy. Secondly, some have highlighted the role of externally induced structural adjustment policies imposing economic liberalization and restrictions in the extent of state regulation and intervention. International institutions have prompted

African countries to join the global drive towards economic deregulation and given high priority to turning the "informal sector" into an engine for economic growth and into a major provider of services.

As Grey-Johnson summarizes it: "The emerging policy thus seems to be one of shrinking government responsibility in providing economic and social protection to the African people and let them fend for themselves". Or as Peattie explains in relation to housing policy, "what appeared in the 1960s as an emancipatory movement has been translated into a language of privatization". Structural approaches have also been concerned with understanding contemporary informalization processes. They have come to focus on the role of global economic restructuring in fostering a proliferation of informal activities across the globe, what has been termed the "informalization approach".

This perspective highlights the ways in which capital is using informal or unregulated ways of operating as part of flexible production practices, and its strategies to reduce costs and protect profits, often with the complicity of the state. From this point of view, an increase in informal activity in the current phase of late capitalism is not interpreted as the liberation of small informal actors but rather seen as the worsening of their working conditions and a downgrading of labour.

This chapter describes the value of the above approaches for understanding the expansion of informality in post-independence Bissau. Pervasive informality in Bissau, I will argue, is a process resulting from the interplay of a variety of actors and pressures, whose complexity is better grasped by combining elements of different perspectives that might seem a priori incompatible. On the one hand, some components of the disengagement perspective lend credit to the struggles and achievements of popular groups.

On the other hand, the informalization perspective gives us the tools to understand current changes and developments in informal economies, including the role of the state and international actors. In Bissau, the politics of informalization has involved instances of both engagement and disengagement. The shifting character of the informal economy and its relations with formal institutions necessitates a definition of informality that is not too narrow or rigid. Here, the informal economy is generally understood to consist of economic activities that evade one or several aspects of existing legislation pertaining to those activities (but not necessarily unregulated or independent from the state).

However, the boundaries delimiting this field are permeable; they encompass a considerable grey zone and are trespassed by categories of actors who operate in both formal and informal spheres. The emphasis here is less on the distinction between formal and informal and more on the relations between the two. The analysis focuses on the food trade sector, which illustrates well the social processes of informalization and is the arena where major struggles between the rich and the poor unfold in Bissau. Trade has been an historically important activity in the city and its importance has probably increased in the last couple of decades.

On the one hand, in spite of an extremely peripheral position in the global economy, growing volumes of international commodities are channelled through the city. On the other hand, increasing numbers of Bissauans rely on trade activities for survival. Indeed, the range of options for income generating activities is narrow. The industrial sector is very small and declining, along with a shrinking public sector. Bissau is a small capital city, with a population estimated at something over 300,000 inhabitants. Beyond the old colonial centre, the urban landscape is dominated by unplanned settlements, including many unplanned market places. The largest of these market places was reported to gather about 3,000 traders in the late 1990s.

The analysis is based on both available literature on the Guinean process of adjustment and my own fieldwork conducted in 1992, 1995 and 1999, when I studied household food strategies, informal livelihoods and social networks among disadvantaged groups in Bissau. A survey of 453 households was conducted in two neighbourhoods in Bissau, covering close to 10 per cent of their populations. The survey included information on the trading activities of household members who headed small trading enterprises. In addition, qualitative interviews were conducted with the heads of about sixty trading enterprises. The majority of these were small traders selected on the basis of the household survey but handfuls were engaged in wholesale and importexport enterprises. Government officials connected to market activities were also interviewed.

INFORMALITY IN THE PRE-ADJUSTMENT ERA

Guinea-Bissau gained independence in 1974 after eleven years of war with Portugal, the colonial power. During this period, the liberation party PAIGC (Partido Africano para a Independencia da Guine e Cabo Verde) succeeded in mobilising a large segment of the population, in establishing alternative systems of distribution of goods and services and in instituting local government structures that functioned more or less democratically. At independence, people's political engagement was high. The single party proclaimed itself as the leading force in society and declared a socialist orientation towards development. The state assumed a leading role in the economy.

Among other things, it largely monopolized external trade and established a network of some 230 commercial outlets throughout the country, the People's Stores. Their function was to collect agricultural produce from peasants and supply consumer and producer goods, at prices fixed by the state. Only a few years after independence, disappointment started mounting.

The state, increasingly centralized and repressive, alienated itself from the masses. The political elite became insulated from popular influence. Mass organizations were controlled by the Party and did not allow for participation in top-level decisions. The government distanced itself from initial social goals and failed to improve the conditions of the population. In fact, government policies turned the terms of trade against producers. In the sphere of distribution, the People's Stores were insufficient in their coverage of the territory. They functioned inefficiently and irregularly and shortages in consumer goods were frequent. The party rapidly lost its political and economic credibility.

The responses of Guineans to these worsening conditions are described in a number of texts, sometimes in a "disengagement" vein. Succinctly, "producers became increasingly unwilling to cooperate and sacrifice to maintain the state", Galli and Jones argue (1987:108). Some emigrated to Senegal and Gambia to grow cash crops there instead. There was a tendency for peasants to cut back on sales of rice, the main staple. Sales of export crops to official outlets also declined sharply, as producers sold their goods at higher prices through clandestine networks.

Acting in the interstices of the state's commercial network, the Dyulas, a group of professional itinerant traders that has been active in West Africa for centuries, continued to move goods across borders and to be a major source of supply for many villages. They offered an alternative to official channels, which paid disadvantageous prices and had frequent supply disruptions. This reportedly intensified smuggling of rice and cash crops across borders.

The far-reaching effects of these popular responses are also discussed by the same authors. Diversion of crops from official channels and the large scale of smuggling deprived the government of taxes but also of export products and thus of foreign exchange. The government losses were estimated at US$14 million in 1983. This decline in domestic revenues eventually contributed to an increase in state dependence on external assistance for importing food and covering the budget deficit, which resulted in a growing external debt.

The disengagement argument often focuses attention on resistance by rural producers. The above analyses on Guinea-Bissau also give little attention to what was happening in urban areas, while rural people were supposedly disengaging. The city of Bissau is mainly portrayed as a consumer of a large share of the national resources, the beneficiary of state policies and an enclave increasingly distanced from the rural masses. The little that has been written allows, however, for some reflections on the problems that urban residents were facing during this period and how they were responding.

Continuing a trend already clear in the colonial time, supply of basic goods such as food to the city was largely dependent on international sources, aid and externally financed imports, as the government seems to have been unable to buy enough rice from domestic producers. Given the trade deficit and the lack of foreign exchange, the government cut down on imports of basic items. This situation resulted in chronic shortages and empty stores in Bissau, where rice shortages were acute in the 1970s and early 1980s.

Ration slips were required to buy imported goods in state stores and a large amount of time was spent queuing to acquire them. The urban population often had to resort to the parallel market with its speculative prices. But urban groups were positioned differently to cope with or even benefit from the scarcities, and were not all affected in the same way. According to the same authors, government employees had priority to food rations. Access to basic items was thus facilitated by having a public job or contacts with the party and party organizations.

Two groups in particular seem to have benefited from chronic food scarcities and the related deepening external dependence for food. These were high rank state officials controlling the flow of imports and the employees in state stores. Bigman refers to "a certain amount of corruption and nepotism" among the latter. Galli and Jones say that shortages were partly due to "increasingly widespread corruption which pilfered supplies and skimmed off profits". State officials took part in large scale smuggling and hoarding of goods and made "them scarce in order to charge exorbitant prices on the black market".

Fernandes (1994) also asserts that basic goods could rarely be found in official stores but circulated through "clientelist networks", originating among state employees and nationalized enterprises. While the latter gradually decayed, he argues, private fortunes accumulated by using informal channels of circulation. These groups thus derived great power from their privileged access to goods in an environment of scarcity as well as from their manipulation of the interface between official and parallel distribution systems.

The majority of the population in the city had no protection against this kind of exploitation by state officials. Some people were in a position to cultivate a relationship with them or with a friend or relative holding a public job. But a large number were recent migrants lacking both access to public work and state contacts, as Bigman (1993) states. This large group had to find ways to survive outside the wage and state marketing systems. Petty trading, especially by women, grew as a way of survival.

The state's attitude to this increasing informal economy was negative. It fought the Dyulas as they were powerful competitors and directly inflicted losses on the state's coffers. Making strategic use of a socialist morality, the state denounced Dyulas as being immoral elements in society. At times, Dyula traders were put in jail for long periods without a trial accused of hoarding and speculation. The government also antagonized other groups trying to make a living in petty trade.

According to Bigman (1993) women who travelled to rural areas to buy produce to sell in the city had to pass intranational checkpoints set up by the government to control contraband. In Bissau the police harassed sellers in the market places, confiscating produce. Even these petty traders were accused of hoarding goods and became the scapegoats for the food shortages.

Both Funk (1991) and Galli and Jones (1987) report that antagonism towards the state and its agents grew. State officials were seen as responsible for the shortages and as guilty of corruption. Political channels were however unavailable for expressing discontent. So when a factional division turned into a military coup in 1980, conditions were ripe for widespread popular support for the new regime. The coup became known as "the rice coup". Some party cadres deeply involved in irregular practices were exposed and purged. However, the change in regime did not put an end to these practices nor did it bring much change in the level of repression or the material conditions of the masses.

Informal systems of distribution on the other hand were gradually taking more and more space while the performance of state institutions weakened. The fact that the government forced journalists to lie about the date of arrival of the next shipment of rice (Galli and Jones 1987) indicates its vulnerability in the face of alternative economic agents. In spite of harassment, Dyulas prospered and petty traders resisted and increased in numbers. These multiple individual responses were having a collective impact.

Thus, elements of disengagement were at work during the pre-liberalization era in the sense that producers and traders were creating a space of autonomy from state channels. Indeed, GuineaBissau and its capital seem to be as good an example of disengagement as those chosen by proponents of the disengagement approach. The similarities with for example Ghana and Guinea (Azarya and Chazan 1987) or Dar es Salaam (Tripp 1997) are many.

But a disengagement account does not provide a complete picture of the process of informalization in Guinea-Bissau. Firstly, as discussed above, parallel to popular responses that were antagonistic to state policies, there was one small group composed partly of state officials who operated in both the formal and the informal economy and thrived on the manipulation of the two. Secondly, the possibility of informal traders attaining a degree of autonomy from state channels and the formal economy probably varied for different groups among them. While those dealing in imported goods were probably directly or indirectly dependent on state officials for supply, those selling local produce may have enjoyed a greater degree of autonomy. Similarly, the possibility of straddling the formal and the informal realms, which may constitute a valuable resource for survival and/or accumulation, seems not to have been open to everyone. Further research is needed to clarify these issues in the pre-adjustment era.

Thirdly, the relations between informal actors need to be addressed. This issue is left blank in the literature on Guinea-Bissau as attention is focused on the contradiction state-society. For example, the relations between Dyulas and rural producers may not have been all that symbiotic. Galli and Jones (1987) state that Dyulas offered better prices to producers than official outlets but also charged high prices for consumer goods and that peasants were annoyed by this but could not change the situation as they could not rely on the irregular official market.

Although the parallel economy in this period in Guinea-Bissau seems to support the disengagement thesis, it is likely that at least one part of those involved in it, i.e. rural producers, would not consider themselves as happily "disengaged". Their supposed disengagement from the state may have meant a forced engagement in other relations of exploitation, such as potentially those with Dyulas.

Finally, one should also point out that people's avoidance of state institutions and policies was nothing new or unique to the post-independence state, as it only continued well established responses from colonial times. In addition, it also involved pre-colonial regional patterns of exchange, as represented by the Dyula traders' networks. This would justify a deeper analysis of how such ancient forms of relations are reworked in a context of disengagement.

THE INFORMAL BOOM IN THE ADJUSTMENT ERA

In a situation of deep dependence on external assistance, the government of Guinea-Bissau negotiated with international financial institutions a first programme of economic stabilization in 1983 and a structural adjustment programme in 1986. As in other countries undergoing adjustment programmes, the Guinean government was urged to liberalize trade, to deregulate and to decriminalize the "informal sector", which instead was to be regarded as a dynamic and competitive sector of the economy. Under the pressure of donors, there was a major change in official policy and discourse towards informal actors.

International institutions advocating these policies were, in this sense, themselves contributing to the expansion of an informal economy. While the state bureaucracy was reluctant to give up its monopoly over trade as this was one of its major sources of power and wealth, the adjustment program would bring new economic opportunities into sight for this group, facilitating its compliance.

The liberalization of domestic and external trade resulted in a more regular and diversified supply of imported goods and in a great increase in commercial activity in the city. This expanding activity has taken mainly an informal character: on the one hand, a part of the operations of larger private trade firms is poorly regulated by the state; on the other hand, there has been a proliferation of petty traders who are denied protection by the state. So I will proceed by looking closer into each of these two sub-spheres within the informal trade sector: that which derives from the accumulation strategies of capitalist merchants and that which results from the strategies for survival of disadvantaged groups.

INFORMALIZATION FOR ACCUMULATION

Structural adjustment policies have imposed heavy costs on the majority of Bissauans. But a minority has benefited greatly, as it was in a position to rapidly seize new economic opportunities emerging in the context of adjustment. There is a consensus among observers of the adjustment process in Guinea-Bissau about whom this minority is and the means by which it attained a position of dominance in the informal trade sector. Firstly, from the early 1980s, exports of a new cash crop, cashew nuts, experienced a dramatic increase.

Import-export firms have made considerable profits by bartering imported rice for cashew nuts with small producers and by speculating on rice prices in the city. Secondly, a large amount of adjustment credits were made available to importers in order to support the balance of payments and sustain the flow of imports of basic goods. These credits were amassed by the state marketing agency (which continued to be involved in external trade for some years), by high rank government officials acting as private importers, and by the new "independent" private merchants.

A high level of default on loan repayment ensued, which several have interpreted as being possible due to an intimate relation between importers-exporters and the government. Firstly, those supposedly independent from the state were reported to be able to count on its protection and privileged access to adjustment credits. Secondly, the overlapping of trade and public functions set in motion a type of liberalization adapted to the interests of traders-officials.

Fernandes (1994) argues that liberalization in Guinea-Bissau turned formerly clandestine private accumulation by bureaucrats into a legitimate one and the state bureaucratic class into a commercial bureaucracy. Thus, one can hardly say that the transition from a state monopoly of the economy with state bureaucrats in privileged positions in a liberalized and informal economy led to a significant decrease in their influence over the economy.

More significantly, this small group that enjoyed the protection of and access to the state and the resources controlled by it came to occupy dominant positions in informal trade, especially in those sub-sectors directly linked with international trade. Indeed, just like former parastatal agents, they seem to have partly derived this position from their ability to operate in both the informal and formal spheres.

With their privileged access to formal institutions such as bank credits and the state apparatus, importers have been able to exert significant influence over the whole chain of distribution of imported goods, determining prices and access to informal credit. Concerning the latter, Monteiro (2001), in a study of the largest market place in the city, discovered that importers dominate the informal financial market in Bissau. Large numbers of traders are seemingly hindered from direct access to bank loans and depend on informal credit suppliers.

Through my own interviews with some six wholesale and

importexport enterprises and key informants I became aware of the hierarchical business networks linking patrons and middlemen in the cashew-rice business. Middlemen who succeed in reaching an informal contract with a patron, i.e. a contract sanctioned by social rather than legal codes, often on the basis of shared cultural norms, kinship or acquaintance, gain access to credit and to a niche in the growth sector of the Guinean economy.

But they also enter a situation of dependency and acquire a subordinate position which greatly decreases their autonomy of action and ultimately works for the benefit of the patron. These vertical networks tend to be exclusivist and tightly drawn and tend to frustrate the efforts of others to penetrate them. In this way, they contribute to a visible ethnic and gender segmentation in the urban market.

Merchants in Guinea-Bissau are able to draw on a large supply of informal labour. At the production end, the cashew harvest is carried out by seasonal workers, including large numbers of Bissauan women, who work on small farms under conditions unregulated by the state. In town, big merchants make extensive use of casual labour. They hire large groups of men for short periods, to load and unload the ships and trucks, as and when they are needed.

As workers themselves have explained to me, they are paid by the day or by task. When the task is completed and payment is made, there are no further obligations between the parties. These short-term, often unwritten agreements mean for the workers that they cannot expect compensation from either employer or the state for periods without work or for accidents on the job. These agreements thus free the employer from any lasting responsibilities towards labour.

In addition to the large numbers of cashew pickers and casual workers, merchants have increasingly made use of informal outlets for retailing their commodities. Gomes (1993) maintains that many merchants imported goods with adjustment loans and then resold the merchandise in the parallel market, allowing them to collect "astronomic profits" by taking advantage of the differences in exchange rates between the parallel and the official markets.

Monteiro (2001) echoes common local perceptions when he states that many informal businesses at the largest market place in Bissau are owned by "invisible" owners who work in the central and local government. In my fieldwork I interviewed some twenty retailers of imported rice who were supplied by wholesale stores. I found that merchants had penetrated peripheral spontaneous market places in the city and subordinated a myriad of small retailers, either through exploitative price practices or credit agreements. For the smallest kind of retailers, often elderly women and young girls, incomes oscillated between very low and nil. Drawn into these international commodity circuits, rice retailers became the lowest link of a vertical network facilitating accumulation at the top.

The emerging picture is one of an informalization process favouring merchants as the informal strategies of well-to-do operators facilitate accumulation while the current form of economic liberalization is not conducive to a regulatory environment that protects the self-employed and informal labour.

In sum, in the context of economic liberalization, accumulation by big merchants operating in international commodity markets is facilitated by their use of informal strategies. At the same time, many unprotected small retailers and casual workers directly linked to those merchants are left on the threshold of survival.

INFORMALIZATION FOR SURVIVAL

The informalization of Bissau's economy is also manifested in an increased reliance by popular groups on informal activities for survival, in the context of the austerity related to adjustment policies, and of a small and declining state regulated wage sector. The household survey elicited data on how household members generated cash incomes. Trade was by far the most common source of income, with 66 per cent of all registered and processed income activities. Retail trade of food items, including prepared food, drinks and charcoal was the most widespread.

All other income activities were much less common. They included brick making, taxi driving, domestic service, dressmaking, car repairs and work at the port. Households also engaged in various forms of food production, including farming and fishing, for their own consumption or for sale. The larger share of the households (57 per cent) had no written contracts for their work, no regular income or paid sick leave, thus conforming to the most common attributes of "informal work".

Only a minority (9 per cent) depended exclusively on regulated wage work while one third relied on a mixture of work situations. The general picture is that the urban households rely heavily on informal trade in goods and services. Within the food trade category, the most common items being sold were vegetables, fruits and locally produced cashew wine. Most traders got their merchandise from other traders or producers or through their own production and a smaller share from wholesalers. Virtually all food trade enterprises (a total of 527 enterprises) were retail enterprises and the majority were one-person enterprises. Food trade shows a gender and ethnic based specialization, with women from coastal ethnic groups and men from the Eastern groups dominating numerically.

Given the lack of alternatives, small scale trade was the source of income most readily available to large segments of the urban population. Unsurprisingly, there has been a true explosion in the number of small scale traders and a mushrooming of market places in the city, as reported by different officials interviewed and other studies. Most of these market places are of a spontaneous kind, i.e. they consist mainly of precarious structures built by the traders themselves.

Most of them offer mainly low cost items, as they cater for poor neighbourhoods. In fact, while spontaneous markets and commercial activity proliferate in the periphery of the city, the old commercial centre in the city core has decayed. Several modern retail outlets selling mainly high cost imported goods have closed down and the Central Market, which once supplied the entire city, is now called "the cooperants' market", which reflects its narrow clientele of aid workers and other expatriates. The locus of commercial activity has clearly shifted to the periphery of the planned city and much of it operates according to informal rules rather than the laws of the state.

These trends require a nuanced interpretation. On the one hand, they reflect the creativeness of small actors and the impressive collective impact of their individual responses. Small informal traders have drastically changed the face of the city in a way clearly beyond the control of the government. In this sense, a number of them may have conquered for themselves a space of relative autonomy. On the other hand, while the efforts of popular groups are impressive, the trends also reflect a darker reality.

Firstly, the rise in demand for retail outlets offering low cost items signals an impoverishment of a large share of the population. Secondly, the growth of informal trade and the informal economy in general can be partly attributed to the burdens that have been placed on the urban population by adjustment related austerity, in the form of retrenchments, frozen and delayed salaries and high inflation. Low rank public workers were forced to seek refuge in informal activities to supplement declining real incomes or to mitigate the effects of redundancy.

For better positioned civil servants, their public contacts and access to public equipment and financial assets have been said to have helped them to become owners of vehicles for collective transport, of repair shops and other informal enterprises. The majority of the urban population, usually not in a position to straddle the two spheres or lacking access to employment or connections in the public sector, has had to multiply its income generating activities in the informal economy.

Some have managed to establish viable businesses. But many traders live hand to mouth. In almost 80 per cent of the 527 food trade enterprises registered during my household survey, respondents said they were not able to make any savings and a large share spent most of their incomes on food. My interviews with some sixty traders, many of whom were women, also revealed many cases in which respondents declared decreased scale of operation and longer working hours in an attempt to attain former levels of consumption.

Their incomes were being crushed between higher costs of operation and a lower purchasing power among their customers, increased competition among an expanding number of small retailers, or, as in the case of rice retailers, exploitation by suppliers. A large share reported that they were frequently unable to recover their small working capital by the end of the day or that they were often forced to spend it on food and other necessities. Sustaining their trading activities was dependent upon assistance from husbands, relatives, credit from suppliers and participation in savings clubs.

Thus, an important share of food traders seemed increasingly marginalized from the accelerated economic growth that has reportedly been taking place in the country. While not much can be said here about the other sectors of the Bissauan informal economy, these findings ressemble those of other studies on trends in informal economies in African cities. Neo-liberal assumptions about the potential of informal work for providing sufficient incomes for the working poor in a context of adjustment have not come true for many of the respondents in this study.

In the context of economic liberalization, the practices of the local government towards these small informal traders are enlightening. Despite a supposedly positive policy towards informal actors, municipal agents have in practice remained essentially hostile to them. Some of the interviewed officials expressed a negative attitude towards spontaneous market places. Municipal collectors operate in all market places including those erected by the sellers themselves.

These markets do not offer any kind of municipal services, but nevertheless charge daily fees that are higher than officially stipulated and are discriminatory for small retailers. When business lags sellers often have to pay repeated fees for the same merchandise, further depleting their meagre income. Relations between sellers and collectors are therefore strained.

The relations between local government in general and trader associations in the largest market place of Bissau, Bandim, have been characterized by Monteiro (2001) as antagonistic; traders complain about the oppressiveness and arbitrariness of public agents as well as their lack of accountability.

Thus a major contradiction between a section of the informal economy and public institutions remains, albeit seemingly in a less pervasive way than during the state monopoly period when public agents determined prices and levels of supply. One way of verifying the popular perception that officials from local and central government are involved in informal ventures would be to identify who is being harassed and who maintains good relations with the municipal agents.

Considering the above trends, it is not surprising that contradictions only increased during the adjustment period within the informal economy and in Bissauan society in general. These contradictions were laid bare in the aftermath of an armed conflict in 1998–99.

In tracing the evolution of informal trade in Bissau in the last two decades, one finds that a combination of processes has been at work; processes which are often analysed separately. During the period of state monopoly over trade, private illegal traders increased in numbers in response to the failures and unfavourable practices of state agencies. They were both escaping government control and posing serious competition to state channels of trade. In this sense, they could be said to be disengaging from the state. In the mid-1980s international financial institutions urged the state to liberalize the economy and to decriminalize informal activity.

In this way they themselves became important actors in the process of informalization. In a liberalized economic environment, informal trade activities grew in Bissau as a result of both popular efforts for survival and strategies of accumulation. Import-export firms have made extensive use of informal strategies which assist them in keeping a foot in the international commodity market. Meanwhile, the majority of the urban population, hit by adjustment austerity, often multiply their survival activities in petty trade, the economic sphere available to them.

Concerning the relations between the public/formal institutions and informal actors, both elements of opposition and symbiosis could be identified, in the 1974–83 periods and from 1983 onwards. Insisting either on a total disengagement from the state or on a complete integration between formal and informal does not take us very far in understanding the politics of informalization. Some informal actors may have antagonistic relations with the formal sphere and struggle for autonomy from it while others maintain alliances with it.

There seems to exist a selective permeability between formal and informal realms, where opportunities for straddling may not be equally open for all. In Bissau's trade economy, a restricted group enjoyed a privileged relationship with the state and seemed to be particularly well positioned to manipulate the formalinformal interface and built their fortunes in this way. The precariousness of their position surfaced however at moments of political upheaval, as in 1980 and in 1998–99.

Some small trade enterprises have been able to expand or find a viable niche in the context of economic liberalization in Bissau. But a large share of the food traders has seen their conditions deteriorate. While data on other sub-sectors of the economy are not available, these findings about small scale food traders in Bissau suggest they have not been "empowered" by the current wave of informalization, as is often assumed in the neo-liberal literature. Rather, small traders continue to struggle on a variety of fronts, including against big merchants and a persistently hostile local government. A pertinent issue for further research would be the ways they organize in order to struggle against the deterioration of conditions and rights in the informal economy.

3

Economic Restructuring in Zambia

The frequent use of the home for economic activities must be seen in the context of an increasingly harsh macro-economic environment. Over the past two decades, Zambia has experienced a severe economic crisis, which has led to high rates of urban poverty. This has been partly the result of a drastic decline in formal employment opportunities mostly due to the poor performance of large state enterprises the bulk of which have since the 1990s been either liquidated or privatized. Increasing proportions of the urban population are no longer able directly or indirectly to rely on formal employment or housing. Cities on the Copperbelt which were established to serve the copper mines have been particularly badly affected.

At the national level formal employment declined from 30 per cent of the labour force in 1980 to less than 10 per cent in 1990. Muneku (2001) reports that formal employment has been declining at an average annual rate of 2 per cent. Between 1992 and 1995 a total of 77,300 formal jobs were lost, while informal sector employment increased from about 1.8 million in 1986 to 2.3 million in 1993. It must be noted that whilst loss of formal sector jobs affects mostly males, women however are less likely to get a formal job in the first place and therefore predominate in the informal sector. In 1993 they represented 53 per cent of the 2.3 million employed there.

Further decline in formal employment is expected as more people lose jobs through the continuing privatization and restructuring of public enterprises, government departments and the newly privatized copper mines. Alongside this shift in the labour market there has been the accelerated growth of poverty. Urban poverty has escalated; the percentage of urban households living below the poverty line increased from 4 to just under 50 between 1975 and 1991. Substantial declines in urban real incomes have occurred. Incomes in the formal sector have often fallen fastest, forcing even those who are in formal employment to seek supplementary incomes within the informal sector.

HOME BASED ENTERPRISES

Hays-Mitchell (1993) has argued that the distinction between reproduction (domestic activities) and production (economic activities) is not clearly drawn in developing country households. Despite this, in many countries including Zambia, planning and land use regulations are designed to promote the separation of these two activities. In Zambia for instance, Hansen (1975:791) describes how, in the early 1970s, even in the low-income neighbourhoods, the use of the home for economic functions was illegal and how people made every effort to hide these activities from the authorities. Despite the desire by authorities to separate the two, home based enterprises (HBEs) continue to proliferate in many cities.

In Zambia, home based enterprises date back to the colonial period when residents of the 'African compounds' would engage in such activities as beer brewing, trading or carpentry. The Central Statistical Office (1997) reported that at least 50 per cent of all informal sector workers in Zambia operate from home. This chapter draws on the work by Lipton (1980:190–91) who describes small scale informal activities as "family mode of production enterprises" (FMPEs) whose key characteristic is the control of the major factors of production (i.e. money, time, space and labour) by the family. Because they are owned by the family, these resources are fungible, i.e. they can be converted swiftly, conveniently and without loss from one use to another.

The flexibility of housing space means that even those without access to serviced industrial/commercial land can afford to engage in economic activities. The fungibility of time means that even those who are unable to work full time, such as women and children, and those who are formally employed but have some spare time or require extra income can also engage in informal income generating activities. Their "extended fungibility" in Lipton's terminology, makes home based enterprises an ideal strategy for making a living and having access to shelter.

As Moser and Holland (1997:50) have argued "Housing can be an important asset that cushions households against severe poverty particularly during times of economic adversity". Because the informal sector survives on family resources, the home and the HBE constitute an important entry point for new informal sector entrants. A lot of work on home based enterprises has focused on low-income neighbourhoods. However HBEs are not restricted to low-income groups. Strassman (1986) for example presents an analysis of HBEs in four different housing categories in Lima, Peru.

Similarly in a study of 172 households in Kitwe, Kazimbaya-Senkwe and Mwale (2001) found that 55 per cent of households in periurban squatter areas, 50 per cent in low cost housing areas, 30 per cent in medium cost, and 34 per cent in high cost areas had an HBE. The spread of HBEs in all housing categories can be taken to suggest either the dearth or unattractiveness of formal employment, a laxity or failure of planning authorities to enforce land use regulations or the spreading of poverty across all social groups.

Olufemi (2000) reports a similar situation in Nigeria where HBEs have spread from low-income to high-income neighbourhoods. An analysis of HBEs therefore presents an opportunity to follow both livelihoods and land use trends through the eyes of those directly affected.

THE COPPERBELT PROVINCE

The Copperbelt Province is the second most urbanized province in Zambia, after Lusaka. Of the province's population 86 per cent reside in 7 urban districts and the remaining 14 per cent in 3 rural districts. The 7 urban districts constitute the economic and industrial heart of Zambia, housing the 7 major copper mines which were owned by the government through the Zambia Consolidated Copper Mines (ZCCM) until March 2000, when they were privatized. Copper accounts for over 80 per cent of the total export earnings of the country.

In 1989, the province had over 355 manufacturing industries ranging from heavy duty engineering to textiles and banking, the bulk of them operating as suppliers to the mines. The province like the rest of the country has been going through a period of economic decline in the last couple of decades. The last 10 years have witnessed significant decline in the formal economy. At the same time, the country has tried to address some of the structural problems in the economy through a World Bank/IMF supported Structural Adjustment Programme (SAP).

Part of the SAP measures have been the liberalization of the economy, which has left many industries exposed to outside competition. This has resulted in the closure of companies that cannot compete and others have rationalized in order to stay afloat. It must be noted that in comparison to the national figures, the Copperbelt Province still has a significant number of people working in the formal sector. For example, in a study of 722 households on the Copperbelt, Malama and Kazimbaya-Senkwe (2001) found that at least 55 per cent of household heads were employed in the formal sector, 36 per cent were employed in the informal sector and the remaining 9 per cent were either in full time agriculture, retired or had no source of income.

The new owners of the copper mines have however indicated that a significant number of the labour force have to be laid off. At the same time, the government plan for the public service is to reduce the number of civil servants from 115,000 in 2000 to about 10,000–12,000 by 2010.

A significant number of these job losses will be on the Copperbelt which houses the second largest number of government departments in the country. However the rate of job creation in the formal sector is very low. For instance a recent study of 207 retrenched miners on the Copperbelt found that only 15 per cent had been able to regain formal employment. With little discussion and no concrete action about redeployment of these retrenchees informal activities are bound to increase.

HOME BASED ENTERPRISES IN KITWE

Kitwe is the second largest city on the Copperbelt and the third largest city in Zambia. The city has a geographical area of approximately 447km, with a population of about 400.000 people and an annual growth rate of 1.1 per cent. The town evolved as a copper mining town in the early 1930s, and like 5 of the other copper mining towns is made up of two townships, one administered by the mining company and the other by the Kitwe City Council, hereafter referred to as Mine and Council Township respectively. The study by Malama and Kazimbaya-Senkwe (2001) referred to above found that only 43 per cent of household heads in Kitwe were formally employed. 50 per cent were in full time informal work while the remaining, either, worked in agriculture, were retired or had no income.

Both the council and mine townships' residential areas have developed on the basis of the income level of residents, namely low, middle and high income. The Mine Township also has one housing estate with 'substandard dwellings'. The Council Township also has two middle-income areas which have been developed as site and service schemes. A total of over 30 squatter settlements are scattered around the city. Home based enterprises (HBEs) are present in all neighbourhoods.

Inspired by the work undertaken by Kellett and Tipple (1997) in India and by Kellett et al. (2000) in Ipusukilo Compound in Kitwe in 1999, a pilot study was drawn up in order to explore how home based enterprises were established, how the home was adapted to house these economic activities as well as the challenges and opportunities presented by working from home. Particular emphasis was placed on describing how workplace and residential activities and spaces were integrated.

The study used in-depth conversational interviews which were recorded on tape and supplemented by notes, physical observation and a follow-up questionnaire, relying on construction of case histories as the central means of data collection and analysis. A research assistant conducted the interviews in January 2000, for 2 weeks. Due to the preliminary nature of the study, the first two available houses with evident home based enterprises were picked in each neighbourhood although a deliberate effort was made to pick two different types of HBEs in each neighbourhood.

A total of 12 respondents (2 from each of 6 neighbourhoods) were targeted, but only 11 interviews were transcribed and analysed, as one respondent did not have time to complete the interview. The interviews were conducted either in the vernacular (Bemba) or English depending on the ability of the respondent to converse in English. The study had three main aims: the first was to define variables that would be used to explain the causes, nature and extent of mixed use in residential areas including the similarities and differences of these between different neighbourhoods. The second was to explore the data collected in order to establish appropriate methods of questioning, data gathering and analysis, and the third to define a set of research questions to be tested in a larger survey, which would provide inputs for policy.

THE CASE STUDY TOWNSHIPS

The neighbourhoods chosen were Ipusukilo, Buchi, Chamboli, Ndeke Village, Nkana West and Riverside representing four neighbourhood types: Ipusukilo is a squatter settlement with over 16,000 inhabitants occupying self built houses on undefined plots and with no access to publicly provided urban services such as water and electricity. Buchi with 9,600 people and Chamboli with over 23,000 inhabitants, are both low-medium income neighbourhoods with houses built by the Kitwe City Council (KCC) and the mining company respectively.

The average plot size in these neighbourhoods is about 300m and house size of about 120m. All houses in Chamboli have a connection to water and electricity whilst most houses in Buchi had until 2001 access only to communal standpoints and up to now still have no electricity. Ndeke Village with a population of just over 8,400 is a medium cost neighbourhood initially planned to house KCC workers but later allocated to private individuals who built their own houses according to council approved plans. Average plot size is about 600m and house size of about 240m.

Main service lines for water and electricity have been provided but each individual household has to arrange to get connected. Nkana West with population of 5,190 and Riverside with 12,000 inhabitants are both high cost neighbourhoods built by the mines and KCC respectively with average plot sizes of 1,500m and house sizes of 375m. Most of the new houses in both townships are however self built. These houses have connections to all public services.

Households from very high-income areas and from substandard settlements were not included in the pilot study. In terms of employment levels in the six neighbourhoods, Malama and Kazimbaya-Senkwe (2001) found that in high cost areas like Riverside only about 20 per cent of household heads were engaged in the informal economy while the rest were formally employed.

The figures for informal employment in medium cost areas like Ndeke Village was about 50 per cent and that for low cost areas like Buchi was over 57 per cent. In the Mine Townships, a study of about 430 households found that 66 per cent were still in mine employment, 14 per cent were retrenched and the rest were either in government or private employment. The study also found that 34 per cent of the retrenched miners were re-employed in the informal sector and only 5 per cent had another job with regular income.

As yet no study has been done in Kitwe or the Copperbelt to show how the different HBE activities are typified in the different house categories or in specific neighbourhoods. However, data obtained by Kazimbaya-Senkwe and Mwale (2001) indicated that in peri-urban, low cost and medium cost areas, trading was the major activity, followed by carpentry, tailoring and chicken rearing. Chicken rearing was the major activity in high cost areas, followed by tailoring and trading. High cost areas like Riverside had a much wider range of activities, 8 types for 28 respondents, as opposed to peri-urban areas, where the 12 respondents were engaged in only two types of activities.

RANGE OF ECONOMIC ACTIVITIES

A wide range of economic activities is undertaken in homes. From the sample of 11 respondents, a total of 8 different activities were identified. All these activities except reed mat making, battery acid manufacture and shoe making were also identified in the Kazimbaya-Senkwe and Mwale study. These activities all fall neatly into the three categories of informal sector activity outlined by Bardouille (1991:24) namely petty trading or retailing, petty manufacturing and repair, and services. In several cases, there was more than one enterprise operating on the premises.

The female tailor for instance was also operating a hair saloon; the male tailor in Ipusukilo was also running a bar and renting out rooms; the mat-maker was also selling some vegetables and the male trader was also running a barber-shop. Interestingly, none of those respondents engaged in manufacturing jobs (i.e. the carpenters and the acid manufacturer) were running other businesses. This finding raises important questions about the relative productivity, as well as the time and capital requirements of different types of HBEs.

Seven of the enterprises had begun operations in the 1990s, the remaining four dated from the 1980s. Two important issues emerge from this finding. Firstly, home based enterprises do not appear to be transient or stop-gap measures, but have been the main lifeline for some households particularly those in the older generation. This notwithstanding, the idea of working from home appears to have increased in the 1990s, linking the HBEs to both the decline in the national economy and the related growth of the informal sector.

Most of the HBEs studied were not registered with any formal institution. The exceptions were the nursery schools, the battery acid manufacturer and the female tailor who were registered with the Registrar of Companies. If legality is the main determining factor, they should not be considered as informal sector activities. However, these activities exhibit other characteristics of informal enterprises in Zambia, such as the small size of the establishment (1–5 persons), and workers working for their own account.

The battery acid maker required a yearly licence from the copper mines to allow him to purchase acid from them. The one HBE which seemed to have a link with the local Council was the young male trader who did not have a licence but somehow paid a 'personal levy' twice weekly to the council. It is difficult from the preliminary results to explain why this is so. Nonetheless, it suggests acceptance of HBEs by different organizations, which may cause confusion if the different organizations do not agree on the status of the HBE. For instance does possession of a Certificate of Incorporation legitimate the use of the house for HBEs?

It also raises the issue of equity between those whose HBEs are approved by authorities and therefore subject to taxes and other regulations and those that are not. It is worth noting that apart from the female trader in Ndeke Village and the tailor in Ipusukilo who indicated being harassed by the Kitwe City Council, none of the other respondents mentioned harassment as a particular problem. In effect, laxity on the part of the planning authority might have contributed to the spread of home based enterprises particularly in formal housing areas.

Home based enterprises are operated by both men and women. In this survey however, 7 of the 11 respondents were male. Other studies have shown that more women are generally engaged in trading activities, but in this study we deliberately sought to include a variety of enterprises. Which ones are easily accessible to women and the gender specificity of various enterprises would need a quantitative survey. In this survey, the nursery schools were operated by women while activities such as carpentry, battery acid manufacture and shoemaking were operated by men. Tailoring and trading were not gender specific.

Studies undertaken by ILO/SATEP (1982), Milimo and Fisseha (1986) and the CSO (1988) found that the average age of informal sector employees in Zambia was above 30 years, but not below 20 or above 45. In this survey, 4 of the 11 respondents were in their early 20s, the youngest being 20, 3 were in their 40s, while the eldest was 55. Another interesting result was that the 4 oldest respondents were engaged in manufacturing. They also had the oldest enterprises.

Seven had attended formal school. Their education levels were however fairly low. The most educated were the nursery school teachers. To run a home based nursery school seems to require some form of tertiary education. These schools are recognized by the local authorities and are thus subject to formal regulations and inspections. All the others had learned their new skills 'on the job' with 3 of them abandoning formally acquired skills. The shoemaker for instance was a trained welder, the carpenter in Chamboli was an electrician, and the male tailor was a marketing clerk.

This result does not suggest that formal training is useless but rather indicates its limited usability outside the formal sector, necessitating informal retraining for new entrants to the informal sector. This preliminary conclusion must of course be verified in a larger scale survey. An important question in the survey was the role of spouses in the HBEs. Eight of the respondents were married. Only one, the shoemaker, indicated that his spouse was directly involved. She had been instrumental in setting up the business, having taught him how to use the sewing machine.

At the time of the survey she was running her own tailoring business but was also responsible for selling the shoes her husband made at the local markets. The wife of the carpenter was a full time housewife but occasionally assisted him with purchasing materials. In all but one of the other 6 cases, the spouses got incomes from other sources, and provided both financial and moral support to their spouses' HBEs. The exception was the husband of the female tailor in Ndeke who was not employed and who was not even involved with the HBE. This finding shows that presently both men and women are contributing to household income. The results also indicate that women still bear responsibility for traditional household chores.

Whilst all the HBE operators were adults, children were in almost all cases involved in one way or the other with the HBE except where they were very young. The shoemaker for instance did not employ any outsider, but relied on his children both to make and sell shoes. Similarly the female tailor worked with her son in tailoring whilst one of her daughters was in charge of the hair saloon. The male trader was assisted by his school-going brothers and sisters. In this way the children learn important life skills which they would not learn in formal school. It also raises a question of the impact of economic hardship on school performance particularly for girls who traditionally are also expected to assist with household chores.

All respondents valued formal education highly and all of them ensured that their school-going children remained in school. Whilst the children were expected to assist with the business, the HBE was not seen as their future employment opportunity. In many instances, the respondents valued the usefulness of passing on their skills to their children as a means of ensuring survival. The question of how children divide their time between assisting with household chores, home based enterprises and school-work is an important one. From another angle, one could also ask whether HBEs have the potential to contribute to the development of better parent-child relationships due to constant interaction.

The HBE operators also relied on informal support networks involving friends and business partners. During the interview with the mat-maker for instance, it soon became clear that she did not work alone but was part of a group of four women, some of whom joined in the interview later. These women had a system whereby at any given time, the whole group made and sold mats for only one group member. The mat women also assisted each other in times of need including paying bills for any member who was unwell. In addition, the women collected the reeds from the river as a group, with some playing the role of watch-women against crocodiles. Mat making was conducted from the house of the oldest woman from whom all the others had learnt their skills.

Similarly, the male tailor worked with his father-in-law and the two were in the process of expanding his tailoring shop to cater for a bar. They also had plans to employ a bar tender, who would sleep in an annex to the bar without paying rent but who would also not be paid for acting as night watch-man. The carpenter in Chamboli was assisted by his neighbours to ensure that the items he displayed by the roadside were not stolen or tampered with by children. And the female trader had a neighbour who looked after her shop while she herself went to church on Sundays.

Seven of the respondents owned the houses from which they were operating. The others were the nursery teacher in Ndeke Village who was renting the house for both domestic and business purposes; the carpenter in Riverside lived in another part of Kitwe but was renting the house in Riverside which he was using as a carpentry workshop; and the nursery teacher in Nkana West and the male trader who were operating from their parents' homes. Given that traditionally houses have been rented out for domestic purposes, it would be worth investigating whether this finding denotes a shift in perceptions of what legally and socially constitutes housing. In addition, it would be interesting to find out whether the traditional view of housing as a domestic sphere limits or prevents those households who are renting from developing HBEs and what alternative survival strategies they use.

Why Are People Involved in Home Based Enterprises? Respondents offered three reasons for why they were involved with HBEs: the need for employment and income, the type of enterprise they were involved in, and the advantage of working from home.

THE NEED FOR EMPLOYMENT AND INCOME

Respondents could be divided into five groups namely:

i. Those who had never been employed in the formal sector and had always relied on the informal sector for their economic survival (i.e. the female tailor, female trader and the female mat makers;

ii. Those who had been employed in the formal sector and then were severed through either retirement or retrenchment (i.e. the carpenter, the battery acid maker, the male tailor, the nursery teacher in Nkana West);

iii. Those that had been employed but severed themselves from the formal sector through resignation (i.e. the nursery teacher in Ndeke Village and the carpenter in Riverside);

iv. Those who were still employed but in need of an extra income (the shoemaker who was still working for ZCCM); and

v. Those who whilst being looked after by their parents still found it necessary to earn their own income. This last group included the male trader who had completed school a year earlier and was waiting to go to college, and the nursery teacher in Nkana West.

Here are both workers for whom the informal sector is seen as an employer of last resort because they have been displaced or are unable to find jobs in the formal sector and workers who by choice separate themselves from the formal sector because of its inadequacies. We see also the failure of the formal sector to provide for its workers when they retire. The carpenter in Chamboli for instance only got K12, 000,000 (US$3,243) as his retirement package after 35 years of employment. The cases of the shoemaker and the male trader also indicate the failure of the formal sector to provide adequate incomes, requiring supplements from the informal one.

It is perhaps not surprising then that apart from the young male trader, who was fresh out of school, none of the others were keen on formal sector employment. When asked whether they would accept a well paying formal job, all respondents indicated that they were better off working for themselves and would only accept a formal job if the pay was very high. Even the shoemaker had handed in his application to the mines for voluntary retrenchment so that he could concentrate on shoe making. The nursery teacher in Nkana West had been called for interviews at a 'formal' school but she decided it was not worth the trouble. This indicates a high level of disillusionment with the formal sector, as its enterprises are not able to meet the income needs of its workers.

The HBE operators in Kitwe were able to make substantial amounts of money. Most respondents were not able to give an accurate breakdown of their expenditure and revenues. The figures are therefore not profits but total earnings.

Although it was difficult to gauge the actual profit from HBEs, it was clear that the incomes from the HBEs compare favourably with wages for formal sector employees, particularly those in the public service. For instance, the average monthly income in the civil service in 1999 was K186, 577.33 (US$64.73). The incomes from the HBEs also seem to compare well with the 'Food Basket' monitored monthly by the CCJP which in 2000 was about K300, 000.

An important issue which fsor lack of information could not be explored here but which would be critical in any larger survey would be to compare the trends of incomes in the HBEs with those in the formal sector and possibly those in other non-home based informal activities. According to the respondents, the manufacturing sector is a better investment in the long term but the service sector is better in terms of providing income for daily sustenance. This was the reason for instance that the female tailor decided to open the saloon to run concurrently with the tailoring business.

TYPE OF ENTERPRISE

Why did the respondents choose particular types of enterprises? Answers to this question included perceived profitability due to either low capital outlays or effective demand. Others chose their enterprises because they either possessed the necessary skills or the equipment required. Others again were just interested in the particular occupation. This was the case with the female tailor who said:

"It attracted me because many times I always wanted to make my own things and then I noticed that I was developing a keen interest. This is what led me to buy the machines and employ people".

Of course all these reasons were supported by other considerations but they were to a large extent the primary ones for choosing the particular type of enterprise. The suitability of the home for the intended economic purposes did not seem to be a consideration for any of the respondents. This supports Lipton's argument (1980) about the flexibility of the house and households to respond to changing situations. Households adapt the house to provide their economic sustenance in the most practical ways available to them. But as they do so, they too adapt to the new environments created by these new uses.

It is only through such adaptation for example that the acid maker, carpenters and shoemaker can ensure that their activities do not pose immediate danger to their household members. Kellett and Tipple (1997) in their work in India also showed how households adapted living space to accommodate economic activities by physically separating the home into working and living spaces. This adaptation in some way also explains why none of the respondents considered the mixed use of the house as a problem except in terms of competition for space and limited markets due to location away from main traffic centres.

ADVANTAGES OF WORKING FROM HOME

Why did people choose to work from the home? In all cases, one of the main reasons why respondents were operating from home was because it was rentfree. The shoemaker and the female tailor had both moved from designated formal places because they could no longer afford to pay rent. The acid maker had tried to get a place in a designated area but was unable to meet the rental obligations. It is important to point out here that while rent was an important determinant for locating at home, the data also seemed to indicate two opposing views on the use of the home.

When asked whether it was better to operate from home or from a designated place, those involved in manufacturing activities e.g. the carpenters, tailors, the acid manufacturer, and the shoemaker perceived the use of the home as necessary for starting the business but not as a permanent work place. On the other hand, those offering service such as the nursery schools, hair saloons and to some extent the traders saw their enterprises as being locally orientated. They were within easy access of their clients. For instance, the nursery teacher in Ndeke Village when asked whether she planned to move to a designated place once her business was fully established said: "No. No. Okay we've got a plot somewhere we are building a house and we are thinking of even putting the classroom outside".

This may be an example of land being a limiting factor in the productivity of informal activities, supporting ILO/SATEP's (1982) argument about the need for relevant authorities in Zambia to make affordable sites available as a means of promoting small scale enterprises. There are questions as well about HBEs that have matured and moved out of the residential areas. On the other hand the home based service enterprises challenge the planners to rethink their current concept of centralising economic activities particularly those providing basic daily services like hair dressing.

At yet another level, the service based HBEs also raise interesting questions about how residents define domestic space and concepts of privacy related to this space. Other factors cited elsewhere such as ease of extending working hours into the night, and ease of combining two jobs at no extra cost, were also cited. One other important factor cited was availability of utility services such as water and electricity which in the case of the acid manufacturer and the shoemaker, had contributed to moving their enterprises from the markets where they had been operating initially.

Studies by House et al. 1993:1210, Humphrey 1992:15, Cordera and Gonzalez 1991:29, Glewwe and Hall 1992:26, and Hays-Mitchell 1993 have indicated that the informal sector is not easy to enter. The ILO/SATEP (1982) study identified similar problems in Zambia. Napier and Mothwa (2000), Olufemi (2000), Titus (2000), Gough (2000) and Kamete (2000), have also identified very similar problems with informal activities generally and HBEs specifically in South Africa, Nigeria, Tanzania, Ghana and Zimbabwe respectively.

This study also seems to support this view, even if informal enterprises do not have to comply with prescribed rules, regulations or standards and do not have to meet specified production targets in order to remain operational. Nonetheless new entrants must deal with a whole set of difficulties and must continuously struggle to stay within the informal sector.

LIMITED ACCESS TO START-UP CAPITAL

One of the main problems was resource mobilization. For all respondents, initial capital outlay was obtained from personal savings, friends or relatives. The young male trader for instance raised his initial capital by doing odd jobs during his free time from school. The male tailor started with no capital outlay but relied on an ancient Singer Simanco 94779 sewing machine which he inherited from his grandfather. The nursery teacher in Nkana West obtained money from her father to start the school.

This lack of start up capital somehow explains why the HBE is seen as "the core of the informal sector". For indeed without the home there would be no money for rent, and by implication, no informal sector activity. It also explains why these activities are small scale familial concerns. None of the respondents had bothered to get a loan because they either did not see the need for it or they were afraid of the risks or did not know where to obtain one.

Informal sector employees in Zambia rarely obtain financial assistance from the banks because they lack collateral. Some soft loans for small- scale businesses are currently available in Zambia, e.g. those offered by the Christian Enterprise Trust of Zambia (CETZAM). However none of the 11 respondents wanted these loans because they were either too small (US$50 for the first loan) or demanded weekly repayments and some form of collateral. This view that US$50 is too small raises interesting questions about micro-finance and small scale informal businesses, not least the potential differences in perception of what constitutes a 'small business' between the creditors and the borrowers.

The second problem with entering the informal sector is related to acquiring skills, which in this study seemed to be a matter of self-determination, selfdiscipline and no little cost to the operators. They had either had to employ trained people to teach them or simply 'learn on the job'. The lack of skills and capital means that development of HBEs takes a lot of time and is undertaken through progressive improvements as and when funds allow. There also seems to be a lot of experimentation in the initial stages of an enterprise until people gets to some fairly stable level.

Most work on the informal sector assumes that the proprietors pass on skills to the younger generation and indeed some do. However, this study demonstrated the repeated incidence of proprietors seeking skills from their employees who in some cases may be much younger. In follow-up research, it would therefore be worthwhile to explore the possibility of a two-way flow of skills, i.e. across generations and possibly across the formal and informal divide.

Because of the easy availability of land in Zambia and the benign climate, most HBE activities were conducted outside the house. Except for in the cases of the nursery schools and the female tailor, the house seemed to be used for storage rather than for production. This is not surprising given that in most residential neighbourhoods in Zambia each house has a significant parcel of free land around it. In this study, even the respondents living in low cost housing had more than 200m of free land on their plots. Many proprietors built 'workshops' either attached to or separated from the main house. The carpenter in Chamboli, the male trader, the male tailor and the shoemaker all had erected sheds outside the main house from which they operated their HBEs.

Only the female tailor had added a room to the main house to cater for her tailoring and hair saloon. HBEs in Kitwe seem to enable participating households to consolidate their housing through either extension of the existing house or construction of new out-buildings. It is interesting to note that in her study of HBEs in Ghana, Gough (2000) found very similar results, i.e. the bulk were undertaken outside either in specially built sheds or in the open. Olumefi (2000) found that in Nigeria women used either the house itself, or out-buildings such as the garage and the servants quarters for their HBEs.

At the same time, Untari et al. (2000) found that HBEs in Indonesia were operated from either inside the house, small sheds attached to the house, out in the open yard or in some cases on plots of land away from the house due to lack of space. Kellett and Tipple (1997) on the other hand found HBEs in India that were completely restricted to the house because of complete lack of alternative outside space. The conspicuous absence of the nursery schools from the list of those who built external work spaces or extensions might be explained by the large capital investment required to construct a classroom block which must be made of approved building materials.

In addition, not very many parents would want to send their children to a school made of 'cheap' materials such as timber or mud bricks. On the other hand, it seems quite acceptable for a small barber shop or local shop, popularly known as 'kantemba', or indeed a local carpentry workshop to be built with either timber or mud bricks. The use of external space also limited the activities of some HBE operators. For instance the mat makers had to stop making mats during the rainy season because they had nowhere to store either the reeds or the mats.

It must be noted though that the seasonality of the mat making was also influenced by the high water levels in the river during the rainy season which made it difficult for the women to both cross the river and to see the crocodiles which were a constant threat. It is also important to note that the mat makers were located in the periurban area and therefore had less access to land and storage facilities compared to their colleagues in the other areas.

HOUSEHOLD SPACE AND WORKING SPACE

Use of external space may explain why having the enterprise based at home does not seem to bother the occupants. Activities such as hammering and chiselling take place outside the home during the day when everybody is busy with their own work, and so do not interfere with daily household activities. Most respondents seemed to indicate that the inconvenience caused by the HBE was bearable as long as it only affected the immediate (nuclear) household members. Even in cases where the sitting rooms had been completely taken over by HBE activity, this was seen as inconvenient only when the household had outside visitors.

It must be noted however that only the proprietors of the HBEs were interviewed. The views of the other household members on this matter may therefore be very different. Although mixed use of the plot was not seen as a problem, most respondents indicated a need for household privacy. There was therefore a sense of distinction between 'HBE space invaded by outsiders' (clients) and 'household space'.

For instance, the male trader would not allow his clients to use the household toilet and he was in the process of trying to build one for them outside. Similarly the teacher in Ndeke Village had two toilets in the house; each painted a different colour to differentiate between the school toilet and the household toilet. Both teachers also stated that they would want to continue operating from home but that the school functions should be separated from the domestic functions. It appears therefore that there are some interesting perceptions on what constitutes home space and work space and that whilst HBEs are accepted; there are limits to the level of outside intrusion that is acceptable.

HOME BASED ENTERPRISES AND INFRASTRUCTURE

Large plots have been helpful to the HBEs. But the state of plots has also created problems for some HBEs, because the city council has become increasingly unable to maintain or expand physical infrastructure such as water, roads and sewerage. People operating HBEs in Ndeke Village for instance suffered erratic water supply. They therefore had to keep water in drums all the time or in dire situations they had to pay some boys to bring water for them from the nearest mine townships. Electricity supply disruptions were also very frequent.

Despite this, the operators got regular bills based on fixed charges from both the council and the Electricity Corporation. The operators in Riverside and Buchi suffered utility disruptions, but the frequency was not as high as in Ndeke Village. Those in Ipusukilo had no access to potable water or electricity. This inhibited investment in electrical equipment, forcing the operators to rely on manual tools. As the tailor in Ipusukilo said when asked how he managed to work without electricity:

Yes, yes that's a very big problem I always face when it comes to working at night. Then I use candles, there's not enough light. So sometimes I have to work in the day only. It's like that. The operators in Chamboli and Nkana West had a constant supply of water, electricity and indeed all other utility services provided by the mining company at a nominal fee. In the case of the carpenter in Chamboli he was not paying anything for all the utilities because he was no longer employed by the mines, which were therefore not able to deduct the Municipal Charge from his salary.

Poorly equipped residential neighbourhoods may thus adversely affect the already disadvantaged, even if they try to get themselves out of their poverty trap. Residents in higher income areas are not only more likely to have a higher financial base for starting their HBE but they also have more land and better access to utilities. In addition, HBEs located in areas with physical infrastructure are manufacturing their goods or services using utility services charged at domestic tariffs. This may give them a competitive advantage but it has equity implications for the unconnected poor, and economic implications for the utility companies.

This chapter has shown that the house is not necessarily just a dwelling place, but may also be a factory floor as well as a storeroom. And in cases where goods produced are not taken to the market, the house also plays a commercial function. It is also a retail outlet for goods produced elsewhere and offers a base for a range of services. Apart from the obvious benefits of not paying rent and tax, households engaged in HBEs maximize all possible income sources by undertaking a variety of activities. Basing their activity in the home enables participants simultaneously to perform both domestic as well as economic functions.

This is of great significance to women who do not have to worry about child minding. Business can be conducted any time of the day at no extra cost. Because their activities are located in residential neighbourhoods, HBE participants are able to use non-monetary exchange neighbourhood networks which would be relatively difficult to establish in specially designated business areas due to competition. In times of extreme difficulties such networks might provide community members with a support system to fall back on. Activities conducted from the house foster free skills training for willing young people, equipping them with basic working skills, which they might not otherwise learn from the formal school.

The minimal income raised from the HBE also enables children to go to formal school. In this way the HBE prepares the young people for future prospects both within and outside the formal sector. HBEs are fundamental to the struggle against poverty. Most of them are encumbered with a myriad of operational constraints and are therefore not very lucrative but offer only a basis for survival for the households concerned. Formalising these activities by locating them in designated land use zones might attract new and unmanageable costs such as rent, transport and in some cases tax, all of which would diminish the viability of the business.

A home is therefore critical for the operations of these enterprises and the survival of the households. As the HBE progresses and brings in extra income, the household is then able to invest in housing improvement both through expansion of the house or separation of economic from domestic functions.

The fact that most operators lack access to financial support re-emphasizes the importance of the house in the survival of those involved in HBEs. Unless they can get funds to reinvest in their businesses, their activities are not likely to expand. But as long as they remain in the informal sector and have no tangible collateral, their chances of getting loans are very limited.

The importance of secure land tenure as well as improvements in housing quality can therefore not be over-emphasized. There are obvious distinctions across gender, generations, income groups and neighbourhoods. For instance physical infrastructure was more readily available in some neighbourhoods compared to others. Men, women and youth seemed to have different areas of interest and opportunity in so far as choosing the type of HBE was concerned. Thus advantages and constraints of operating economic activities from home will vary from one group to another.

Last but not least, it is important to seriously examine the social aspects of HBEs, in particular the potential of HBEs to contribute to developments in gender and generational relations at household level. These relationships no doubt have a bearing on the development of the HBE to the extent that they represent a rearrangement of household structure to enable HBE activities. Whilst this study has focused on the economic aspect of HBEs their physical implications must in no way be underplayed.

There is no doubt that development of HBEs has led to a change in the landscape of many residential areas. The continued development of sheds for workshops and retail outlets will give a different outlook from that envisaged by the planners. A question then is whether this trend should be stopped or simply regulated. Whatever decision is taken must be based on a clear understanding of the economic reality of the people who live there and perhaps a rethinking of concepts of land use zoning and plot usage.

This study has shown that housing is indeed fundamental to the fight against poverty. If this argument is accepted, should we then discard all planning and land use regulations in order to assist the HBEs? Or should we perhaps treat the phenomenon as a transitional phase in city development? There are of course no straightforward answers to these questions. But one thing which is obvious is that there is a need to broaden the conceptual categories of home use to include income generating activities as valid and normal within the domestic environment.

Home based enterprises challenge us to re-evaluate our definition of what is acceptable within the home. Strict land use controls can no longer be taken as the norm without jeopardising the lives of hundreds of city residents. What we need is a better, research-based understanding of HBEs and to identify the areas where planning can play a role both to assist their development and also to mitigate their negative impacts. There will of course be variation of needs and problems between different social groups and between neighbourhoods.

For informal areas for instance a priority concern might be provision of infrastructure services, whilst for formal areas priority concerns might be with mitigating negative environmental effects. For the youth and women priority might be access to start-up capital and maybe a place to work from, while for the men it could be skills training and markets for their goods. Whatever the problem and however they are dealt with, it is clear from this study that HBEs have become an important part of the urban landscape from both their physical as well as economic aspects. With the levels of formal job losses forecast in the public sector, it can only be assumed that there will be more not fewer such enterprises in the foreseeable future.

More importantly, the HBEs have 'thrived' regardless of planning regulations designed to prevent their growth. It is therefore fair to conclude that if urban planners want to be relevant to the urban development agenda, then they should rethink their fixation with master planning ideas which hitherto has limited their role in the development of the informal sector. They must adopt approaches in which solutions do not come from master planning text books but rather are developed with the people concerned, using planning tools that respect the economic reality of the city and the voices of other stakeholders. The essence of planning after all should be about people and not buildings. Only in this way can planning make a positive contribution to enhancing people's lives and be made relevant to the economic and social context of today's developing city.

4

Call Centres and the Prospects for Work in the Developing World

Geographers have long been interested in the tendency of firms to (re)locate low value-added or mature manufacturing activities in less developed regions of advanced countries in order to take advantage of lower input costs. More recently, interest has grown in the trend toward locating such activities 'offshore', often in less economically developed countries. By contrast it has generally been felt that few service activities could be located in this way, because of the need for the co-presence of the producer and the customer during service transactions.

Over the past few years, however, it has become clear that developments in information and communications technologies have the potential to alter this position. Freeman and Soete, for example, suggest that:

Information technology, almost by definition, will allow for the increased tradability of service activities, particularly those which have been most constrained by the geographical or time proximity of production and consumption. By bringing in a space or time/ storage dimension, information technology will make possible the separation of production and consumption in an increasing number of such activities.

Once service production and consumption are separated,

firms can, at least in theory, locate their activities at a distance from their core markets, and so take advantage of lower costs and exploit spatial divisions of labour. There is now a growing body of case study evidence suggesting that certain kinds of service work are being relocated to cheaper production locations 'offshore' and then 'exported' to richer markets. This is occurring within Europe, but also between continents. Unfortunately, there is no statistical evidence that would allow us to say how widespread this tendency is, particularly at the international level, though on-going research by the author suggests that it is no longer only the leading-edge companies that are transferring work offshore.

Two sets of service activities have received most attention in terms of international relocation: routine 'back-office' data processing work and software production, with locations such as Bangalore and Mumbai in India attracting work from the US and Europe. This process of sending work offshore is not, however, confined to firms based in the northern hemisphere. Firms within the Pacific Basin are also seeking lower-cost locations for production activities. Wilson (1995), for example, sites the case of Singapore Airlines, which outsources much of its computer software services from Mumbai.

These service activities can be carried out either in-house, through firms setting up (or acquiring) direct subsidiaries, or through outsourcing them to third-party firms, which are required to meet standards laid down by contract. This chapter is concerned with a relatively new set of mobile service activities, namely teleservices, which are increasingly carried out in a new kind of production site known as the call centre. Teleservices refer to service functions carried out over the telephone, replacing or complementing face-to-face interaction with the customer.

Call centres are offices, usually fairly large in scale, in which most of the telephone functions of a company (or particular types of telephone functions, such as sales or customer care) are concentrated in order to create economies of scale. After a description of these new activities and their rapid growth in Europe, there is a discussion of the locational requirements of call centres.

It is suggested that some of Europe's less favoured regions are benefiting from the relocation of these activities. The potential for call centre activities to relocate to developing countries, servicing European markets at a distance, is then discussed. It is pointed out that there may be a number of barriers that will impede this process, though it is suggested that some call centre activities may be so transferred. Finally, consideration is given to the implications of call centre work for economic development.

DRIVERS OF TELESERVICE GROWTH

In the 1970s and 1980s business became increasingly aware of the potential of information and communications technologies (ICTs) to enhance the efficiency of their operations while at the same time cutting costs. During this period firms tended to focus on internal, mostly data, communications and on establishing data communications with preferred suppliers and customers. By the early 1980s, firms in the US were beginning to explore the potential for ICTs as a means of offering their services to a wider range of customers, both business and consumer. Since the beginning of the 1990s, a similar trend has emerged in the UK and, albeit more slowly, appears to be emerging in the rest of Western Europe. Several factors have led firms to increase their use of the telephone for customer interface:

- Competitive pressures have led firms to seek new, more cost-effective, service delivery channels.
- Telephony has been transformed through information technology, and the emergence of digital exchanges and 'intelligent networks' have radically transformed its functionality, reliability, and performance.
- Telephony costs have fallen rapidly and new customer-oriented services, such as toll-free, local call, and premium services, have been introduced, utilising the intelligence in public networks.
- Telephone penetration is high in the key markets of the advanced industrial economies, and individuals and businesses are therefore familiar and comfortable with it.

- Complex and relatively rich information can be communicated over the telephone and clarification and recapping can take place in real time, with follow-up instructions sent by fax or e-mail if necessary.

SECTORS AND ACTIVITIES AFFECTED BY TELESERVICE GROWTH IN EUROPE

Firms are increasingly using the telephone to interface with customers across a range of activities, but the areas in which the telephone is being most regularly used in a strategic manner are:

- Sales
- Marketing
- Technical upport
- Appointment setting
- Lead generation
- Brochure fulfilment
- Market research
- Reservations
- Order taking
- Customer enquiries
- Membership renewal
- 'Customer care'

Most of these activities occur in a range of sectors, including:

- Travel and transport
- Computing (hardware and software)
- Marketing
- Financial services
- Distribution
- Hotels
- Telecommunications
- Retail
- Utilities
- Government services

THE RATE OF TELESERVICE GROWTH IN EUROPE

There are no consistently derived and standardised figures which allow us to state precisely the rate of growth of call centres in Europe, but by drawing on a range of consultancy reports and research by the author, however, we can say something about the order of magnitude of growth, and it is clear that significant growth is occurring. A report by the business consultants Datamonitor (1996) suggests that the call centre market in Europe grew by 40 per cent in 1996, and that this rate of growth is likely to continue until the end of the century.

These findings are broadly supported by other consultancy studies, and by sectoral and areal studies. Growth rates have varied among European countries, with the UK in the forefront and southern countries such as Spain and Italy lagging.

EMPLOYMENT GROWTH IN TELESERVICES IN EUROPE

There is no agreed-upon figure for the numbers employed in teleservices, largely because of the paucity of official data in this area. One survey calculated that 800,000 people, or around 3 per cent of the UK workforce, were employed in what it termed 'telebusinesses' in 1994. Here, however, we are concerned only with teleservice workers employed in call centres, and a recent study by Datamonitor (1996) suggests a figure for that group of 270,000 in Europe (covering the UK, France, Germany, Benelux, Spain, and Italy); 125,000 of those workers are in the UK. The report anticipates that that figure for Europe will be 670,000 by the year 2001, representing 1 per cent of the total working population.

When face-to-face interaction is replaced by the telephone, there is obviously less need for production to be located in physical proximity to the customer. In many cases this means that activities that were previously most sensibly carried out in small local offices close to the customer-for example, bank and insurance branches, travel agencies, small sales offices, and local technical support offices-can now be concentrated in large offices, at one or a few sites, covering a national or international territory, where significant cost savings can be made.

Similarly, when new firms enter markets or create new markets through the use of teleservices, they tend to establish single/few site operations rather than distributed operations. These new large offices are designed to be ICT-intensive, quasi-Taylorised operations, and can be thought of as 'customer service factories', though in the industry they are known as call centres. Concentration of teleservice operations into call centres presents a number of advantages to firms. These include:

- The reduction of property costs, moving from high-cost sites, rationalising property portfolios, making more cost-effective use of space, and reducing space management costs.
- Reducing unit capital costs by using technology more intensively (indeed, office technologies such as automated call distribution and power dialling systems are being designed specifically for these large-scale operations).
- Management and supervisory costs can be reduced; once again, expensive and sophisticated office technologies can assist in this process.
- Most importantly, technology-intensive large sites present labour cost savings through economies of scale.
- Standardisation of product and service; better management control of the process, through training and building a shared culture.
- Creating a critical mass of knowledge, leading to complementarities and synergies within the workforce.

Further economies of scale can be gained through outsourcing call centre work, and there are now a significant number of firms emerging to serve this market. At present, however, it is estimated that only about 10 per cent of agent positions in Europe are outsourced, and, although the absolute numbers are anticipated to grow to around 62,000 (from about 30,000), the percentage figure is likely to remain the same

(Datamonitor 1996). One factor that potentially limits the growth of outsourcing in call centre work is the desire of many firms to keep control of the client interface.

TELESERVICES AND THE CHANGING LOCATION OF CUSTOMER SERVICES

The growth of the telephone as a method of conducting business with the customer opens up new locational possibilities for firms engaged in teleservices. In addition, the industrialisation and routinisation of the work process that are also features of much teleservice activity provide the opportunity to move work to areas where supplies of less skilled, lower-paid workers are located, perhaps at the same time side-stepping problems such as trade union opposition to restructuring.

Many firms will take advantage of these new possibilities. However, the new locational possibilities are not limitless and remain constrained by the uneven availability of factors of production, particularly labour. The following list illustrates, in broad terms, the key locational attractors considered by firms involved in teleservices when deciding where to locate call centres.

- Advanced telecommunications suitable for data and voice transmission and capable of hosting intelligent network services. Telecommunications costs must also be considered, particularly when call centres can be located in several countries.
- A pool of labour of sufficient quality to carry out the particular tasks required in the locating firm's call centre, bearing in mind that the call centre may have to be manned 24 hours a day.
- An advantageous labour cost/quality ratio.
- Fiscal and grant incentives.
- A living environment able to attract management and other key staff.
- Low occupancy costs (rents, rates, servicing, parking costs, etc.).

- Access to good local public transport and, in some cases, to national and international transport.

Obviously, firms considering where to locate a call centre will have to balance the factors listed above against each other, as it is unlikely that any single location will offer all these advantages. The two principal locational factors are telecommunications infrastructure, without which teleservice firms cannot operate, and an advantageous cost/quality ratio of labour, without which firms will not relocate.

Fiscal incentives are usually regarded as an added bonus, though these incentives usually occur where labour is cheaper in any event. Of course, as with all locational decisions, 'rational' economic criteria may be relegated from the forefront of the process. During the course of the research reported here, several examples were found where the locational decision was ultimately based on the living preferences of senior managers or on the accessibility of the site for senior managers from headquarters.

Another crucial factor was senior management's demand that a call centre be set up immediately; here the crucial criterion becomes the availability of suitable real estate. Real estate may also be a factor where a firm's existing property portfolio is under-used but has little resale value.

TELECOMMUNICATIONS INFRASTRUCTURE AND SERVICES

The call centre industry's success relies on there being a sophisticated ICT infrastructure, both where the consumer is located and where the call centre is located. In order to create a market for call centres, the consumer must have access to a good publicly switched telecommunications network (PSTN) with the required 'intelligence' to host advanced services, through which he/she can contact call centres at low or no cost (for example, through freephone or local call-rate numbers).

The call centre needs to be effectively linked to that PSTN. It can, however, be located in a region that does not have a generally advanced telecommunications network; but to be cost-effective and robust there must be a local digital telephone exchange, and the firm must be able to lease a high-bandwidth line from the telecommunications provider, through which voice and data traffic can be sent speedily. For example, one firm that has located its call centre in rural Scotland to take advantage of lower labour costs 'gathers' calls from customers in London, made via the PSTN, at its London office and switches them to Scotland over leased lines.

The firm sends its internal data in the same way. This strategy adds to telecommunications costs, but these costs are more than offset by lower labour costs. As liberalisation of the telecommunications market takes place within Europe, the falling costs of voice and data traffic make this sort of arrangement more feasible on a pan-European basis. Interviews suggest that a number of telecommunications factors beyond those mentioned above are taken into account.

Not surprisingly, given the dominance of US firms, the existence of a competitive environment with the presence of more than one telecommunications supplier is regarded as important. Beyond this, the precise mix that firms require will depend on the nature of the business-for example, the balance between in-bound and out-bound calls, or whether international toll-free numbers are to be offered to customers. Considerations will include the costs of setting up private circuits, line rental, cost of national and international phone calls, and so on.

LABOUR AVAILABILITY AND COSTS

The availability of advanced telecommunications infrastructure is, then, a crucial locational factor for teleservice firms. Beyond this, it is the traditional locational factors that remain important; and the most important of these is labour. The precise nature of labour requirements for any particular teleservice operation will depend on the type of activity undertaken and the products and geographical markets served. Call centre agents can be conceptualised as the interface mechanism between a firm's information systems and the customer.

For all call centre activities, firms will attempt to standardise information and embed product knowledge in the information system. There are limits to how far this is possible, however, and agents may be required to 'add value' to the information by mentally manipulating, reconfiguring, and customising it to suit a particular customer. Other activities require additional skills, such as selling, marketing, and 'customer care' skills. Activities such as technical support, which are most advanced in the IT sector, require higher-order skills, and even within these activities the level of skills will vary depending on the complexity of the product and the sophistication of the customer.

For firms wishing to establish internationally oriented call centres, there is a further requirement for a workforce that is multilingual. A number of points regarding location emerge from the studies upon which this chapter is based. First, call centres in western Europe are mainly, though not exclusively, urban-based. This is due to the fact that telecommunications investment tends to be most advanced in urban areas, and that a larger labour pool is available there. The majority of call centres require a large labour pool for a number of reasons:

- Most call centres need a sufficient number of workers to staff 12, 18, or even 24 hour operations, including 'unsocial' hours, without necessarily paying the extra costs normally associated with such work patterns.
- Many call centres operate four-hour shift patterns, the idea being that lunch hours and tea-breaks are thus not paid for by the employer, and that productivity declines after four hours of intense telephone activity in any case; this requires a bigger pool of labour from which to choose.
- Call centres have relatively strict recruitment criteria, even for lower-level activities, involving telephone and face-to-face interviews and a number of proficiency and psychometric tests.

As previously indicated, call centre growth in Western Europe has been very rapid. The data do not exist to allow us to map in detail how this growth has occurred across space.

What is clear, however, is that certain less favoured cities and regions are attracting these activities. At the national level this is probably most striking in the UK, where regional disparities in income are pronounced. Telecommunications infrastructure provision in most parts of the UK is now sufficiently sophisticated to allow call centres to operate. The key question thus becomes the cost of labour.

As can be seen, those areas beyond the core South-east region offer the lowest-cost labour. The partial exception to this is Outer London, an area which has long been the recipient of back-office work from the capital, and which has a ready supply of female clerical-type labour. The lower-salaried regions, as would be expected, tend to be those with fewer alternative job opportunities. As a result, labour turnover is also lower, thus contributing to lower training and recruitment costs. Many of these areas are also able to offer a number of property and labour-related fiscal incentives.

UK banks have chosen to locate telebanking centres in cities in the north of the country. Area studies by the author suggest that these cities and regions are succeeding in attracting a range of call centre activities beyond telebanking. Call centres are primarily an urban phenomenon in Western Europe, but they do locate in less urbanised areas where adequate telecommunications infrastructure is available.

In the Highlands and Islands region of Scotland, for example, which is classified as an Objective 1 region by the European Commission because of its peripherality and low-income status, an advanced network has been installed and the region has attracted a number of call centres by providing a highly educated, low-cost workforce (and, it should be said, considerable financial assistance). There exists a great variety of call centre activities, ranging from very simple information-giving to relatively complex tasks, such as computer software support. In some sectors there is also a growing trend toward pan-European call centres requiring multilingual staff.

These centres tend to be smaller, but the jobs can be more challenging and better rewarded. The range of locations open to firms operating such centres is obviously more limited than for those addressing lower-skilled, single-language tasks. In the UK it is likely that the majority of these centres will locate in or around London to take advantage of its uniquely cosmopolitan character. Similarly, in the Netherlands most multilingual centres are located in the Randstadt.

Again, however, less favoured regions have been able to capture some of these activities. In the UK, the cities referred to above in the context of national call centres have had some success in attracting international centres as well. Ireland, which is on the geographical periphery of Europe and is classed as an Objective 1 region by the European Commission, has been particularly successful in attracting (mainly US) call centres operating on a pan-European basis, through a combination of low-cost, highly educated workers (including many multilingual workers), and fiscal incentives. These centres are, however, predominantly located in and around the capital, Dublin.

In considering the prospects for less favoured regions in Western Europe benefiting from the growth in call centres, the evidence suggests that this growth has created opportunities for export-oriented employment in some less favoured regions. To date this appears to be mainly an urban phenomenon, though the evidence suggests that more advanced rural areas (in terms of education, etc.) can benefit if they have the telecommunications and support infrastructure required. I now turn to consider whether the growth of call centres represents an opportunity for developing countries.

Call centre growth and export-oriented work: opportunities for the developing world? This is concerned with the relationship between Europe and the developing world. I will, therefore, concentrate here on the possibilities of call centre activities aimed at European markets creating export-oriented employment growth in the developing world. Before doing so, however, three points need to be made:

i. For the more advanced developing countries, the growth in call centre work may well be internally generated, rather than export-oriented. The evidence from Europe certainly suggests that international trading in teleservices remains relatively limited.

ii. Export-oriented call centre activity may well be confined to the global region in which a particular country is situated. Unpublished research by the author suggests that firms are not in favour of a single-site call centre serving the globe, preferring to have at least one centre in each of the three global regions (the US, Europe, and Asia). Examples of inter-regional activity do exist, but they are at the margin.

iii. In attempting to forecast call centre trends globally, Europe is probably not the best place to start, since most call centre innovation has tended to emanate from the US.

There are two possibilities for developing countries in creating exportoriented work around call centres. The first is to use this channel to promote the products and services of indigenous firms. This route is more likely to lead to sustainable economic development. It is also, of course, the more difficult to achieve. One example of a firm in a less favoured region in Europe doing this is the leading accountancy software firm in the UK, Sage, a company based in the North-east of England, which has grown into an internationally successful business through selling and supporting products via its call centres.

In order to do this, however, a firm must first have a marketable product and the capacity to market it. This can be difficult from the periphery of Europe, and it is likely to be even more difficult from outside Europe.

If export-oriented call centre activity aimed at European markets is to occur on any scale in developing countries, it is likely that, at least initially, it will be based on attracting inward investment, predicated on a perception by European (or US) firms that their European business and consumer markets can be served from these countries. The next section turns to consider the possibilities for, and barriers to, attracting such investment.

OPPORTUNITIES FOR ATTRACTING EXOGENOUS EXPORT-ORIENTED CALL CENTRE WORK

There are a number of reasons to suggest that at least some call centre work may follow service operations of the type referred to in the introduction to this chapter offshore:

- Many developing countries represent a cheaper locational option than less favoured regions in Europe.
- Reinforcing the previous point, there are signs of wage inflation and increasing turnover in some successful call centre regions in Europe.
- Call centres with higher skill requirements, such as network software help desk centres, are experiencing skill shortages, and this situation is likely to be exacerbated as economic growth in Europe recovers and skilled workers' expectations increase.
- Many lower-cost regions in Europe appear not to be particularly well placed to attract call centre work, lacking the telecommunications infrastructure and/or the requisite labour skills.
- Many firms that operate call centres have long experience of locating other activities offshore, and are therefore comfortable with the concept.
- Some of these firms have their own global telecommunications networks, which would facilitate the establishment of offshore activities at a minimal cost in terms of telecommunications.
- Outsourcing of call centre work is growing; a number of firms in the developing world have already demonstrated an ability to undertake other forms of outsourced service work.

BARRIERS TO ATTRACTING CALL CENTRE WORK TO DEVELOPING COUNTRIES

There are, however, also a number of barriers to call centre work going offshore, and there may also be limits to the number of countries capable of attracting this work. Many of these barriers may be based on misperceptions by European managers, but in questions of locational choices, perceptions are important. These (perceived) barriers can be divided into technological, regulatory, organisational, linguistic, and cultural.

TECHNOLOGY BARRIERS

Much of the service work transferred to developing countries in recent years has not, in fact, required advanced telecommunications. Much of the data sent overseas for processing have been in the form of paper-based records sent by air. Indeed, so far as we can tell, much offshore processing work appears to be concerned with transferring historical data from paper to electronic form. The electronic data can be returned on disk, by air.

Hence air connections have been more important than ICT links. A variation on this practice is to send hard copy by air and to return copy electronically 'across the wire'. More recently, data have been sent offshore in electronic form and, after processing, have been returned electronically. Such transactions require either a cable connection or a satellite link.

Until now most service activities that have gone offshore involve a transaction between the client company and the third-party company (i.e., the company undertaking the outsourced work). But offshore, out-sourced, call centre work would involve transactions between the third-party company and the client's customers, either business customers or consumers. As was pointed out earlier, firms can locate in less favoured regions in Europe, regions that do not have an advanced telecommunications infrastructure, and still access the customer so long as there is a digital exchange to switch the traffic and wide-bandwidth leased lines or some other mechanism for accessing calls gathered through the PSTN.

On an intercontinental basis it would be possible for customers, say from the UK, to call a UK number; the calls would then be 'gathered', either by the firm itself or within the intelligent network, and transmitted to the location in, say, India. This process could be extended, with calls from

European customers from a number of countries being gathered centrally in Europe, and then transferred to a developing country. However, the link between that central point and the developing country would have to be a fixed link, that is, a cable link. Satellite would not be generally acceptable; because the 'slap-back' delay associated with satellite telephone calls would be frustrating for customers. Except for companies that already have a leased-line link between Europe and the appropriate developing country; this would be a very expensive option.

Perhaps more importantly, in the customer service environment questions remain over the reliability of long distance electronic links. In processing or software activities, work can continue while a telecommunications problem is being fixed, and the output transmitted later. In a call centre environment, work would come to a halt and the customer is lost.

REGULATORY BARRIERS

There are two potential regulatory barriers to call centre work going offshore from Europe. First, there is the question of regulations covering telecommunications. Call centre firms in Europe (particularly US firms) regard a competitive telecommunications environment, with a number of competing suppliers, as important to their locational decisions. Several reports claim that a key element in the UK's rapid growth in teleservices is its competitive telecommunications environment.

Many developing countries remain heavily regulated in this area, and are therefore unlikely to be attractive to teleservice firms. Regulation may also have implications for flow of voice and data traffic and for the cost of communicating data between nation states. In addition, the author has noted a perception in several firms that local telecommunications companies in many developing countries would not have the competencies required to operate the required network.

A second set of regulatory questions concern certain sectors such as banking. For example, in financial services within (a supposedly single-market) Europe, there are key regulatory differences between countries. Even when those regulatory differences decline, their historical legacy and resulting cultural expectations remain to be overcome. So although the financial services industry is the most developed sector in its use of call centres, there are few examples of cross-border servicing of customers.

ORGANISATIONAL AND COMMERCIAL BARRIERS

One of the principal reasons why service firms go offshore is to speed up the production process. The case of the insurance company processing new policies and claims overnight by sending them across time-zones, thus making it possible to provide the customer with documents the next day, is well documented. Thus, in addition to potential labour cost savings, exploitation of time-zone differences gives competitive advantage. But despite the fact that many European teleservice firms offer 24-hour-a-day service, the vast majority of calls are still received during traditional office hours, and demand for service outside 8.00 am to 8.00 pm remains limited.

Conceivably, call centres in the developing world could act as overflow points for calls received outside traditional European office hours, perhaps acting as a bureau on behalf of a number of European firms. A call centre in a developing country could also adapt its working hours to provide a service that covered European office hours, though there would potentially be cost disadvantages and other disincentives (such as problems of access to public transport) in doing so.

Another potential barrier to work going offshore is managers' perception of loss of control of the production process. This concern is particularly pronounced in the call centre environment, since firms see successful customer relations as a key area in maintaining competitiveness. The majority of firms in Europe still operate their own call centres and see them as a key competitive weapon. This situation may change over time, however, and outsourcing may grow.

LINGUISTIC BARRIERS

Language presents both an opportunity and a barrier for developing countries in attracting call centres. In most areas of customer service, a common language is required. The evidence from Europe suggests that, by and large, customers want agents to be able to speak the customer's own language and to speak it well-they do not want to have to struggle to communicate. In a limited number of areas, for example, where a customer phones a help desk when his/her computer is down, he/she will be prepared to speak in a second language, usually English.

In most areas, however, and particularly in sales, a customer will not accept a second language. This is a key reason why the growth in pan-European call centres remains limited. Firms that set up pan-European centres would ideally employ multilingual staff, thus generating economies of scope and scale; but this is not easy to do, given the relatively low wages for these jobs, and many firms end up importing native speakers to overcome this problem. This can be an expensive solution, however, as turnover tends to be high.

This situation may present opportunities for developing countries that have large pools of people who can speak a European language well, perhaps based on former colonial connections and residual educational links. The experience in the UK tends to suggest that customers (on both sides of the Atlantic) are amused by the idea of being answered by someone at a distance. The broader European experience suggests customer resistance to call centre agents who speak the customer's language but are obviously not from the customer's country. For example, it was commonly reported that French customers were not happy dealing with French-speaking Belgians, notwithstanding the geographical proximity of the two countries.

CULTURAL BARRIERS

Two sets of cultural factors might be important in determining whether to set up a European market-oriented call centre in a developing country: the work/employment culture and the customer-relations/consumer culture. Here I focus on the latter. Cultural differences between countries are much harder to define than linguistic differences, but they may form an important barrier to some forms of call centre activity going offshore. Evidence from Europe suggests that there are significant problems with marketing and selling goods across borders.

Many pan-European call centre managers expressed the view that there were cultural nuances which an agent has to understand. Again, this often means using as agents natives of the countries that a firm is targeting. Furthermore, firms went to considerable lengths to keep agents up-to-date with events in the consuming countries, for example, bringing in newspapers and magazines.

There is also a perception of cultural differences in the way that consumers from different European countries use the telephone-Germans, for example, being business-like and to the point, Italians being more relaxed and talkative. The perception of managers is that cultural differences across continents will be even greater. One major third-party marketing firm that attempted to serve a South-east Asian market from London found problems coping with the range of attitudes and ways of using the telephone, and in the end decided to establish call centres in Japan and Singapore to service that regional market.

As with the language barrier, cultural barriers are likely to be less pronounced in certain areas of call centre activity, particularly business-to-business operations. For example, the computer industry has its own culture, which transcends local cultures to some extent. Other areas where cultural nuances would have less impact are those such as air travel, where the information exchange is fairly straightforward and the 'language' and procedures have become universal.

There are, then, a number of barriers to call centre work being transferred from Europe to the developing world. Nevertheless, with the sector growing so rapidly, countries that can provide the required telecommunications infrastructure, even within a restricted part of their territory, may be able to attract certain call centre activities. This section considers what economic benefits may be derived from attracting export-oriented call centres.

The evidence from Europe's less favoured regions suggests that call centres provide significant benefits in terms of net new jobs. Some city-regions in the UK, for example, claim to have attracted over 10,000 call centre jobs in just a few years, and most of the output of this work is 'exported'. It should be added that regions that fail to attract export-oriented call centres are increasingly likely to import these services over the telephone, thus impacting detrimentally on local employment.

Call centres can also bring new skills to a region. Call centre work offers the opportunity for workers to familiarise themselves with new technologies. However, many of the jobs that call centres bring in are fairly low-skilled. Except for a few activities, agents tend to be overqualified for the mundane tasks they have to handle. The jobs can be boring and repetitive, but at the same time are much pressured. Furthermore, the 'new' skills are fairly basic, and are not of the kind that would permit less favoured regions to 'leap-frog' more developed ones, in the manner suggested by some of the more optimistic commentators on the information society.

One problem with low-skilled work, of course, is that it tends to be the first to be automated. There are already ranges of evolving technologies within the call centre environment that are leading to fewer workers being required per unit of output. This is likely to slow the growth in employment, and eventually to result in a decline. Other technologies, such as the Internet, are also likely to have this effect. If call centres can act as a 'point of departure', providing workers with skills that can be upgraded as new technologies eliminate basic call centre jobs, then the employment benefits can be long-term. Otherwise, many call centre employees will find themselves redundant, as did low-skilled industrial workers.

Although the majority of call centres offer what can be seen as low-grade jobs, they may provide wages above the local norm. Certainly, there is evidence in Europe's less favoured regions that these centres provided reasonable incomes in the context of local labour markets. A survey of workers in several call centres in the Highlands and Islands region of Scotland showed that these centres brought genuinely new employment opportunities, not only in terms of numbers of jobs, but also new kinds of jobs, and with better earnings potential.

Furthermore, sectors such as IT do provide more sophisticated work and higher wages; and given the international nature of IT and the dearth of skills in Europe at present, this is one of the sectors that might transfer work to certain developing countries. A larger concern is the lack of career structure in call centres, which seldom bring high-level management tasks to a region. Call centres have a flat hierarchical structure, and there is only limited opportunity for promotion beyond supervisory level.

Even management and technology support functions tend to be limited, though call centres in developing countries may host more support management, given their distance from their parent/client organisations. On the whole, however, call centre work represents a job rather than a career. There is some evidence from Europe that, in a limited number of sectors (IT again being a case in point, but also in sectors such as chemical and pharmaceuticals), individuals can gain experience that allows them to advance into other parts of a company.

Although this is good for the individual, it probably means that the individual's skills are lost to the region, since the higher-order jobs are located elsewhere. The lack of prospects for worker advancement must be a serious concern, given the amount of time, grant aid, and fiscal relief that is likely to have to be provided to attract these firms. On the plus side, what management there is in these centres may bring with it innovative techniques and practices, either directly or by influencing local third-party firms.

And it can be argued that these techniques may contribute to the longer-term economic development of a country or region, though they may also force workers into more intensive and regimented ways of working. Another potential advantage of attracting call centres is that they bring gains in terms of capital investment, particularly IT investment. It is likely, however, that in order to attract these activities, considerable local (probably public) investment will be required in telecommunications infrastructure. This is likely to mean diverting resources from other areas of investment to create 'hot-spots'; and there may be little overspill to other parts of the territory.

The overarching question, of course, is whether less favoured regions, whether in the north or south, should allow themselves to become so dependent on external capital, whether through direct inward investment or through undertaking externally controlled, outsourced work. In this respect call centres appear to present an information age analogue to the industrial branch plant.

Regions that become over-reliant on this form of investment are likely to face the problems that branch plant economies faced in the past, including low growth in support services, a lack of research and development capacity, a concentration of low-skilled jobs and a lack of entrepreurial initiative. Given the short-term benefits on offer from call centres and other low value-added activities, however, it is difficult to see how, on the eve of the 'information age', many less favoured regions will be able to avoid going down the inward investment route and perhaps replicating the mistakes of the industrial age.

5

Globalization and Economic Management

An important lesson of experience is that the strong markets created by globalization need strong states. Both markets and states need not only competitiveness, but, perhaps more important for the long-term survival of the system, they also need collaborative partnerships. These partnerships are most effective with the active involvement of outsiders. In this chapter, the focus turns to national economic management and globalization. The emphasis here is on the productive sectors of the economy and how they are organized and managed to take advantage of, and protect themselves from, the adverse effects of globalization.

All countries in the world- those in support of or opposed to globalization-support the concept of economic growth and development. Growth means the opportunity for wealth creation and income generation. Support for economic globalization is based on the realization that it enables nations, governments, societies, enterprises, and individuals to create more wealth and generate more income through more efficient modes of production, consumption, and exchange.

Increases in wealth and income give rise to higher standards of living and improved quality of life. Without a growing productive sector of the economy, it is not possible to sustain higher levels of wealth creation or income generation. Questions of inequality are related to how wealth and income are distributed among and within countries. Here, the emphasis is on how to create the necessary macroeconomic enablers and on the organization and management of the country's productive sector for more wealth creation and income generation through globalization.

MACROECONOMIC ENABLERS

Supporters of globalization also advocate for an open, free-enterprise capitalist economy. For most developing countries and economies in transition with a history of socialist government central planning and control and ownership of productive enterprises, this requires significant changes in defining the role of the state in the management of the economy. It does not mean total abdication of the state in economic ownership and management.

Rather, it requires evolutionary changes in the dominant ideology, mind-set, institutional capacities, and private–public partnership arrangements. The key challenge is to create and sustain an enabling environment for the development and competitive performance of the productive sector. It starts with a national governance system, and is based on the need for the establishment of effective, functioning, and productive private–public partnerships.

The central driving force for the macroeconomic enabling framework is the productive enterprises sector, which actually creates wealth and generates income. The productive enterprises sector is supported by a credible national integrity and regulatory system; a functioning infrastructure; a competitive environment; a system of professional, trade, and business associations; and ongoing institutional sociocultural change, development, and innovation.

PRIVATE–PUBLIC PARTNERSHIPS

Throughout history, one of capitalism's greatest assets has been its ability to establish beneficial partnerships between or among family members, private sector entrepreneurs, or with individuals or institutions in the public sector. Corporate law recognized this at the very beginning and established standard rules and procedures for conducting business under sole proprietorships, partnerships, private corporations, and public corporations. These forms of business organizations are on a progressive scale of partnering designed to account for the increasing complexity of the relationships and to protect the interests of all parties under law.

Indeed, from the early days of the Industrial Revolution through to the period of European explorations, private companies joined kings, churches, and other wealthy civic organizations to launch expeditions in search of fortunes in far away places. From the days of Christopher Columbus in the New World through to the British and Dutch East India Companies and even King Leopold's brutal adventures in the Congo, all these enterprises were made possible by complex partnership arrangements within and across the private–public sector divide.

During the Cold War, industrialized countries used combinations of imperialism, diplomacy, militarism, religion, and superior access to capital and technology to facilitate formation of partnership arrangements, which helped their private sectors to win markets in their areas of influence. Japan's Ministry of International Trade and Industry is a good example of a private–public partnership; it helped Japanese businesses to dominate world markets in a relatively short period of time.

A close look at the deregulation and privatization of industry in developing countries and transition economies reveals how Western businesses use the partnership model to win contracts and buy foreign assets. Deregulation and privatization of industries-ranging from telecommunications (for example, in Indonesia, Brazil, and Thailand) to oil and gas (for example, in Nigeria and Mexico) to banking (for example, in Indonesia and Argentina)-show that Western companies worked very closely with their respective governments to win contracts.

More recently, high-technology firms have benefited from private–public sector partnerships championed by competing governments. Ireland is a good example. Until recently, Ireland has been regarded as one of the poorest countries in Western Europe. Heavily dependent on natural resources, with a population of only 3.7 million, the country suffered from high unemployment of 17 percent and a mass emigration of young people, resulting in serious brain drain.

It had a national debt of about 123 percent of GDP. With new leadership and a redefinition of the essence of the state, Ireland has been able to transform itself through a series of three-year agreements with trade unions and big business. These institutional arrangements, similar to Southeast Asian deliberation councils, focused on setting new strategic directions for national economic recovery and development. By putting in place very practical macroeconomic enablers and incentives such as tax cuts, investments in education, and the digital infrastructure, Ireland has been able to attract leading high-technology firms including Microsoft.

By the year 2000, Ireland had emerged as the world's largest exporter of computer software, producing about two-thirds of all personal computers sold in Europe and one-half of the Pentium chips sold in the world. Because of the partnership nature of the transformation, Ireland took a balanced approach, creating a society that is both competitive and compassionate. Accordingly, spending on health care was increased by 50 percent, and university education was heavily subsidized. Mindful of the power of intellectual capital, Ireland hopes to produce as many information technology graduates as Germany, which has a population of 80 million.

If Ireland can do it, so can many other countries that have been too long in the doldrums. The key is the leadership and vision and the development of effective private–public partnerships that create incentives and socioeconomic enablers. Let's review some of the advantages of private–public partnerships. First, they provide an institutionalized arrangement for bringing together leaders from different sectors of society (for example, political, business, civil service, civil society, academic, unions) to get to know one another and develop common understanding, shared values, mutual respect, and trust.

The development of a shared mind-set provides the foundation for joint decision making and collaborative partnership. Second, they provide opportunities for joint deliberations of public policy analysis that result in broad-based government policies acceptable to the wider society, thus making them easier to implement or modify as the need arises. Third, they facilitate joint action planning and joint resource mobilization. By working together a government can assist the private sector in obtaining capital through loans, grants, concessions, contracts, taxes, and other forms of guarantees and subsidies.

Fourth, the partnership can provide practical solutions for eliminating impediments to competitiveness (for example, by eliminating red tape), supporting productivity improvements (for example, through training and development, research, development and commercialization, innovation, improved labour–management relations), and promoting international trade (for example, through joint negotiations, Internet technology). Partnerships also help to improve the country's national integrity and regulatory systems by making sure that the right laws, rules, and regulations are enacted fairly and are consistently enforced.

This helps reduce corruption and protect the environment. Finally, these partnerships can be extremely valuable in times of national crises or emergencies. They can be used as an early warning system to prepare the country for foreseen crises, and they can be used as a vehicle for mobilizing domestic and international support and resources in the preparation and management of crises or emergencies. Unfortunately, some newly globalizing countries do not have a critical mass of credible private sector organizations for effective partnerships.

There are additional advantages for globalizing developing countries to establish and sustain effective private–public partnerships. In times of uncertainty and change, the partnership arrangements provide leaders with mutual support and common understanding, unity of purpose, and sharing experiences and learning new roles and rules, as well as reinforcing the values and principles of globalization. Gathering strength for globalization becomes less onerous in partnership.

On a global scale, most of the actors in developing countries, in both the private and the public sector, are small: Governments have smaller budgets, businesses have smaller operations, and civil society organizations have fewer members, volunteers, and donors. Partnership provides them with the opportunity to scale up and to enjoy synergy, economies of scale, and clout. This is particularly important when dealing with foreign firms that are used to handling large-scale transactions or doing business with large organizations.

In terms of policy analysis, formulation, and implementation, partnerships can be particularly important for developing countries and countries in transition. These countries need growth-oriented policies as part of the overall strategy for the development of macroeconomic enablers and incentives for domestic and foreign investment. They need joint policies and strategies for rapid accumulation, including capital formation, high rates of saving, investment, and rapid growth; trade and investment, including creating an export push; productivity improvement, including technology and innovation; and public sector reform, including democratization, civil service reform, private sector development, and poverty alleviation.

For most developing countries and countries in transition, the most difficult challenge is effective implementation of macroeconomic policies. By working together through private–public sector partnerships, these countries increase their chances of effective policy implementation through improved ownership, commitment, shared learning, and joint mobilization of resources. Private–public partnerships are so important that they have become an important acid test for readiness, openness, competitiveness, and globalization.

Countries, societies, institutions, businesses, and individuals who cannot sustain or be part of effective private-public sector partnerships are not ready for globalization. In addition, the exhibit describes what these councils do, how they work, their composition, and where they have been particularly effective in putting in place macroeconomic enablers and incentives for economic development and globalization. This is not to suggest that other countries should necessarily emulate the experiences of Southeast Asia and start their own deliberation councils.

Rather, the purpose is to provide models by which other countries can extract general principles and lessons of experience relevant to their own situations. They can then draw on these experiences to establish and sustain private-public partnership arrangements most appropriate to the prevailing realities on the ground. In Southeast Asia where deliberation councils were used as part of the Asian model of economic development, there were several deficiencies that became obvious during the 1997–1998 economic crises. These included structural weaknesses in the banking system; poor corporate governance and ownership of enterprises; incestuous relationships among business, politics, and the military; lack of public accountability and transparency; and a general absence of political freedom.

Although these deficiencies do not apply equally to all countries, the region as a whole continues to experience difficulties in its attempts to implement effective post-crises institutional reforms. In industrialized countries, some of the private–public partnerships can be improper, unethical, or illegal. By choosing winners and losers, a government can stifle competition and innovation through public policy instruments such as awarding contracts, loans, grants, concessions, tax cuts, and protectionist subsidies to select businesses.

Examples of this include European and U.S. subsidies to farmers and protective tariffs to their domestic textile and steel firms, thus keeping away producers from developing countries and transition economies. Recently, Canada and

Brazil accused each other of unfair and illegal trade practices as a result of government subsidies to their respective aircraft industries. Japan has often used private–public partnership arrangements to keep foreign competition out.

In the competitive world of globalization, there are no angels. That is why it is very important to have an independent, an impartial, a credible, and a competent system of dispute resolution, both domestically and internationally. In developing countries, this should be an integral part of the country's national integrity and regulatory system. One of the key functions of the WTO is to resolve disputes between or among nations arising from government business practices, which are forbidden according to international law and trade rules and procedures.

NATIONAL INTEGRITY AND REGULATORY SYSTEM

Corruption transcends history and geography. All countries and all societies have experienced (and continue to experience) some form of corrupt, unethical conduct by their political, business, and civic leaders as well as ordinary citizens. Differences occur in how different societies tolerate corruption or how much they are prepared to punish the perpetrators. As a result of globalization, there is a growing universal intolerance of high-level corruption among public officials. In any case, our interest here is not to moralize across cultures but, rather, to discuss the relationships between corruption, openness, competitiveness, economic management, and globalization.

Studies show, and practical experience confirms, the widely held view that corruption impedes the development of a positive sustainable macroeconomic enabling environment for globalization. Evidence from the United States seems to suggest that corporate corruption is related to the business cycle. Boom times, associated with inflated wealth creation, provide corporate executives with opportunities for greed and fraudulent conduct. Regulatory systems are lax and unable to keep up with the growing volume of business transactions. Yet, the misconduct of large U.S. corporations, such as Anderson, Enron, Global Crossing, and Worldcom, hurts more than just their employees, customers, and shareholders-they hurt globalization.

To understand the concept of a national integrity and regulatory system (NIRS), it is important to understand corruption first. According to Transparency International, corruption can be defined as the "misuse of power for private profit ... behaviour on the part of officials in the public sector, whether politicians or civil servants, in which they improperly and unlawfully enrich themselves, or those close to them, by the misuse of the public power entrusted to them." To this must be added actors in the private sector because corruption is a transaction between giver and taker, and therefore, confining it either to the public or private sector alone misses the transactional nature of the disease.

Consider the analogy of disease. The chairman of the Chinese Communist Party called corruption a disease; Dr. Mahathir, the prime minister of Malaysia, called it a cancer with all its pervasive implications. The NIRS is the country's institutional and societal response to fighting the cancerous disease. Like the global fight against cancer of the body, the NIRS is aimed at:

1. Protecting society against corruption (the disease),
2. Treating those already inflicted with the disease,
3. Removing from the environment cosogenic agents that cause the disease,
4. Preventing outsiders from catching the disease, or bringing in foreign strains,
5. Ultimately finding a cure or vaccine for the disease.

The disease spreads faster and new strains come in when the borders are porous. This is particularly the case as countries begin to deregulate and open their economy to the outside world. Experience shows that the first wave of foreigners who come to do business with previously closed economies includes many with questionable business ethics. For example, Nigerians have always complained that foreign business representatives are largely to blame for the country's corrupt image because of their willingness to offer irresistibly big bribes to public officials.

A recent World Bank report on corruption in Uganda found that in 1987 "more than 1,200 birds were smuggled out of the country, more than 280 tons of ivory were illegally exported, and 550 crocodile skins were sent overseas, mainly to Italy and France." Therefore, it is very likely that public officials and private businesses, both in Italy and France, participated in illegal activities and corrupt practices together with Ugandans. Under globalization, an NIRS must develop the institutional capacities and human competencies for dealing effectively with the international dimensions of unethical behaviour and corrupt practices in both the public and the private sectors.

These include institutions at the highest level of government (Executive and Legislative branches), judiciary and law enforcement (for example, courts, policing, legislation), anticorruption agencies (for example, the inspector general of government), central agencies and regulatory boards (for example, the central bank, competition bureau, office of the auditor general), operating line ministries, departments, and agencies (for example, education, health, defense), local authorities, public enterprises, and private sector organizations.

The role of the private sector as an integral part of the NIRS is extremely important. Government alone cannot fight the disease. The two sectors must work together, share experiences, and build a system of institutions, societal values, and promote collective professional conduct designed to uphold the law and the highest level of ethical conduct by those in positions of power and influence in both the public and the private sectors. In this regard, the business sector is particularly critical because they have the resources, and are strategically positioned, to leverage their resources: either to perpetuate or eradicate corruption.

Reporting from Kekku, Myanmar, Blaine Harden wrote about a conversation he had with a local business executive in November 2000 who said that corruption in Myanmar is so bad that citizens are not free to travel abroad without paying bribes for passports, cannot import cars without paying bribes for import licenses, nor can they run businesses without the generals extorting profits. Most transnational corporations provide extensive managerial training in ethics and have developed codes of conduct for their employees and business associates both at home and abroad. An increasing number of businesses are posting copies of their codes of conduct on their Web sites.

General Electric and Nortel both have elaborate codes of ethics. Business, trade, and professional associations can also be instrumental in the fight against corruption by working directly with their members and the clients with whom they do business. Professional associations for auditing, accounting, purchasing, and engineering could refuse to certify work or bid on contracts if laws or rules of conduct have been broken. Some of the big NGOs are also concerned about corruption and have taken steps to play their role in protecting their employees, volunteers, donors, and aid recipients. For example, the Red Cross has established rules of conduct for employees and volunteers going overseas.

The international community is particularly active in containing corruption because of its pervasive global costs. James Wolfensohn, president of the World Bank, has been particularly active in the campaign against corruption by persuading others, including the European Union, to join in the fight. In a recent publication on corruption, he had this to say:

Corruption is a problem that all countries have to confront. Solutions however, can only be home-grown. National leaders need to take a stand. Civil society plays a key role as well.... We will support international efforts to fight corruption and to establish voluntary standards of behaviour for corporations and investors in the industrialized world.... The Bank Group will not tolerate corruption in the programs that we support, and we are taking steps to ensure that our activities continue to meet the highest standards of probity.

This statement is particularly important because it recognizes that the bank, as well as many international organizations with lots of money, is part of the problem when it comes to corruption of senior government officials. They are indeed the supply side of the equation. A few years ago, an international consultant who is also a U.S. citizen told me that he had to stop working on a World Bank road construction project in a South American country. Mindful of the U.S. Foreign Corrupt Practices Act, he was afraid that he could be liable to criminal prosecution because of the way the World Bank task manager and the local contractor were conducting business.

Other international organizations, bilateral donors, and foreign governments belatedly are taking steps to confront problems of corruption within their own ranks. Donors are pushing hard to achieve levels of accountability acceptable to their domestic constituencies. Still, it can be argued that due to the multiple roles these organizations play as lenders, donors, consultants, and clients, they often find themselves in compromising conflict-of-interest situations with governments, corporations, and even NGOs, which render them biased and ineffective in dealing with ethical questions and problems of corruption.

All available evidence points to the inevitable conclusion that corruption is bad for globalization. In general, corruption is bad for globalization because it weakens the state, undermines the market, demoralizes society, and alienates the outside world. It weakens the state through poor governance, reduced government revenue, lack of public respect, lost integrity of public officials, and overall institutional decay. A weak state is not good for globalization.

Corruption undermines the market by creating and perpetuating artificial market imperfections and preventing the normal functioning of competitive market forces. For example, a recent study of privatization in one of the Commonwealth of Independent States (CIS) found that formerly state-owned construction firms were sold to politicians, civil servants, and close associates who run the construction sector as a cartel rather than a competitive business. Worse still, corruption undermines the market by discouraging the growth of SMEs and the indigenous private sector. This is very harmful to the economy because these firms are best known for job creation, innovation, risk taking, and promoting overall competitiveness and entrepreneurship. SMEs cannot compete with big business when it comes to doing business by bribes.

Corruption demoralizes society in many different ways. It denies the people the opportunity to be the best they can be. It undermines their self-esteem and confidence in public institutions and private enterprise. It impoverishes and disempowers them. It forces them to live a life of dishonesty and lies. It alienates them from one another and creates social discord. It tears society apart. A disconnected society with so much pain does not have the necessary collective capacity for competitiveness, innovation, and equitable globalization. It is unrealistic to expect citizens to respect law and order when they are being brutalized by their own government.

Finally, corruption keeps foreign capital away. International capital goes where it is needed, but stays only where it feels welcome. Corruption discriminates against foreign business interests because local businesses are much closer to the politicians and civil servants. In another CIS example, public officials worked closely with local hotel owners to prevent foreigners from opening hotels in the country. By labeling certain industries as "strategic" meaning that they are of national strategic importance-many developing countries in Africa and elsewhere have kept foreign capital out, deprived the economy of badly needed foreign investment, stifled innovation, and retarded growth and competitiveness.

Corruption adds to the cost and risk of doing business and makes the corrupt country less competitive for foreign investment. The CIS study showed that in one country, foreign investors estimated that up to 40 per cent of the cost of doing business in the first year of operation was spent on corruption. This explains why foreign investors ask for such high rates of return when they invest in chronically corrupt countries. This message is very clear. Any country, society, institution, local government, business (small or large), and individual, if you are seriously interested in active and lasting participation in the global economy and global society, eradicate corruption first.

INDUSTRIAL POLICY IN A GLOBAL ECONOMY

In a globalizing economy, industrial policy formulation and implementation is key to wealth creation and income generation for society as a whole. Yet, this remains one of the most difficult public policy challenges for government and the private sector. There are a few reasons for these challenges: First, as the role of the state changes in economic management, corresponding market-friendly changes are required in the values, attitudes, and behaviour of politicians, public servants, and civic leaders.

In many cases, these changes have been slow to take root, and senior officials have not been consistent in their support for market-friendly industrial policies. Second, there has often been confusion and misunderstanding about the exact nature of the new role of government in an open globalizing economy. The idea is not for government to abdicate its responsibility for providing leadership and strategic direction as would be suggested under pure laissez-faire conditions. Indeed, no country in the world practices pure laissez-faire economics.

Therefore, the new role requires government officials to work as facilitators and champions of the overall strategic directions of the country's industrial policy and development. The role of the government is to remove the impediments to industrial policy development and implementation and to work closely with the private sector and the international community to ensure a positive sustaining enabling environment.

A third area of challenge has been the absence of a capable and credible private sector to work with. Countries emerging out of Communism, socialism, colonialism, or conflicts do not have a viable private sector. In some cases, the emerging private sector is a reincarnation of the old regime in support of the old ideology and is connected to reactionary military, traditional, or criminal parts of society. When this happens, governments become both unable and unwilling to open up the economy for fear of being overthrown or taken over by reactionary or criminal forces.

This list is a useful guide for both government and the private sector to assess the current industrial policy for the economy, to set specific goals and objectives for each of the strategic directions, and to develop a practical and realistic plan of action. For example, if the objective is to change the industrial policy from import substitution to export growth, specific objectives can be set and monitored through trade and export performance of the economy. Second, changing the direction from central planning and government ownership and control to a private sector–led economy can be achieved through privatization and private sector development.

If the goal is to invite and encourage foreign ownership and participation in the economy, this can be assessed by looking at the legal and administrative systems in place, the extent to which it welcomes or discourages foreign investment, and the actual participation of foreign capital, technology, and management in the economy. Before globalization, most developing economies depended on a few commodities for exports and domestic cash economy: in Ghana, it was cocoa; Brazil, coffee; Malaysia, rubber; and Australia and New Zealand, wool and mutton.

With globalization, the economy needs to be diversified by using modern technology to create high-value-added goods and services sold to the global market. Indeed, successful globalizing economies are those which diversify their export portfolios and lessen their dependence on natural resources or commodities as the key exports. This does not mean neglecting traditional agricultural exports as Nigeria did with groundnuts; it means using the traditional exports as the basis for diversification. Malaysia provides a good example. At the time of independence in 1956, the country depended almost exclusively on commodities for exports.

Today, its export portfolio includes electronic equipment, petroleum products, and textiles. For Nigeria, apart from petroleum products, it has no high-value-added goods or services in its export portfolio nor is it diversified. Equally important is the diversification of trading partners from a few trading partners to increasing participation in the worldwide trading system. Many developing countries have historical ties to one or a few major trading partners resulting from former colonial ties. As the world trading system opens up and becomes more global, these countries need to diversify their trading partnerships and move closer to the global system. In some cases, this may start with one or several regional trading arrangements.

Indeed, the world is now divided into regional trading blocks: in North America (NAFTA), Europe (EU), Asia (ASEAN), Pacific Rim (APAC), Africa (COMESA, ECOWAS, and TPA), South America (MERCOSUR), and South Asia (SAARC). These regional groupings have generally been positive in promoting openness, competitiveness, and trade, although some have been more successful than others. Yet, they should be seen as an interim arrangement toward a more worldwide trading system under the WTO. While developing countries benefit from and must be encouraged, and where necessary supported, to join a regional trading block, ultimately the objective should be to become active participants in the worldwide trading system.

Globalization requires significant policy changes in labour and employment. While the traditional approach is to draw on large pools of unskilled cheap labour and to support labour-intensive industries, with globalization, and given the need to produce high-end value-added goods and services, the emphasis changes to skilled technologists and knowledge workers. Technologists are those workers who combine both technical knowledge and manual skills.

They are usually trained in community colleges or specialized technical schools, rather than academic universities. Examples include different types of technicians, automobile mechanics, health-care workers, and computer programmers. They are highly skilled and provide industry with a competitive comparative advantage. Developing countries unable to produce enough technologies are at a disadvantage because they do not have the human resources needed for producing nontraditional high-value-added goods and services.

In fact, it has been argued that industrialized countries will continue to maintain a significant competitive edge over and above emerging economies as long as they educate and produce more technologists than the competition. Before globalization, the tendency is for the economy to be dominated by SOEs and selected invited MNCs. With globalization, the state gets out of direct productive and operational aspects of business, thus reducing the role and significance of SOEs. These are replaced by the emergence of indigenous SMEs run by independent entrepreneurs.

As well, by opening up the economy, more foreign firms, big and small, become active participants, reducing the monopoly previously enjoyed by the select few multinationals. These changes encourage openness, competitiveness, and entrepreneurship-all of which are good for globalization. Globalization brings greater pressures on industry to become socially responsible and to protect the environment. It is no longer acceptable for industry to pollute the air, water, and/ or soil or otherwise harm the environment for industrial development and job creation. Government must make sure that it has the appropriate legal framework to protect the environment, the institutional capacity and human capital to enforce the rules, and the political will to punish the offenders.

An increasing number of global businesses are beginning to take environmental concerns seriously and are taking practical steps to ensure that their operations are environmentally sound. Environmental audits have become an important part of corporate governance and reporting. Businesses that pollute the environment in the name of global competitiveness do more harm to globalization than the anarchists who demonstrate openly in opposition to globalization. Civil society-the press, NGOs-has a role to play in keeping government and business accountable and transparent in dealing with matters of environmental awareness and protection.

Finally, globalization changes the industrial policy environment from relatively stable and predictable to rapidly changing, complex, and uncertain. Therefore, managing change and transformations becomes an important capacity for all the players in bringing about the changes identified. All these changes are interconnected and bring about both intended and unintended positive and adverse effects on different segments of society. In some countries, previously isolated villages have responded to openness by selling their produce to the outside market.

While this has significantly increased their cash earnings, it has also made them more vulnerable to food shortages because nobody advised them of the need to keep some food in reserve instead of selling it all for cash. A government, in cooperation with the private sector, needs to develop sophisticated management systems and practices in order to anticipate and effectively manage both the expected and the unexpected changes and transformations resulting from changes in industrial policy for globalization. Risk assessment and management is a necessary critical competence for globalizing economies.

OVERCOMING IMPEDIMENTS TO INDUSTRIAL DEVELOPMENT

In many cases, developing countries fail to pursue pro-globalization policies for industrial development, not for lack of good ideas but because of systemic impediments to policy implementation. One of the most serious impediments has to do with societal values and institutions. In many developing countries, societal values do not support the underlying values and principles of competitiveness, privatization, capitalism, individualism, and an economy largely driven by the private sector.

In South Africa, Vietnam, Cambodia, and some of the Arab and Muslim countries, privatization and other related strategies of economic reform are slow and tentative because governments fear that these policies do not enjoy popular societal support. In the case of South Africa, the ruling African National Congress (ANC) has a long history of socialist ideology, has members of the Communist Party in its cabinet, and is strongly supported by the trade union movement COSATU which, like most unions the world over, is anti-globalization.

As well, historically, the South African black population always associated capitalism with apartheid. Local industry is also dependent on cheap unskilled labour, especially in the mining and agricultural sectors. Accordingly, resistance to industrial transformation comes from all sides of the South African society. Therefore, it is imperative that government provides leadership that will bring about changes in societal values. This is not easy and cannot be done overnight.

Values can and do change through carefully designed programs such as public awareness, education, demonstration and pilot projects, various incentives, opportunities for influential community leaders and decision makers to travel abroad, and exposing society to different frames of reference. Participation is a very powerful instrument for bringing about sustaining changes in personal and societal values, attitudes, and behaviour. As the old saying goes, "Tell me and I might forget, show me and I might remember, but involve me, and I will understand."

Involving various segments of society in those aspects of industrial development for globalization which affects them most will help transform values, belief systems, attitudes, and behaviour. In southern Africa where there is increasing pressure on the land, local communities are often in conflict with wildlife conservation because there is not enough land for both human settlement and wildlife. In response, several countries have started to experiment with involving the local community in wildlife conservation and management.

The communities are asked to share the land with wildlife, and in return, they participate in making wildlife management decisions and share in the resulting economic benefits. As a result, wildlife resources become community resources, and the community becomes the best frontline agent for conservation and fighting poaching. For the weaker nation-states, especially those categorized as P2, a key impediment to effective implementation is political instability, lack of political will, and poor or misguided leadership. Here, any efforts at overcoming these impediments must start with peacemaking and peacekeeping initiatives.

These initiatives are usually supported by an international or U.N. force. The last quarter of the twentieth century witnessed many nation-states either totally collapsed (for example, Somalia) or on the verge of collapsing (for example, Afghanistan, Sierra Leone, Cambodia, Haiti, Liberia, Congo, Rwanda). These countries are in no position to participate meaningfully in the global economy. Unfortunately, they are also in no position to stop the illegal globalization of their economies.

This is done through the illegal exportation of minerals (such as diamonds), wildlife, drugs, human beings, and arms as well as other illegal trade. Under the Taliban regime, Afghanistan contributed 90 per cent of the heroin sold on the streets of London. There are no short-term solutions or quick fixes for such weak states. Here, the international community must intervene and help build national institutions, develop new leadership, encourage change in leadership, and introduce new policies in support of rehabilitation and eventual development toward legitimate globalization.

After the war, Vietnam's wounds were deep, industries weak, technology backward, infrastructure deplorable, and the country was unable to manage globalization to its advantage. For such countries, it may be advisable to close them off from the global economy until they have reestablished a strong state with credible governance systems. The third impediment identified is the existence of a weak indigenous private sector. Before globalization, many developing countries were hostile to their own indigenous private sector, and many years of official harassment and unsupportive public policy have left the local private sector small, unorganized, poorly resourced and managed, and lacking in public esteem and respect.

Globalization is not possible without a vibrant local/ indigenous private sector. Steps can be taken to support the development of the sector; the most important of which is there must be a significant change in government policy and public support for the private sector. It is not enough for government to retreat from active participation in the economy; it must also make sure that it is replaced by a private sector with the capacity to perform and deliver results and the reputation, credibility, and support from the citizens it serves. Therefore, it may be necessary for government to undertake confidence-building measures between the private sector and the general public.

The fourth impediment is lack of management know-how in either the private or the public sector. The simplest way to address this is through management consulting contracts. There are many global management-consulting firms providing a wide range of expertise. Some developing countries have developed their own local consulting firms and may not need to buy the services on the open market. Some other countries prefer a combination of local and foreign consulting firms working together and reinforcing each other's areas of strength. No matter what mode of application a country chooses at different stages of development, it must understand the challenges and limitations of using management consultants.

Other strategies for overcoming lack of management expertise include management training and development, staff interchange and use of volunteer executive services from other countries. With many schools offering MBAs at various locations and on the Internet, the opportunities for management training and development have never been greater and are becoming less expensive. For most developing countries interested in managing globalization, there is room for more creative use of executive interchange both domestically-within a country but across sectors, industries, or regions-and internationally.

In addition to lack of management expertise, many developing countries experience generalized lack of capital, resources, and capacity for policy development and implementation. The strategies for overcoming these impediments are listed and include better mobilization and utilization of resources both at home and abroad, increased government revenues through a more efficient tax collection system, economic growth, wealth creation, and income generation. They also include building institutional capacities for policy analysis and implementation and attracting foreign capital and FDI (capital, technology, management).

Even after a country has taken steps to overcome these impediments, it may still find itself unable to effectively implement its industrial development policies or enjoy the benefits of globalization. This may be due to a group of impediments collectively referred to as "exogenous variables". These are "external" factors over which the country has no direct and effective control. The sources of exogenous variables are many and varied. As I have discussed, for weak states they may be associated with internal discord and the inability of the government to hold the country together let alone implement industrial development policies.

They may be caused by acts of God, as often happens with small island and coastal states that periodically suffer from massive floods (for example, Bangladesh, India, Mozambique), hurricanes and typhoons (for example, the Caribbean), earthquakes (for example, Turkey), droughts (for example, Ethiopia), land slides (for example, Venezuela), or diseases such as HIV/AIDS or Ebola.

Exogenous variables also include changes going on elsewhere in the world that have profound effects on the fortunes or misfortunes of other countries. These may be technological, economic, political, or sociocultural changes. For example, changes in technology that makes it possible for the world to produce cheaper and almost equally attractive synthetic products have profound negative effects on producers of natural products. Recent examples include wool (for example, Australia), leather (for example, the Middle East), ivory (for example, Africa), hardwood (for example, Ghana, Brazil, Indonesia), cotton (for example, Egypt), and rugs (for example, Iran).

When this happens, the affected country needs to make immediate and fundamental changes to its industrial development policies and strategies. Technologically advanced countries with strong economies and institutional capacities can make these changes in a relatively short period of time with minimal adverse effects to the majority of the citizens. This is what happened, for example, when Switzerland lost world leadership in the production and marketing of watches to the Japanese when they invented digital and more functional watches. But the Swiss economy did not collapse.

The affected watch-making firms and communities either adjusted to the new technological changes by producing and marketing watches that would compete with the Japanese or simply exited from the industry and invested in other sectors of the economy. Unfortunately, firms and communities in developing countries have very limited resources and capacities to make the necessary adjustments to technological change.

Changes in the world economy can also cause several exogenous variables, making it difficult for developing countries to effectively implement industrial development policies in support of globalization. These changes could cause the value of the U.S. dollar to go up significantly relative to the local currency, interest rates to rise, world oil prices to sky-rocket in response to political changes in the Middle East, or commodity prices to rise or fall as a result of unexpected weather conditions in key producer countries.

Any of these factors or combinations thereof can directly affect the country's capacity to pursue industrial development policies in support of globalization. Economic downturns in the United States and other industralized countries cause economic hardships to many developing and transition economies. What strategies can a country use to protect itself against these exogenous variables? There are no easy solutions or quick fixes, especially for the weaker developing countries. Perhaps, the first and most important strategy is to create public awareness about the realities and possible advance consequences of exogenous variables. Economic crises are most painful and destructive when they are least expected.

This is what happened to the Southeast Asian economies because before 1997–1998 they were considered "miracles" and therefore not subject to the normal economic cycle. On the other hand, when the government and its institutions, businesses, civil society, and the public in general are made aware of the likelihood of unanticipated events and their possible negative consequences, they can take individual and collective measures to protect their interests. The evidence from China supports this: Scientists have been able to predict earthquakes with increasing accuracy, thus allowing citizens to take defensive measures and reducing loss of life and property.

Other possible strategies against exogenous variables include modeling, risk management, strengthening planning systems at all levels of society, environmental scanning, and developing a national emergency management system. Modeling is commonly used in management and economics. In macroeconomics, it can be used to predict the effects on the national economy or parts thereof of changes in the value of the U.S. dollar, interest rates, oil prices, or terms of trade. For example, if a country has a large percentage of its external debt in U.S. dollars, modeling external debt management at different levels of exchange rates can reveal to the debtor the net effects on their cash flow and the levels at which it becomes impossible for them to keep up with debt payments.

RISK AND EMERGENCY MANAGEMENT

Risk management provides tools and techniques for controlling the effect of exogenous variables. It involves risk assessment-determining the level of risk associated with a given event or activity-and risk management, which involves taking steps to protect individuals or collective interests in line with the level of assessed risk. Everything we do in life involves a certain level of risk, but in most cases, we consider the risk involved so low that we hardly think about it. In other cases, the risks involved are considered high enough to necessitate taking practical steps to manage such risks. For example, crossing a residential street is considered a very low risk event, and for most people, no special steps are taken to manage the risk.

On the other hand, driving a car and taking a plane trip are events associated with high enough levels of risk to require special risk management undertaking. In both cases, we buy insurance policies for protection, and for driving we are required to take training, driving tests, and certification for additional protection. Likewise, globalizing government institutions, societies, businesses, and individuals should assess the risks associated with various activities and take the necessary risk management measures as protection.

Businesses buy insurance against operational losses, farmers buy insurance against crop failures due to a range of natural or human-made causes, and most individuals buy life insurance as protection against premature death. It makes sense for anybody in the public or private sector actively involved in globalization to take risk management steps, such as buying insurance, as protection against predictable and unintended adverse effects of globalization. To do otherwise is to expose oneself to dangerous and unacceptable levels of risk.

It is also possible to control the effects of exogenous variables by strengthening planning, monitoring, and evaluation systems. This can be done at both macro and micro levels involving the national government and its institutions, subnational governments, business firms, NGOs, or individual citizens. Planning is one of the most effective management tools business organizations use to mobilize resources and to achieve unity of purpose. Management sets strategic directions, develops business plans and operational targets, determines objectives, and establishes individual performance goals. Regular ongoing reporting is used to monitor performance, compare achievements vis-à-vis planned targets, and take corrective measures.

Management is always looking for opportunities for continuous improvements. The public sector can learn and draw lessons from business organizations and use planning, monitoring, and evaluation tools to control the effects of exogenous variables on various aspects of globalization. While most public agencies do a fair amount of strategic and operational planning, they tend to be less rigorous when it comes to monitoring, evaluation, and taking corrective measures for continuous improvement. They tend to assume that plans are deterministic rather than probabilistic.

Planning is not an exact science, and all the facts and important factors cannot be known at the time of planning. So every plan is associated with a probability that it may not be accomplished either in its entirely or parts thereof. This is why monitoring and evaluation are so important-as a basis for drawing out lessons of experience, which should inform subsequent planning and operations. One of the reasons why public agencies shy away from continuous monitoring and evaluation is because the results are often used for finger pointing rather than problem solving. Public servants feel threatened because feedback is used to punish employees rather than to encourage creativity.

Therefore, it is necessary for government agencies to create conditions for the development of learning communities/ organizations as part of the management of globalization. A learning community refers to having the capacity to adapt to changes in the environment and to respond to lessons of experience by making changes to the way the community functions and people behave. Developing emergency management systems would help developing countries in dealing with the effects of exogenous variables. Most developing countries are susceptible to emergencies and crises. While some of these are due to natural causes, many are due to weaknesses in the systems and structures that exist in these countries.

For example, the physical infrastructure is often weak, overworked, and underserviced with minimal and infrequent repairs and maintenance. The technology used is often old, and new technology may be pirated. There is often a shortage of experienced technologists, and management is also in short supply. Opportunities for skills training and upgrading are limited. Budgetary limitations make it difficult to upgrade equipment and to undertake necessary repairs and maintenance, especially if these require foreign currency expenditures.

Therefore, as part of their industrial policy for globalization, developing countries need to develop multilevel emergency management systems in preparation for emergencies or crises. These systems should be able to deal with disasters, epidemics, industrial accidents, food and gasoline shortages, rationing, factory closures, massive layoffs, liquidity problems, political unrest, and economic crises.

Once again, government needs to work in partnership with the private sector, other levels of government, civil society, and the international community to ensure that effective practical arrangements are in place and that all sectors of society are actively involved in the design and implementation of the country's emergency management systems. If developing countries cannot rule out the likelihood of emergencies and crises arising from activities associated with globalization, the least they can do is put in place effective emergency and crises management systems. These measures would not prevent crises from taking place but would help to mitigate their negative consequences.

DIVERSIFICATION

Another exogenous variable is diversification. Diversification as part of industrial policy is not new, but with globalization, it becomes much more significant. Diversification as part of a country's industrial development strategy means that a country develops capacities, competencies, and competitive advantages for producing a wider range of marketable goods and services. Its advantages include distribution of risks and rewards and providing a broader industrial knowledge base and competitive advantage, broader export base, more trading partners, and more opportunities for spin-offs and entrepreneurial development in different sectors and regions of the economy.

Diversification strategies can be developed by industry, sector, or region. Within industry, it is common to think in terms of the new (high-tech) economy, and the old economy. While developing countries can pursue opportunities in the new economy such as international call centers and data processing in India and electronic assembling in the Philippines and Costa Rica, they should not forget opportunities in the old economy. The old economy such as textiles, food-processing ser vices, and light manufacturing is still important and continues to offer these countries greater competitive advantages and niche opportunities.

Indeed, it appears that the more successful globalizing developing countries are pursuing this strategy. For example, while pursuing industrial opportunities in the new economy, Thailand continues to export high-value agricultural products such as seafood and rice and provides attractive world-class tourist services. Likewise, Chile's economic recovery and growth is largely based on the old economy of mining, especially copper that makes up almost 40 percent of exports by value, and high-value-added agricultural products including wine, fruits, and high-quality wood products. At the other end of the spectrum, the challenge for globalizing countries, such as Ghana, is to diversify the economy, especially the export base.

Ghana continues to depend on exports of mining (gold, bauxite) and agriculture (cocoa) with a rather small and underdeveloped tourist industry. What the country now needs is to develop niche specialization, which will allow it to produce high-value products or services marketable to the global market. The third area of diversification is by region. Many developing countries have large territories or landmasses with a variety of natural and human resources.

These provide opportunities for regional diversification of industrial development for globalization. Coastal areas rich in marine life and tourist attractions, interior forests teeming with plant and animal life, dry desertlike lands with rolling sand dunes, and mountain ranges capped with snow all year round all provide fertile grounds for the development of regional economic specialization. One of the subsectors that offers developing countries greater but as yet unexploited opportunities is agri food for the global market. These countries have interesting variations in topography, soil types, and climatic conditions and an abundant supply of freshwater.

They have a large supply of inexpensive labour: young, eager to work, and easy to train. On the demand side, there are a number of factors that also work in their favor. The world population is growing, and almost all of this growth is in developing countries. More people are moving into urban areas where they are increasingly dependent on commerce for food supplies. Many of the world's hungry and those who do not get adequate nutrients in their diets are in developing countries.

As income rises, tastes and eating habits change, and people seek high-value, specialty food for enjoyment. With globalization also comes multiculturalism, which means that foods previously found in one part of the world are now successfully marketed globally. Examples include Mexican food, Italian pasta, Chinese and Thai food, and Indian curry. Looking for niche markets in the agri-food business, developing countries can draw on and take advantage of various technological advances and management know-how in areas such as biotechnology, genetic engineering, marine science, farm management, international marketing, and transportation including canning, packaging, and shipping. Recent experiences seem to suggest that the agri-food business is relatively easy for developing and emerging economies.

Witness how fast Eastern Europe has been able to revive its wine industry in a relatively short period of time. Competitive wines are now available on the world market from Bulgaria, Hungary, Croatia, and Romania. South African exports include wine and other agri-food products. Countries such as Brazil, Argentina, Sudan, South Africa, Iran, Indonesia,

Syria, and Ukraine have a lot of potential for producing specialized high-value regional goods and services for the global economy. What developing countries need is diversification that cuts across industrial, sectoral, and regional dimensions and brings together private–public partnerships drawn from both the indigenous private sector and international business.

PRIVATIZATION AND PRIVATE SECTOR DEVELOPMENT

A lot has been written on privatization and private sector development by academics, journalists, governments, and international organizations. Most of the literature is not neutral; rather, it speaks either for or against privatization. The keen interest and intensity is quite understandable. Privatization is at the core of political and socioeconomic reforms for all globalizing countries. It is controversial in terms of ideology, objectives, processes, and results.

It significantly changes the role of the state from owner and manager of productive assets to partner, facilitator, or enabler of economic development. Like globalization, it produces winners as well as losers. Needless to say, the ideological debate is not about to be settled anytime soon. Our interest here is not to review the literature on privatization and private sector development or to weigh in on the ideological debate. Rather, the purpose is to discuss briefly the relationship between privatization and private sector development and globalization.

The question of interest here is whether developing countries and transition economies enhance their capacities for meaningful participation in the global economy through privatization and private sector development. We are also interested in drawing out lessons of experience from privatizing countries for the benefit of others. It should be pointed out at the outset that privatization is not an issue only for developing countries. Rich, industrialized countries also face challenges of privatization, although the net impact may be greater for the poor countries. The three common forms of privatization are:

1. Partial or complete sale of SOEs to new private sector owners,
2. Private provision of public services,
3. Alternative service delivery arrangements.

Most of the discussions on privatization focus on the sale of public enterprise (SOEs) to the private sector. For most developing countries, this form of privatization is the most practical manifestation of public commitment to reform and, ultimately, to globalization. During the period 1980–1991, a total of 2,162 SOEs were privatized in developing countries representing all regions of the world-Latin America and the Caribbean (37 per cent) and Eastern Europe (37 per cent) had the largest percentage and sub-Saharan Africa (17 per cent), Asia (6 per cent), and the Middle East and North Africa (3 per cent) had the smallest percentage.

With all its economic, management, legal, technical, and social problems, privatization-sale of SOEs-on the whole has benefited the countries and their citizens. Private provision of public goods and services is an extension to the privatization of SOEs. Here, instead of the government selling public assets, it invites the private sector, through a process of competitive bidding, to provide a defined set of public services for profit. These may be social services such as health care and welfare administration; utilities such as water, roads, and electricity; or security services such as prisons, or in the case of weak states, private military service.

These services are usually provided under contract, which, among other things, specifies the expected level of performance, the cost of providing the services, and the duration of the contract. The government retains responsibility for the management of the contract and the supervision, monitoring, and evaluation of the services. The contract can be suspended or cancelled if the private contractor does not meet performance specifications, and contract renewal is subject to review and competition. The private sector contractors may be drawn from the local business community, NGOs, academic institutions, foreign companies or institutions, or combinations thereof.

Sometimes, government agencies can also bid to get their jobs back through a competitive process. They can do this individually or in partnership with private sector organizations. Alternative service delivery (ASD) is derived from the idea that there is no one simple best way of managing and providing services to the public. As part of the new public management paradigm, ASD is a creative attempt to find solutions to the government challenge of meeting the growing and changing demands and expectations of the citizens, within the context of increasing citizen awareness of service delivery options and value for money.

ASD can be defined as a creative and dynamic process of public sector management and restructuring that aims to improve the delivery of services to citizens or clients by sharing governance and operational functions with individuals, community groups, business organizations, and other government agencies. Some of the common delivery options include co-location, single-window service centers, common-service providers, special operating agencies, and other forms of government-owned but commercially operated organizations such as airports.

Although they may have different operating rules, all these arrangements share one common characteristic: They are still managed and directed from inside government. Therefore, ASD mechanisms combine some of the aspects of privatization (private operators) and the private provision of public service (government ownership). They are also different in that they deliberately treat the citizens as an informed and active participant and decision maker in the design and delivery of important public services.

ASD is a form of private–public partnership arrangement. It facilitates the pooling together of resources, capacities, skills, and experiences from all sectors of society instead of depending only on government agencies. The tools associated with ASD mechanisms allow governments to tailor various options to meet prevailing needs on the ground, challenge traditional hierarchical structures, and allow public servants in partnership with others the flexibility to adapt to the changing environment of public administration and economic management.

Having defined the parameters of privatization, let's now address the question of how all this relates to globalization. First, all three types of privatization-sale of SOEs, private provision of public service and ASD-reduce the burden of administration to the state. SOEs traditionally lose money and are a constant drain on the national treasury. Selling them reduces the financial burden of the state, including foreign debts and contingent liabilities. The other two types of privatization also reduce the burden of management for the state as private sector operators take over some of the functions and responsibilities previously handled by the state alone.

Contracting out public services usually contributes to a smaller and more streamlined public service. The social burdens arising from privatization can also be shared with the private sector, which can provide creative solutions or social safety nets for those who are left behind. The more these burdens are removed from the state, the more politicians and senior civil servants are freed up to concentrate their efforts on good governance and creating an enabling environment for globalization.

Privatization contributes to enterprise efficiency, creativity, transparency, and accountability. There are many examples in which money-losing SOEs have been privatized and turned into profitable ongoing enterprises. Privatized enterprises provide better services, operate more efficiently, introduce more new products and services, and have a better and regular reporting relationship with their stockholders. This commercial approach to enterprise management contributes to the development of a local business-like climate and a culture of entrepreneurship. These developments help to prepare the local population for globalization and make the country attractive to outside investment.

Privatization also generates revenue for the treasury. Sales of SOEs generate millions of dollars, whereas the other two types save governments money by providing services at reduced costs. The additional revenue allows the government to spend more on social services and to build up the national infrastructure. Both of these are necessary preconditions for effective globalization. Privatization also encourages and prepares the ground for the development of a local indigenous private sector. Some countries, such as Indonesia, insist on local participation in the privatization of SOEs, government contracting, and ASD.

Foreigners with capital, technology, and management expertise are required to form alliances with local businesses in order to qualify to bid on large government contracts or sales. Although this can lead to abuse by the government choosing winners, if done openly and competitively, it has the potential of providing local businesses with the boost they need to grow and to become globally competitive. It also provides foreign businesses the opportunity to work in partnership with those who are intimately knowledgeable about and experienced with the local political economy, culture, and business practices.

The partners give each other a window into the unknown: Foreigners learn about the local society, and the local partners learn about international business and the global economy. These personal relationships can be instrumental in subsequent development of outside contacts for globalization. Privatization also has the added advantage of bringing together various sectors of society to learn to work collaboratively in partnership. The private provision of public services and ASD are particularly good in advancing private–public collaboration because they both seek organizational arrangements that facilitate participation from across institutions, sectors, and regions.

This gives rise to the development of institutional capacities and human competencies such as corporate governance, negotiations, conflict management, dispute resolution, organizational restructuring, change management, and cross-cultural decision making, information sharing, and joint problem solving. All these capacities and competencies are necessary for managing globalization.

The first lesson speaks to the need for planning. The reform followed a long process of technical, economic, social, political, and managerial planning by Indonesians with the help of outside experts. This process allowed the government to evaluate different reform and privatization options before deciding on a course of action. For example, the use of a joint operations scheme and division of the country into separate telecommunications market areas was aimed at ensuring development of telecommunications services in rural, remote, and isolated areas.

It was also aimed at responding to local pressures for indigenous participation by insisting on local leadership for each bidding consortium. The JOS also ensured international competition because each of the five consortia would include a foreign telecommunications firm with the necessary capital, technology, and management expertise. This was important because directly and indirectly, through donors and financing agencies such as the World Bank, Indonesia was getting pressure from powerful and influential countries such as Japan, the United States, Australia, the Netherlands, and Germany for their national telecommunications firms to get a piece of the action in the Indonesian growing market.

The president-director of PTO described the corporate plan as the fastest infrastructure expansion ever attempted anywhere in the world. The strategy for achieving the plan targets was multifaceted, involving the resources of nearly a dozen countries and specific areas of expertise from more than five countries. Yet, control of PTO was to remain in Indonesian hands for reasons of "national security." Challenge: Despite all the reform measures, the physical expansion and service improvement were not keeping up with the rapidly growing and changing telecommunications demand for the Indonesian economy and society. Performance measures such as call completion rates, telephone failure rates, and teledensity were all below ASEAN averages.

A more serious challenge was the realization in 1994 that there was serious underutilization of new telecommunications infrastructure, suggesting that PTO did not have the necessary institutional capacity and human competencies to meet the targets of its corporate goals. (Note: The term call completion is used in telecommunications to refer to the rate at which calls are successfully completed on first attempt.) Joint Operations Scheme: In response to PTO's challenges, the supervising ministry established a JOS whose purpose was to provide an institutional framework to screen and select domestic and international private sector partners with whom PTO would have to work to achieve its corporate goals. JOS made the following arrangements:

- The country was divided into twelve telecommunications service areas (WITELS) each with separate targets, but these were later collapsed into five large markets in order to attract foreign investors.
- Excluding Jakarta and Surabaya, a total of 2 million new line units were to be added at an estimated total cost of U.S.$2.4 billion.
- JOS participants were to come from national private sector companies, national or provincial SOEs, cooperatives, NGOs, or MNCs.
- Interested partners were to organize themselves into consortiums, each with a maximum of five corporate entities.
- Indonesian companies were required to lead the consortium.
- A consortium that included a cooperative or a local small- or medium-size company would receive special consideration from the government.
- Each consortium had to include a reputable telecommunications company with the necessary capital, technology, and management expertise.

- Each consortium was to perform the following functions: planning, engineering, construction, operations, human resource development, and technology transfer. Operations included marketing, maintenance, and related operational management functions.
- Each consortium would share revenue with PTO in the ratio of 70:30.

Source: Based on the results of a field research project in 1994, partly published by Moses N. Kiggundu, "Capacity Development for Managing Telecommunications Reform and Restructuring: A Corporate Approach from Indonesia," Journal of Asian Business 13, no. 12 (1997):19–57.

Another important lesson from the Indonesian experience is the importance of having the right legal framework for deregulation and privatization. Indonesia reformed the PTO's legal framework by upgrading it from a government department to a corporate entity. Corporatization gave it the autonomy and responsibility to conduct business with local and foreign firms and to pursue its own corporate mission and business objectives, separate from the supervising ministry. It sent out the message to the outside investors that government was serious about reform and privatization.

Yet, PTO still remained as a state monopoly. Private investors could not operate in the country independently-they needed to be licensed through PTO. The supervising ministry still controlled PTO, its operations, and investments. The government took out as much as 50 percent of PTO's profits for general purposes, leaving the corporation with a shortage of investment capital. Therefore, while the reform of the legal framework was moving in the right direction, there were serious impediments to corporatization and privatization that needed to be addressed.

The Indonesian experience also teaches us the importance of time and the need to learn from reform experiences. Things did not happen as fast as the planners had hoped. PTO did not have the institutional capacity or the human capital for the effective implementation of the five-year corporate plan.

For example, a March 1994 report by Japan's Overseas Economic Cooperation Fund concluded that:

> Problems or difficulties ... remain unresolved ... in asynchronization among subsystem expansion programs, poor quality of services and low productivity.... [D]iscrepancy of numbers between installed switching capacity and newly installed subscribers is considerable due to unsatisfactory coordination and synchronization among subsystem expansion programs and inaccuracy of demand forecast. One of the major causes for unsatisfactory coordination among subsystem constructions comes from separately planned programs.... OSP (outside plant) and transmission were planned separately with separate funds.

The president-director of PTO seemed to agree with this assessment when he admitted to a local telecommunications gathering, "My minister asks me, 'Are you ready for competition?' I say yes, but my 43,000 employees are not yet ready." A detailed study of capacity assessment identified many operational and managerial gaps where PTO needed significant improvements.

These included improvements in network management; service, repair, and maintenance; contract management; managing domestic and international alliances; and change management especially relating to strategic management of major business shifts and internal corporate changes. PTO had no sales or marketing experience because, as a monopoly, it did not have to compete for customers, but instead maintained a ten-year waiting list for residential telephone installations. PTO needed resources and times to build the necessary institutional capacity and human capital to undertake the necessary reforms and to meet its corporate goals and objectives.

One of the advantages of corporatization is that it helps to introduce competitiveness and a business-like culture, know-how, and discipline with modern management. For PTO, this included the development of a corporate and business plan for the first time and learning to focus on the market and the customers instead of focusing on technology and the bureaucracy only (internal operations). PTO started taking human resource development seriously and was measuring performance by results rather than inputs. Still, one area that needed much improvement was the management of all the private sector alliances arising out of the JOS. Some thought that these were marriages of convenience, whereas others were concerned that they perpetuated cronyism rather than reform.

With Mozambique, there does not seem to have been adequate local planning and consultation with the various private-public interest groups. The government of Mozambique seems to have relied almost exclusively on outsiders for information, analysis, and advice-as it turned out some of the advice was wrong. The failure to bring together the cashew farmers, traders, and exporters with various government departments and agencies (for example, industry, finance, agriculture) meant that there was no local common understanding and commitment to reform.

As expected, the lack of consultation on the ground bred resentment and resistance to reform. This made it difficult for the government to manage and deal with the adverse consequence of the reform. Another lesson from the Mozambique experience is the apparent lack of direct involvement of private sector foreign investors with intimate knowledge about the cashew business in a global economy. While the major telecommunications companies of the major industrialized countries were actively lobbying for active participation in Indonesia's telecommunications reform, there were no equivalent foreign private investors seeking to participate in restructuring of the cashew industry in Mozambique.

As often happens with most of the weaker developing countries (P2 countries), Mozambique depended too much on the advice of the U.N. agencies rather than drawing on the practical expertise of the relevant international private sector. Consequently, Mozambique's reform program did not make a serious attempt to modernize the industry by means of new capital, technology, and management expertise. The changes in taxation were perhaps necessary but not sufficient to bring about the needed changes in the cashew industry and to make it globally competitive.

It is also clear that both the government and the industry-farmers, traders, factory owners, exporters-did not have sufficient understanding and capacity to sustain the reforms, modernize the industry, and become globally competitive. Unlike the Indonesian case, no serious attempts were made in Mozambique to develop the local indigenous private sector. Mozambique represents many cases, especially in weak developing countries involved in premature deregulation and privatization.

When the local key players, in both the public and the private sector, are not ready for reform and if no attempts are made first to bring them together, enhance their understanding, and build capacities, moving ahead with deregulation and privatization can create opportunities for exploitable globalization. This is when smuggling, tax evasion, and other criminal activities including civil war become the inevitable consequences of premature globalization.

It is important for globalizing countries to experience successes early on in the process for positive reinforcement. Unmanageable negative consequences do more harm than good, not only to the directly affected individuals and institutions but also to the entire society and its overall support for openness and globalization. International assistance and intervention, carefully conceived and implemented, can help mitigate the dangers of false start.

6

The WTO
Challenges for Developing Countries

As the 1990s came to a close and the new millennium began, the WTO became the leading international symbol for or against globalization. Yet, ten years before, nobody had ever heard of the WTO, and only academics and senior trade officials, mainly in industrial countries, paid much attention to its predecessor, GATT. Today, no serious discussion on globalization is complete without a close examination of the role of this controversial organization and its impact on the global economy, different regions and countries of the world, and ordinary citizens. This chapter begins by providing the history, mission, structure, and governance of the WTO.

It then looks at the relationship between the WTO and developing countries, focusing on current issues important for developing countries. The chapter concludes with a discussion of the strategies needed for developing countries to develop the necessary human competencies and institutional capacities to deal effectively with these and future emerging issues and to enhance the quality of their participation in the WTO and related institutions.

Like most international organizations, the WTO owes its origins from the time immediately after World War II when the Allies were creating new institutions for a world order that would promote peace, reconstruction, and development. At the time, a suggestion was made for the creation of an international trade organization, but opposition from the U.S. Congress blocked the idea. Instead, the world had to settle for less institutional arrangements and less legal and moral force under GATT.

In 1947, GATT was a relatively small organization with only twenty-three member states. This was because most of today's nations were not yet born. The purpose of GATT was to negotiate trade rules and to negotiate down tariffs and other trade barriers. It conducted its business in sessions called "rounds." The first round, started in 1947, covered approximately 50 percent of world trade and lasted for two years. The second round, started in 1949, involved only thirteen trading nations. For the next twenty-five years, there were several rounds involving various countries.

The most famous of these is the eighth round called the "Uruguay Round," which lasted for seven years, was concluded on December 15, 1993, and was signed into force in March 1994. By this time, more countries had joined GATT, so the Uruguay Round involved 117 nations, especially the developed countries and the big emerging markets (BEMs). The Uruguay Round was the most comprehensive international trade negotiations the world has ever undertaken. It involved more nations and a higher percentage of world trade.

It covered not only tariffs and other trade barriers but also trade agreements in a wide range of sectors and topics including agriculture, services, manufacturing, and intellectual properties. The Uruguay Round is famous because it created the WTO. Unlike GATT, the WTO is not just a "general agreement," instead; it has legal status and powers to enforce its decisions and rulings. It was also given powers to enforce the general agreements made under GATT.

GATT started out as a trade club for the rich industrial nations, and although it eventually broadened its membership to include some of the advanced developing countries, it never truly reflected the serious concerns of the poor developing countries (P2), who generally had minimal involvement in GATT's governance, negotiations, or decisions. Yet, all GATT's decisions were passed on to the WTO. Therefore, as far as developing countries are concerned, the WTO inherited the problems of GATT and passed them on to the developing countries.

As the only multilateral organization dealing with global rules of trade between and among nations, the WTO is charged with the responsibility of ensuring that trade flows as smoothly, fairly, freely, and predictably as possible. After the fourth Ministerial Conference in Doha, Qatar, in November 2001, membership in the WTO stood at 143 nations of which about 110 were developing and transition economy members. More than three-quarters of the members are developing or least-developed countries; special provisions for these members are included in all WTO agreements.

Yet, while all members of the WTO may sleep in the same bed, they have different dreams. The trade, investment, and development dreams of developing countries and transition economies are significantly different both in content and context than those of the rich industrial countries or their trading blocks. Therefore, the WTO's greatest challenge is to bring to bear greater understanding of these differences and to reconcile the often widely divergent interests among member states in a way that is fair and technically and politically credible. Future prospects of the WTO depend on its ability to do so.

In terms of structure and governance, WTO's highest authority is the Ministerial Conference which is made up of one representative from each member state and meets about once every two years. The first conference took place in December 1996 in Singapore. The second was in 1998 in Geneva, and the third was the infamous meetings in Seattle, Washington, from November 30 to December 3, 1999. The fourth meeting took place in November 2001 in Doha, Qatar. The conference acts as a governing council and sets the agenda and program of work for the organization.

The administration of the organization is overseen by the General Council, which is headed by the director-general who is appointed for a six-year term. The council performs two broad administrative tasks: dispute settlement and trade policy review. Decisions are made by consensus, but when voting is required, each member has one vote. A two-thirds majority is required to amend provisions of the multilateral agreements and to admit new members.

WORLD TRADE ORGANIZATION MEMBERSHIP

It also lists thirty-seven countries that sent observers to the conference and fifteen countries-the isolates-that stayed away. The list of members is testimony to the support the world community has given to the WTO as an agent of globalization. The WTO represents mainstream countries of the world: big and small, rich and poor, from all continents, races, creeds, and cultures. Most of the nonmembers are former Communist states such as Russia, Vietnam, Cambodia, North Korea, and Yemen; Islamic states such as Saudi Arabia, Libya, Iran, Iraq, and Syria; and post-conflict states such as Bhutan, Tuvalu, Micronesia, and East Timor.

Overall, these countries make up a small fraction of the total global economy and world population. Most of the observer countries are actively taking steps to join the WTO. For example, President Vladimir Putin of Russia has asked for American support in his bid to become a member of the WTO and other international organizations. Over the years, it is expected that many more countries will seek membership in the WTO, and those who do not will become isolated from the global economy and global society.

As the world becomes more global and as trade becomes the driving force for growth, wealth creation, poverty alleviation, innovation, entrepreneurship, openness, and globalization, there is need for a credible multilateral system of regulation and enforcement to create, protect, and preserve a level playing field for all nations, big and small, rich and poor. The WTO is supposed to form the core of this global regulatory and enforcement system.

It also provides a mechanism for settling disputes among trading nations, and if the recent experience is indicative of future challenges, dispute settlement and enforcement is becoming the most active and important work of the organization as more and more members seek to settle their trade disputes using this multilateral system. As well, the WTO is expected to promote transparency, accountability, and respect for the rule of law, thus contributing both to global economic and global democratic/political development.

There is also concern about the relationships between the WTO and the developing countries, especially the small and weak least-developing countries, which are not currently major beneficiaries of global trade. Western trade unions are also opposed to the WTO because they see it as facilitating the export of jobs to low-cost developing countries. Others, especially on the right, do not want to see the WTO getting involved in environmental protection because of its implications for industrial operations and production. Membership in the WTO can be used as a scapegoat to explain away problems caused by internal economic weaknesses such as high unemployment, runaway inflation, business bankruptcies, and currency depreciation.

WORLD TRADE ORGANIZATION CALLS FOR REFORMS

Among the avid supporters and opponents, there are reformers. Reformers accept the need for the WTO but point out that it needs fundamental changes, both as an organization and as a multilateral regulatory institution. Reforms have been proposed in various areas including structure, function, and governance; leadership and succession; litigation and negotiation; regionalism; and relationship with developing countries and transition economies.

At the governance level, it has been suggested that the WTO lacks a board of directors, steering committee, or similar structure for providing vision, strategic direction, and long-term planning. The proposed body should not have executive decision-making authority; rather, with broadly representative and rotating participation, similar to the rotating membership of the Trade Policy Review, it could provide the full membership with nonbinding, thoughtful advice and council.

It would also take some of the pressure off the Ministerial Conference, which is inherently political in its composition. Drawing from corporate governance, the Ministerial Conference would become something like a biannual meeting of shareholders. It has also been suggested that the dispute settlement mechanism (DSM) should be reformed to make it simpler, more inclusive and participative, transparent, and speedier. According to the WTO's current rules, the proceedings are private, exclude third parties including NGOs, and on average last thirty-four months from start to dispute settlement.

The costs are more than most developing countries can afford. Reformers have also suggested that the WTO should streamline its processing of applications for new membership. By the end of 2000, there was a long queue for new nations wishing to join, especially developing countries and transition economies. While membership has its costs, it also bestows status, voice, and respectability. It also sends a powerful message to the rest of the world that the new member is ready for globalization. In September 2001, China was admitted as a full member, but important countries, including Russia, are not yet members. Therefore, it is important for the WTO to stream its membership procedures and make them faster and affordable.

The WTO's leadership and succession problems are political and geopolitical in nature, but they need to be addressed because they affect its functioning and credibility, especially in the eyes of the developing countries. These problems are perhaps best illustrated by the organization's short history of the appointment of its director-general. The first director-general, Renato Ruggiero, an Italian, served only one four-year term to April 1999. A European could not succeed him because the position has to rotate among the major regions of the world. Each of the four world regions proposed a candidate. North America proposed a Canadian, Roy McLaren, because an American would not have had a chance.

South America proposed Mexico's former President Carlos Salinas de Gortari, but scandal made his candidacy untenable. Africa proposed Morocco's Hassan Abouyoub; and Southeast Asia put forward Supachai Panitchapakdi of Thailand. Finally the Oceania region proposed New Zealand's Mike Moore. After a period of intense lobbying and failing to come up with a broad-based acceptable candidate, a compromise solution was reached. Moore was finally appointed as the WTO's director-general only on the condition that he be replaced by Panitchapakdi of Thailand halfway between the mandates.

With this kind of compromise solution, the industrial countries and the developing countries each win half the battle, but the WTO loses in leadership and institutional continuity, especially at a time when it is beginning to get its feet wet and has so much to do to win the confidence of the world. Regarding litigation and negotiation, since 1994 the WTO has functioned more like an international trade court than a forum for trade negotiation, harmonization, and development. This is because of the increasing number of disputes coming before the WTO from both industrial and developing countries. The biggest trade blocks are mired in bilateral trade disputes only the WTO can help to settle. For example, both the EU and the United States are involved in trade disputes harmful to overall global trade.

They are depriving developing countries of trade opportunities, which would otherwise help their economies and citizens. Nick Stern, chief economist of the World Bank, describes protectionism as "a rip-off of the rich consumers, a rip-off of rich-country taxpayers, and intensely damaging to the poor of the world." Since the end of the Uruguay Round in 1993–1994, with the exception of sector-specific and side agreements in areas such as financial services and telecommunications, no new rules have emerged from negotiations. Rather, new global trade rules from the WTO have so far resulted from dispute settlement panels.

By refusing to engage in meaningful multilateral negotiations, the world leaders are depriving the world of the evolution of a sound global trading regulatory system based on a balanced consideration of technical trade matters as well as political needs and realities of the majority of the member states. The way the WTO has been operating for the first seven years of its existence is akin to a country being taken over by a dictator, closing its legislature, and governing by the law courts. The world leaders, especially those from the leading industrial countries, are abdicating their global leadership responsibilities in trade matters, and this hurts the long-term interests of developing countries and transition economies.

Reformers have also suggested that the WTO should be concerned about the growing trend toward the emergence of regional trading blocks. The debate about regionalism and global trade has not yet been settled. There are those who support the development of regional trading blocks on the grounds that they are more "home grown" and more sensitive to local, national, and regional issues. Others support them as an evolutionary stage and learning process in preparation for global trade participation. It is also argued that Europe (EU), Southeast Asia (ASEAN), and North America (NAFTA) have become avid global traders because of their respective regional trading blocks.

These regional trading blocks have provided member states with the opportunity to develop institutional capacities and political support most useful in managing trade both at the regional and global levels. Yet, WTO reformers are concerned that too many regional trading blocks undermine the authority of the WTO as the single authoritative global regulator of trade. As of 2000, there were about 172 existing regional trade agreements, with another 70 or so under negotiation or discussion. Because the third Ministerial Conference in Seattle ended in failure, there are renewed fears that most nations resort to regionalization as the only realistic option for trade negotiations and development. This would be a disservice to globalization.

Perhaps the most important area of reform for the WTO, as far as its potential effects on the majority of member states and citizens of the world, is the relationship between the WTO and the developing countries. Here, it is important to note that some of the reformers have argued that none of these reforms deal with the fundamental problems facing developing countries.

For example, J. Michael Finger, lead economist for trade policy of the World Bank, has argued that the transaction costs associated with membership in the WTO are too high for most of the least-developing countries to afford. Furthermore, the WTO, as a trade organization, does not have the mandate or the institutional capacity to promote development among the poor countries. Yet, for most of the developing countries, what they need more than anything else is development. Undoubtedly, trade and development are positively correlated, but a development agenda is not necessarily identical to a trade agenda, especially for poor countries with weak infant economies and fragile political democracies.

LESSONS FROM SEATTLE

Before discussing the relationship between the WTO and developing countries and the issues most important to these countries, it is important to look briefly at the impact of Seattle on the future of the WTO. First, it is important to note that the highly publicized thousands of anti-globalization demonstrators who successfully battled police and forced the city to shut down did not cause the failure of the Seattle ministerial meetings. Rather, the failure at Seattle was because the third Ministerial Conference, dominated by member states from developing countries including among the poorest countries of the world, could not agree on the agenda for the next round of negotiations. It had been expected that a new round, called the "Millennium Round," would begin in the year 2000 to coincide with the beginning of the new millennium.

The Millennium Round was expected to be even more comprehensive and far more reaching in its scope to regulate different forms of merchandise trade and tradable services. The Ministerial Conference failed to approve the agenda for the Millennium Round because the developing countries voted en masse to block the proposed agenda. As a result of the substantive failure of the Ministerial Conference and in response to the highly publicized protestors' demonstration, Western leaders appeared to distance themselves from the WTO and its ambitious proposals of the Millennium Round. For example, President Bill Clinton publicly supported the demonstrators because many in the labour and environment movements are traditional supporters of the Democratic Party and 1999–2000 was a presidential election year.

At the same time, the political leaders from the developing countries did not seem to have paid any political cost back home in their political constituencies. Either the long-term implications of the failure of Seattle were not fully understood in the developing countries or the general opposition to globalization provided cover for these failures. Either way, the WTO and the ideals of free trade were the immediate losers. Only seven years old, the WTO looked like an orphan with no champion, no defender, and lots of bashing. As a result of Seattle, the WTO became widely known all over the world, but it also lost credibility and remains badly wounded.

Seattle also taught us some other lessons of experience. As the WTO begins to assert its authority, it will need to find an acceptable balance between external pressures for greater openness, transparency, and accountability and the member-states' insistence on privacy and confidentiality. No organization can be completely open in all its transactions, but after Seattle, the WTO is forced to respond to the legitimate demands for greater openness. Another lesson coming out of Seattle is the new power of numbers that developing countries have acquired in the governance of the WTO.

With a system of one nation–one vote, no major decisions can be made without the support of the developing countries, and Seattle confirmed this. It is not clear how this newly acquired power will be used in the future. One hopes that it will be used facilitatively and will not always lead to failure or deadlock. In any case, it is a very different global trade-negotiating environment than the one that existed during the GATT period (1947–1993) when industrial countries called the shots.

Another lesson of experience for the WTO that came out of the Seattle conference is the realization of the complex nature of global trade. Both the failure of the conference and the demonstrations outside the conference underscore the point that trade is not only a technical macroeconomic and administrative matter; it is also a social, political, geopolitical, and cultural matter. To become a competent, credible champion and institutional home for global trade, the WTO must become a center of excellence in all aspects of trade. The failure to predict the failure of the Ministerial Conference and the extent and damage of the protests and demonstrations suggests that the WTO has a lot to learn beyond the technical dimensions of global trade.

Supporters of free global trade must also learn from Seattle. For example, it became clear after Seattle that public awareness and reactions to the events in Seattle were different in industrial and developing countries. In the developing countries, there was only limited discussion and awareness of the significance and long-term consequences of the Seattle outcomes. If trade is so important for the overall development of developing countries, why didn't the public put pressure on the leaders to work for the successful conclusion of a new trade agenda for the Millennium Round? The wider implication for this is that trade negotiations do not take place only in Geneva, where the WTO has its headquarters; rather, they take place first and foremost in every constituency of every country.

Most developing countries, especially the least developed, have not started or championed the process of discussing and debating the merits of global trade in their domestic constituencies. It is as if they have no mandate to negotiate on behalf of their people. This must change. There must be active and informed trade discussions and debates within each of the developing countries in order to develop the necessary domestic support for international engagement and negotiations. Once again, the international community has a role to play in helping these emerging weak countries develop a trade-positive, enabling domestic environment. Seattle has taught us all that trade is too important to be left only to the experts.

The private sectors of the developing countries must also draw instructive lessons from both the hotel conference rooms where the delegates of the failed Ministerial Conference were meeting and the city streets where the demonstrators and the uninvited representatives of the northern private sectors were promoting their respective alternative interests.

Private sector includes all the different civil society groupings including NGOs, labour and trade unions, the media, environmental activists, traditional chiefs, academics, youths, professional associations, reformists, the business community, and so on. From the streets of Seattle, the private sector from the developing countries learns at least two things: One, is that they, too, have a role to play in shaping trade policy and implementation in their respective countries and regions; and two, their interests are not necessarily identical to the interests of the northern protestors. Therefore, they must develop their own strategies and responses to the WTO and global trade based on an informed assessment of the economic, political, social, and cultural realities on the ground.

While northern counterparts can and should provide technical support and advice, they should never dictate the agenda for how the civil society in the developing countries responds to the WTO and global trade. Two examples- labour and the environment- help to explain the different policy interests between northern and southern opposition to the two issues and global trade. Northern trade unions are opposed to global trade because they fear that jobs will be exported to low-cost developing countries. The natural extension of this logic is that the trade union movement in developing countries should support trade-positive public policies because of the opportunities to create well-paying jobs in the private sector.

Likewise, some northern environmental activists are opposed to global trade because industry destroys the natural environment and pollutes the air, water, and soil. Yet, while southern environmental activists are also opposed to pollution, they see much more clearly the relationship between poverty and environmental degradation.

Therefore, to the extent that trade and industrialization help to alleviate poverty, southern environmentalists should be supportive of trade-positive public policies. This said, northern anti-globalization groups are beginning to link up with their like-minded southern counterparts.

For example, in January 2001, the first meeting of the newly formed Global Social Forum, representing more than one hundred countries, took place in Brazil's southern city of Pôrto Alegre. The timing and location were deliberately chosen by the organizers to show solidarity between northern and southern anti-globalization forces and to demonstrate against the meeting of the Global Economic Forum that was taking place in Davos, Switzerland. The demonstrations in the summer of 2001 in Quebec City against the Free Trade Area of the Americas also included many NGOs from the south.

The private sector business community in each of the developing countries must become more actively involved in promoting trade and investment in their respective countries or regions. Global trade is good for business, even for those firms that are not yet actively involved in the export–import sector. In every globalizing developing country, business leaders should take up the challenge to explain to the public, especially the rest of the business community, the relationships between the WTO and global trade and the practical implications for their respective countries.

Traveling through some of the small and weaker less-developed countries, one gets the impression that many business leaders are not adequately aware or informed about matters of global trade and trade policy. This must change because in any globalizing country the business sector constitutes a very important part of the national institutional infrastructure for managing global trade.

IMPORTANT ISSUES FOR DEVELOPING COUNTRIES

Following the successful conclusion of the Uruguay Round and the establishment of the WTO, concern has been expressed that the issues and needs of developing countries and transition economies have not been given serious consideration, let alone finding practical solutions to problems. As a result, in preparation for the third Ministerial Conference that took place toward the end of 1999, various publications came out identifying trade and development issues most important for developing countries and transition economies.

Some of these publications focused on single sectors such as agriculture or financial services, others looked at specific regions such as Latin America and Central and Eastern Europe, others looked at specific topics such as participation and commitment, and others talked about all developing countries in general. This section highlights the most important trade investment and development issues for developing countries. As I have emphasized previously, developing countries are not a homogeneous group, and globalization is making them even less so as some countries seem to adjust to global competition faster and more successfully than others.

The periphery was divided between the advanced developing countries (P1) and the least developed countries (P2). In the discussion of foreign direct investment (FDI), a subgrouping of successful developing countries-the BEMs-was also identified. P1 and BEMs are almost identical groups, and their issues and concerns regarding the WTO, global trade, investment, and development are different than the P2 or least-developed countries. The issues and concerns I will discuss apply to all developing countries, but they are more serious, severe, and limiting for the P2 least-developed countries than for the P1 countries or the BEMs.

Most of these have been discussed in great technical detail by U.N. experts and World Bank staff. For example, in preparation for the Seattle conference, a group of U.N. experts met in September 1998 and identified ten of the twelve issues listed. As is evident, some of these issues relate to specific sectors such as agriculture and tourism; others deal with technical matters relating to the administration of trade such as tariffs, standards, antidumping, and competition. Other issues deal with specific agreements such as TRIPs (trade-related intellectual property rights) regulations, technology such as E-commerce, and special treatment and consideration for developing countries (special and differential [S&D]) treatment.

There are also issues related to questions of national ownership, commitment and capacity for managing trade, and taking an integrated approach to trade, investment, and national development. The least-developed countries are particularly most challenged because they lack the necessary national human capital and institutional capacity to implement the obligations arising from GATT agreements and to make the necessary technical and political preparations for future negotiations.

Agriculture is a very important economic sector for developing countries because this is traditionally the area in which these countries have enjoyed competitive trade advantages. Yet, there are serious issues associated with market access, export subsidies, and domestic support, all resulting from protectionist behaviour of developed countries. Agriculture also illustrates the differences among developing countries in terms of their trade policies and interests.

Three groups can be identified among developing countries: exporters of tropical products, exporters of temperate products in direct competition with Europe and North America, and importers of food stuffs and grains who are also the ones least likely to have the capacity to produce for export any agricultural commodities. One of the key differences in interest among developing countries lies between those who are not importers of food grains (P2 countries) and those who are net exporters such as the BEMs.

Exporters are interested in opening up more market access for their commodities and devising rules to prohibit export taxes, quotas, and other forms of trade protectionism. Therefore, they are, at least in principle, in support of the WTO and the resulting agreements and rulings. These are mainly the twenty to twenty-five countries that grated in the multilateral trading system. They participate actively in the WTO, abide by are mostly BEMs, middle income from Asia and Latin America, and are almost fully intethe rules, use similar types of trade remedies, such as antidumping, as the industrial countries do, and take full advantage of the opportunities offered by the WTO's trade DSM.

Then there are the fifty to sixty least-developed countries members of the WTO who are net importers of food. They are mostly concerned with increases in the price of imported food, the negative impact on their limited foreign exchange earnings, and the net impact on their poor populations. They want to keep the option to support domestic agriculture with export subsidies in the future should they then have developed the capacity to export. Most of these countries are not yet effectively integrated in the multilateral trading system.

They have only minimal participation in the WTO and little or no national capacity to implement the Uruguay Round commitments, WTO rulings, or the preparation of future negotiations. They tend to focus on the S&D aspects of trade negotiations. Although they enjoy exemptions under the aggregate measures support for agriculture as provided for the urban and rural poor and a ten-year grace period for full implementation of commitment, they still resist trade liberalization because they are not ready.

In terms of agriculture, the small, poor developing countries are subjected to negotiating pressures from three powerful forces. First, there is the United States that is seeking improved market access for its wide range of agricultural products, while at the same time protecting its domestic producers of commodities such as sugar. Second, there is the EU that is seeking to maintain import restrictions, export subsidies, and domestic support in accordance with the

Common Agricultural Policy.

Third, there is the Cairns Group that is pressing hard for agricultural liberalization and removal of all tariff and nontariff trade restrictions. The poor developing countries with limited technical capacity and negotiating clout are hard-pressed to counter these powerful forces and to identify, articulate, and actively pursue their legitimate long-term agricultural interests. Several other issues point to the qualitative differences between the advanced developing countries such as the BEMs and the least-developed members or prospective members of the WTO.

Examples of such issues include phytosanitary standards; movements of natural persons; TRIPs agreement, ownership, and commitment; and national capacity. SPS standards require that exporters of animal products such as beef build and maintain technical facilities to guarantee quality and sanitary safety of the exports. The advanced developing countries such as Argentina and Brazil are interested in discussing and sharing their experiences with other exporters under the Uruguay Round to ensure that any changes made to the regulations are aimed at improving SPS standards and not a disguised form of trade protectionism, especially by the industrial countries.

On the other hand, the facilities required to meet the GATT/WTO SPS standards are well beyond the means and capacities of the least-developed countries. A World Bank official estimated that such facilities would cost about U.S.$150 million, which is more than the entire annual capital development budget for many of the small and poor countries. He also observed that almost ninety countries were in violation of the SPS, customs valuation, and TRIPs agreements and are not likely to meet their commitments any time soon.

Liberalization of services is another trade issue that differentiates the interests of the BEMs from the less-developed countries. An important aspect of the service sector is the movement of natural persons so that citizens of developing countries can move freely to work in other developing or developed countries. In addition to the various professional areas, construction is one industry that is important for developing countries. Countries such as Turkey, South Korea, and China have the capacity to export construction services, providing they can bring in temporary workers.

There are examples of this already happening, especially in the Middle East where oil revenues have attracted construction services from South Korea and other BEM countries. Once again, the small poor countries have not developed an exportable construction service industry and issues of access are not important to them. Instead, they are more concerned about the brain drain implications of liberalization whereby their technical and professional nationals, already limited in number, would leave and seek employment opportunities in the more competitive countries.

After the end of the Uruguay Round, several sectoral negotiations were undertaken. By the end of 2000, four such negotiations had been undertaken on market access. Maritime transport negotiations reached no agreement and were suspended. Negotiations on the movement of natural persons have not achieved much, especially for developing countries. The only two service areas in which successful negotiations have been beneficial to developing countries, especially the more advanced BEMs, are basic telecommunications and financial services. Domestic reforms of the latter two sectors are of particular advantage to globalizing developing countries and transition economies.

NATIONAL CAPACITY DEVELOPMENT FOR TRADE AND DEVELOPMENT

It is now clear that most developing countries, especially the least developed ones (P2), lack the capacity to take full advantage of the opportunities offered by a liberalized global trading system as well as their membership in the WTO. Without building the necessary national capacity, the majority of P2 countries will continue to focus on maintaining S&D treatment as their protective negotiating strategy instead of moving toward openness, liberalization, and gainful participation in trade and globalization. This would be bad for everybody. The areas particularly difficult for these countries in terms of technical capacity include TRIPs, SPS, TBT, and Customs valuation.

These countries need to develop the necessary capacity and take a strategic approach to trade and development that is goal directed focused, systemic, long term, and national in scope. Evidence of the lack of capacity to manage trade and its negative consequences for P2 countries comes from various sources. Their participation in world trade seems to be declining as their share of total global trade is falling even in primary commodities such as agriculture, mining, and textiles-areas in which they have had a historical comparative advantage.

The African, Caribbean, and Pacific group has lost or are in the process of losing market access as a result of dilution of preferences previously enjoyed in the EU countries. Lack of capacity explains why these countries are unable to meet their obligations arising from the Uruguay Round and the WTO rulings within the given transition period and why they are unable to prepare for and engage in effective trade negotiations. Mindful of this problem, the 1998 Ministerial Conference expressed concern about the increasing marginalization of the P2 countries and called on WTO member states to address the issue and come up with practical solutions to reverse the trend.

To that end, the WTO draft preparatory document for the 2001 Ministerial Conference clearly stated: "We recognize that the further integration of the least-developed countries (LDCs) into the trading system requires combined and inter-related action at three levels namely, market access, trade-related technical assistance and capacity-building, and LDCs' domestic reform." One area in which these countries are at a serious disadvantage is the DSM established by the WTO. According to the procedural rules, only government officials are allowed to participate in panel hearings.

Yet, most P2 countries do not have enough government officials with the necessary knowledge, skills, and experience to provide effective representation and negotiation. Lacking the necessary background in areas such as international economics and legal knowledge and experience, these countries often fail to identify and defend their interests in WTO disputes. At the same time, they cannot hire foreign legal consultants because of the rules limiting participation only to government officials. Indeed, from the perspectives of these countries, DSM rules are legalistic, obstructive, and not sensitive to matters of equity.

The lack of an effective national capacity for trade and development manifests itself in many important areas: weak or no representation at the WTO, failure to develop a domestic trade-positive institutional infrastructure, inability to conceptually and operationally link trade to overall national development, maintaining a low profile and low prestige of the trade profile within the public service, and weak interdisciplinary academic, research, and training in areas relevant for managing trade and development.

TRADE REPRESENTATION AT THE WORLD TRADE ORGANIZATION

One of the best indicators of a country's effective representation and participation in the global trading system is the quality and quantity of representation at the WTO, or before at GATT. Developing countries have always complained about the outcomes of the Uruguay Round because they were poorly represented. For example, when the round started in 1987, there were sixty-five developing countries belonging to GATT. Twenty of these countries did not have representation in Geneva. Fifteen of the twenty were represented by their embassy staff stationed elsewhere in Europe, and the other five were represented from their national capitals where distance and poor infrastructure make effective commu-nication and consultation difficult.

In contrast, the industrial countries and the BEMs were much better represented in Geneva. For example, the EU had ten trade representatives plus fifty-seven from the individual member European states; Japan had fifteen, and the United States had ten. Among the BEMs, Korea and Mexico each had seven, Brazil and Indonesia had six each, and Thailand and Hong Kong had five each. By contrast, of the tweny-nine least-developed countries, which are members of the WTO, only eleven maintain permanent delegations in Geneva. Part of the reason is that it is expensive to maintain a permanent staff in Geneva, especially for P2 countries.

A senior Canadian official once told me that it costs about U.S.$150,000 annually to maintain a trade officer and his/her family in Geneva. Therefore, a staff of seven would cost more than U.S.$1 million, which is more than most P2 countries can afford. Another reason for poor representation is because of the low priority that most of these countries give to matters of global trade.

Since they are not fully integrated in the global trading system and since most of their foreign capital comes in by means of overseas development assistance (ODA), rather than trade and private sector investments, the public policy makers of these countries do not see the need to invest in trade and development. It took China fifteen years of hard technical, diplomatic, and political work before being admitted as a full member of the WTO. Many developing countries and some of the transition economies do not have the capacity to persevere.

Out of the forty WTO member states listed, nineteen (or almost 50 per cent) did not have any representation in Geneva; another twelve had only 1–3 trade officials, and only six had 4–5. It is interesting to note that the countries that attract the most FDI among those listed in the table-Nigeria, Egypt, and South Africa-each had six or more trade representatives in Geneva. South Africa, as a newcomer to the global trading system, and as a member of the Cairns Group, needs strong representation at the WTO.

They are the least integrated in the global trading system and have the least liberalized trading system. They need to improve their participation and increase their share of benefits from trade and the WTO. They need to become active trading nations. Yet, they are, at best, only minimally represented in the international forum where important trade and investment decisions and rulings are made.

Without effective representation and participation in these decisions and rulings, these countries cannot guarantee that their individual and collective interests will be protected and preserved. In fact, recent experiences seem to suggest that they are losing out. This is one area in which critics of the global trading system, in general, and the WTO, in particular, has a strong economic and moral justification. When these P2 countries lose out, everyone loses. Global trade is not a zero-sum game, and therefore, it is imperative that the WTO and other international organizations work in partnership with the P2 member states to build a win–win global trading system.

There is a link between representation and participation, on the one hand, and understanding, commitment, acceptance, motivation, and support, on the other hand. With minimal representation and participation, P2 governments and their publics enjoy a low level of understanding of the strategic importance of trade, and consequently, their levels of commitment, acceptance, and intrinsic motivation to support liberalization is low. This, in turn, leads to limited political will to push for trade and liberalization, which in turn results in lack of ownership or weak identification with the ideals and practical realities of the WTO and the global trading system it represents.

The sentiments and lessons of experience are similar to those of the 1980s when most of the same P2 countries were required to implement political and economic reforms such as structural adjustment programs without the necessary national commitment, political will, or institutional capacity. Drawing from the lessons of the earlier experiences, it is clear that each of the P2 countries must develop a sustainable national capacity for trade and development as a prerequisite to effective globalization.

There are several efforts by the international community and several specialized UN agencies to help developing countries enhance their individual and collective capacities to become more effectively integrated into the global trading system. The WTO, and GATT before it, makes special provisions for developing countries, especially under the S&D treatment. The special provisions either involve positive action by developed countries and/or international institutions or they are exceptions to the overall rules contained in the agreements that apply to developing countries in general, or more specifically to the less-developed developing (P2) countries.

In general, developed countries support S&D by extending preferential access to their markets, primarily through the voluntary provisions of the Generalized System of Preferences, implementing the agreements and rulings in ways that are beneficial or least damaging to developing countries, and providing technical and other forms of assistance. As well, developed countries have accepted the need for the developing countries, especially the P2 countries, to undertake policies that limit access to their markets or provide support to domestic producers and exporters, which would otherwise be prohibited under WTO agreements and rulings.

Developed countries are also willing to give the weaker developing countries more time before they are required to fulfill their WTO obligations and commitments. The United Nations Conference on Trade and Development (UNCTAD) is a specialized agency that provides technical support to developing countries in the areas of trade and development. Historically, most developing countries have always found UNCTAD more sympathetic to their special circumstances than the more hard-nosed GATT/WTO. According to Rubens Ricupero, UNCTAD's secretary-general, UNCTAD's new mandate is to help developing countries, and particularly the least-developed countries (P2), to better integrate into the global economy and the global trading system. To fulfill its mandate, UNCTAD must assist these countries to:

1. Identify and take advantage of trading opportunities;
2. Fulfill their multilateral trade obligations;
3. Formulate and pursue development strategies within the framework of these obligations;

4. Protect, defend, and preserve their acquired trading rights;
5. Set objectives and affectively pursue them in trade negotiations.

In addition to organizing conferences, UNCTAD works collaboratively with the WTO and other international organizations-such as the World Bank, IMF, UNDP, ILO, Food and Agriculture Organization of the United Nations (FAO), and World Health Organization (WHO), as well as bilateral donors-to provide training and other forms of assistance to developing countries either individually or in groups. The World Bank's International Trade Center has been particularly active in providing traditional forms of training and development. The Swiss government provides subsidies to selected developing countries to support their trade missions in Geneva.

Still, the general conclusion is that so far these initiatives are necessary but not sufficient to overcome the problems of marginalization, alienation, and inadequate national capacity for trade and development, which characterize more developing countries. There are many reasons why the results of these initiatives have been limited thus far. They are primarily focused on the WTO and Geneva, taking a rather narrow technical approach to trade. Like the earlier efforts at capacity building, following the introduction of SAPs and other reforms, they are essentially externally donor driven with limited meaningful local participation or national ownership.

They do not take a holistic approach to integrating, trade, investment, and overall national development. They tend to shy away from confronting the domestic political, administrative, social, and cultural impediments to liberalization and trade. They also tend to focus on government-to-government relationships with minimal and superficial involvement of other sectors of P2 societies such as the business community, the labour movement, the media, academic institutions, and the NGO sector. In other situations, the developing countries have not paid enough attention or given high priority to the WTO and global trade. Instead, they have been preoccupied with short-term domestic problems of survival, confrontation, or open conflict.

The countries with no trade officials in Geneva, such as Sierra Leone and Rwanda, or that are not members of the WTO, such as Sudan, Liberia, Somalia, and Ethiopia, are characterized by internal conflicts or civil war. It is also the case that developed countries have not been consistent in their support for developing countries in the area of trade and development. For example, while providing technical and other forms of assistance to developing countries, developed countries have sought to use labour and environmental standards, antidumping, and countervailing duty to target the exports of the more successful exporting developing countries.

As well, in the area of SPS, developed countries have shown less flexibility in accommodating variations in systems structure and performance in developing countries. While showing an increasing tendency to be cooperative in the areas of technical assistance and international development, developed countries have become uncompromisingly competitive when dealing with developing countries in the areas of trade and investment.

This schizophrenic approach has not been helpful for developing countries wishing to integrate trade into their overall national development nor has it helped in the overall efforts to build a national capacity for the effective management of trade and development. Developed countries seem to have given with the left hand and taken away with the right. This message was driven home in January 2001 when the fourteen countries of the Caribbean community (CARICOM) and Canada held a summit to discuss trade. Canada and the Caribbean have a trade agreement already in place that was signed in 1986. P. J. Patterson, the prime minister of Jamaica, explained that the agreement was not working in favor of the small island Caribbean nations because of Canada's protectionist policies.

While 95 percent of Caribbean exports are supposed to

enter Canada duty-free, exceptions imposed by Canada on clothing, footwear, and agriculture mean that only a tiny fraction of about 7.3 per cent of all Caribbean goods in fact qualify as duty-free. It should be noted that these are the areas in which the Caribbeans, like other developing countries, have competitive advantage over Canada and other rich industrial countries. The message from Canada to the CARICOM countries seems to be that: You can bring in your exports duty-free as long as they do not compete with Canadian producers. Not surprisingly, the Caribbean nations are lukewarm about the Free Trade Area of the Americas.

This "mixed-signals" approach to international cooperation and trade on the part of industrial countries is further evidenced by the British government's recent White Paper on globalization and poverty alleviation. On the one hand, the government promised to work with others to strengthen the capacity of developing countries to participate in international negotiations and to take advantage of new trading opportunities, including through improved infrastructure and transport links. This is commendable. On the other hand, the United Kingdom, together with other members of the EU, still retains the same tariff and nontariff barriers, which keep tradable goods and services from developing countries out of these markets.

A MODEL FOR NATIONAL CAPACITY DEVELOPMENT

The case has been made for the need for developing countries, in general, and the least-developed ones (P2), in particular, to develop a sustaining national capacity for the effective integration and management of trade and development. In this section, a model for such capacity development is proposed with a brief discussion of its main attributes, overall goal, objectives, and expected results.

This model is mainly developed in response to the special trade development needs of the least-developed P2 countries. At the same time, some aspects of the model may be of interest to the more advanced developing countries and transition economies. The proposed model for capacity development for trade and development is strategic, national in scope, integrative, holistic, dynamic, and participative. It is strategic in the sense that it is goal directed, results oriented, and long term.

It is long term because of the realization that most P2 countries do not have the capacity to initiate and sustain drastic changes. It is national in scope because of the need to ensure the understanding and active participation of various segments of society and institutions both in the public and private sectors. It is integrative because of the need to make both conceptual and practical links between trade, investment, and development. One of the problems facing countries with a history of minimal involvement in the global trading system is a general lack of understanding and appreciation of the role trade plays in attracting foreign capital and investment, poverty alleviation, and economic and overall national social development.

The proposed model is also holistic in that it looks at the whole global trading system in several ways. First, it recognizes that building the necessary capacity is not only a matter of technical training and physical infrastructure. Perhaps, more important, in the long run, corresponding trade-positive capacities must be built in the political, social, cultural, and administrative sectors of the country.

Political capacity building for trade is particularly important partly because of the dominant role politics continues to play at WTO and global trade negotiations and partly because most politicians and rebel leaders of the least-developed countries do not consider trade liberalization a matter of national priority. The model is also holistic because it attempts to ensure that what happens in Geneva at the WTO is perceived as having relevancy for development back home as well as internationally. If the governments of the P2 countries do not see any practical relationship between the priorities in Geneva and those in their capital, they are much less likely to support the development of the necessary capacity for trade and liberalization.

This holistic approach is intended to ensure effective coordination between the Geneva delegations and the relevant agencies in both the public and the private sectors. Finally, the proposed model is both dynamic and participative. It is dynamic because of the changing circumstances within each of the developing countries, among groups of developing countries, within the global trading system, and within the WTO as a multilateral trade organization.

One of the biggest challenges of the least-developed countries is that they lack the capacity, the resources, and the tools to keep abreast of changes in the global economy. Therefore, it becomes difficult for them to plan and take advantage of changes and developments in the global economy and its trading system. Within the individual countries, changes are also taking place. For example, as a country begins to liberalize and the economy becomes more competitive, it requires different trade policies and policy management capacities and institutional arrangements.

The dynamic aspects of this model ensure that these changes are constantly monitored and the results are reflected in changes in the overall strategy and plan of action for national capacity development. Critics argue that China is not ready for globalization or membership in the WTO beyond Beijing and the eastern provinces. The model is participative because experience has shown that governments cannot succeed in building national capacities alone.

In addition to the role currently being played by the international community, it is suggested here that the private sector must play a much more active role than is presently the case in most developing countries. There are four groups of stakeholders whose participation in national capacity development for trade is crucial: members of civil society, municipal and local governments, the local private sector, and the international private sector. Civil society should participate in sensitizing the public to the issues of trade and raising the general level of awareness, understanding, and debate about trade, national trade policy, and people's standards of living and quality of life.

The institutions most likely to be active here are the trade unions; the mass media; professional associations; academic, educational, and research institutions; youth organizations; women's organizations; and other NGOs operating in areas such as the environment, poverty alleviation, and human and social services. Without their active participation, it would be almost impossible to mobilize the population and to develop national consensus on the essence of trade and development.

The participation of municipal and local governments is necessary because they are closer to the people than the central government, and they can help develop nationwide political capacity for trade. They are also interested in promoting growth and development in their areas through trade and globalization. Some day, local government authorities may play a direct role at the WTO and may be allowed to have their own trade representatives.

The third aspect of participative capacity development is the role of the local business sector. It is proposed here that the business sector should form a partnership or close working relationship with the government in the development of the national capacity for trade and investment. The business community should be involved in developing informed opinions about global trade within its ranks, working with the government in the formulation of trade policy, and developing the necessary capacity within both the business and the public sectors.

The business sector may have resources, tools, and competencies necessary for capacity development that the public sector needs but does not have. Likewise, the public sector may have information or competencies that the business sector needs to build its own trade development capacities. Therefore, the partnership would be mutually beneficial and reinforcing. One of the novel ideas proposed here as part of the capacity development model is the active, direct involvement of the international business community, especially the global corporations.

These corporations have the resources and the expertise and it is in their long-term best interest for more countries to liberalize trade and become active, integrated participants in the global trading system. While the active participation and assistance of global corporations makes sense, issues relating to incentives and mechanics by which they can become meaningfully involved need to be discussed. Here, it is proposed that a multilateral organization such as the WTO, UNCTAD, UNDP, or the World Bank–IMF should develop an "Adopt a Nation Global Program." The purpose of the program would be to get global corporations directly involved in working with the least-developed countries and assist them in developing the necessary national capacities and competencies for their affective liberalization and integration into the global trading system.

One or two carefully selected global corporations could be matched with one or a group of neighboring least-developed countries and their respective private sectors to work together and identify capacity gaps in which the corporation's resources and expertise could be both useful and useable. Global corporations would be required to make their training, management, facilities, and other resources available to the matched P2 countries for the development and maintenance of their national capacities for trade.

Obviously, such a program would be voluntary on both sides and would have to be carefully monitored and supervised by the sponsoring multilateral organization. If, however, a number of high-profile global corporations got involved initially with highly publicized positive results, it could become popular among both the global corporations and the least-developed countries. The model proposed here can benefit from the experiences of similar initiatives in international cooperation. For example, the fight against river blindness (onchocerciasis) in West Africa is regarded as one of the most successful programs in the history of international cooperation.

Before the program started in 1974, more than 1 million people were infected with the disease, and more than 100,000 people were blind. By the time the program ends in 2002, 34 million people will be protected, 600,000 cases of blindness will have been prevented, and 5 million years of productive labour will have been saved. The program was successful because it was strategic, long term (lasting almost thirty years), and involved the active participation of local, national, regional, and international partners.

The partners in the program included eleven African governments, local communities, international organizations, bilateral donors, foundations, NGOs, and corporations. Merck Corporation, a global drug company, was the lead corporate partner in the program, providing medical advice and the drug ivermectin for free. This is the kind of multipartner, strategic approach developing countries need to develop their trade sectors, human capital, and institutional capacities for global competitiveness.

As for incentives, in addition to selling the program as part of corporate global social responsibility and long-term self-interest, developed countries could demonstrate direct support to the least-developed countries by providing tax credits to the participating global corporations. As well, the reforming countries could eventually develop business opportunities of interest to the participating global corporation. The participation of the leaders of the local business community would also provide opportunities for building business relationships and eventual partnerships. This would be an important side benefit because it would promote the development of the local private sector. The success of this program would be based on quality, not quantity.

As of 2000, there were about five thousand global corporations. If 10 percent were targeted and invited to participate, that would give an estimated pool of about five hundred global corporations. In the same year, there were about twenty-nine least-developed countries listed as members of the WTO, indicating their willingness to undertake liberalization for globalization. If only 10 percent of the five hundred global corporations agreed to participate, that would mean a total of fifty corporations available to be matched with twenty-nine countries.

Specifically, the exhibit provides a brief statement of the model's overall goal, purpose, and expected results. The overall goal is the development of a homemade national capacity for the country to be able to achieve effective integration and ongoing management of its global trade, investment, and development. The holistic approach proposed here differs significantly from the narrow functional approach to capacity development often associated with SAPs.

The intended results go beyond the narrow technical capacity often undertaken by international organizations and include local political, social, and cultural considerations at both the national and subnational levels. Most important, it gives the private sector, especially the business sector, which is the vanguard for global trade, a direct role in the development of the national capacity for liberalization, trade, and globalization.

A recent UNCTAD report concluded that a policy of cheap labour combined with currency devaluation is no longer sufficient for developing countries to achieve continued export success. Drawing on case studies in the textile, garment, and electronics industries for Korea, Taiwan, Thailand, Indonesia, and Vietnam, the report recommended that learning and developing technological capacities are critical for sustaining competitiveness for developing countries.

REQUIRED SKILLS AND CORE COMPETENCIES

Although it is widely believed that most trade representatives of the least-developed countries lack the necessary qualifications to perform their duties effectively, no attempts have been made to spell out the required skills set and core competencies for these positions. This information is necessary for effective human resource management and institutional development as part of the overall capacity development.

For example, this kind of information is critical for the effective recruitment, selection, placement, training and development, motivation, retention, and promotion of the trade representatives in both the public and the private sectors. Four dimensions of the required skills set and core competencies are presented: areas of specialized knowledge, practical work experience, specific job skills, and areas of general working knowledge.

USING SECTORWIDE APPROACHES

Building effective and sustainable capacities for development remains one of the most daunting problems facing developing countries, especially the least-developed ones. Various attempts by governments, donors, and the international development community have often produced mixed results. The capacity development model proposed for trade and development runs the risk of facing serious implementation problems. To minimize these risks, it is proposed here that the sectorwide approaches (SWAPs) be considered in the implementation of the model.

This section provides a brief description of SWAPs, their current applications in development, and why they are considered particularly appropriate for capacity development, especially for P2 member states of the WTO. SWAPs are used in international development in an attempt to move away from project-specific aid and technical assistance to focus on an entire sector.

They are a mechanism by which the donors, government, and other invited stakeholders agree on sectorwide priorities, develop a sectoral national strategy and plan of action, determine the resources required and the action to be taken, outline the responsibilities for implementation, and monitor the results and the procedures by which decisions are to be made and disputes resolved. All this is usually outlined in a working document available to all parties.

SWAPs have the advantage of mobilizing significant resources from the recipient government and from the donors and channeling them to a single identified priority sector or subsector. The recipient government takes the leadership role in priority setting and implementation, and the donors agree to use government procedures for program management, including budgeting, disbursements, and overall accountability.

Donors like the SWAPs because they allow them to work together toward common goals (without invoking the unpopular memories of aid coordination), reduce donor transaction costs, enhance local ownership, and help the recipient government build its own capacity in the priority sectors. Governments of developing countries like SWAPs because they make it easy for them to mobilize and channel donor support in areas of their choice. They also see it as a sign of donor support for the UNDP's approach of "national execution."

It is important to note that SWAPs are basically a general approach to technical assistance, not a blueprint. Therefore, they are quite flexible. SWAPs are fairly new, having been started in the 1990s. They are almost exclusively used in highly aid-dependent poor countries with weak physical, digital, and institutional capacities for development policy formulation and implementation. These are essentially the P2 countries where, historically, donors have experienced difficulty in the successful implementation of aid programs.

Likewise, these are the same countries needing a lot of help from the WTO and the international community. Therefore, the lessons and experiences gained in SWAPs should be useful for these countries as they begin the process of capacity development for trade liberalization and development. As of 2000, there were eighty SWAPs programs in various stages of implementation. Of these, 85 per cent were in sub-Saharan Africa and the rest were in Asia and Latin America.

The countries most actively involved include Bangladesh, Ethiopia, Ghana, Tanzania, Uganda, Vietnam, and Zambia. Most of the programs are in social services (health and education), but other sectors such as agriculture, the environment, energy, roads and transport, water, and urban development are also represented.

Various international donors-Department of Foreign and International Development (DFID; United Kingdom), Danish International Development Agency (DANIDA), Canadian International Development Agency (CIDA), Irish Aid, Dutch Ministry of Foreign Affairs and International Development, United States Agency for International Development (USAID), and Norwegian Agency for Development (NORAD)-are working together using the SWAPs framework to provide technical and financial assistance to Uganda's educational sector, especially the Universal Primary Education national initiative launched in 1997.

As of the year 2000, there were no SWAPs programs aimed at trade as a sector. This may be a reflection of the low priority that both donors and governments of P2 countries give to trade and trade development as an instrument of poverty alleviation. One of the advantages is that SWAPs are deliberative, creating a mechanism for key stakeholders to come together in a spirit of partnership to discuss various aspects of sector-specific development and to come to a consensus regarding the priorities and how to address them.

This deliberative aspect is particularly important for national capacity development for trade because most of the P2 countries still need to undertake a national dialogue on trade, its priority within national development, and the strategies by which to address it. The presence of outsiders is also useful because, as proposed in the model, P2 countries will need a lot of direct participation from the international community.

THE WAY FORWARD: DOHA AND BEYOND

Unlike the third Ministerial Conference held in Seattle, the fourth Ministerial Conference held in Doha succeeded in getting WTO members to agree to launch a new round of trade talks and to keep the global economy on track toward freer trade and investment. Coming only two months after September 11, 2001, in the middle of the global fight against terrorism in Afghanistan and elsewhere and with the world economy on the verge of a recession and mindful of the catastrophic failure in Seattle two years earlier, the delegates knew that failure at Doha could be fatal for the WTO as an organization, which would be a major setback for the multilateral economic system.

Accordingly, both developing and rich countries made last-minute compromises in order to reach a deal: The conference agreed to establish a Trade Negotiation Committee under the authority of the General Council and to conclude negotiations by January 2005. This is very ambitious given the many outstanding issues and given that the Uruguay Round, with a smaller and less-diverse WTO membership, took seven years to negotiate.

Doha was good for developing countries in several ways. First, they benefited from the failure of Seattle because the WTO would not have survived two Ministerial Conference failures in a row. Therefore, Doha paid a lot more attention to the needs and concerns of the developing and least-developed countries. Second, China and Taiwan were admitted as full members of the WTO, thus strengthening the voice and representation of the developing countries in all future negotiations.

China, with a population of 1.3 billion people and one of the fastest growing economies in the world, is likely to change the balance of power at the WTO negotiating table, mostly in favor of developing countries. Third, Europe, America, and Japan agreed to negotiate the opening of their markets to goods and services from developing countries. Finally, the rich countries promised to help the developing countries build their competencies and capacities for more effective membership in the WTO and gainfully participate in the multilateral trading system and global society.

Still, developing countries remain suspicious because they remember the Uruguay Round when most of the benefits went to the rich countries. They also fear that the rich countries could use environmental concerns and labour standards as nontariff barriers to trade. Concerned with the difficulties of implementing earlier commitments, developing countries need firm commitments from the international community for practical assistance to build their capacities.

It was agreed that priority be given to negotiating outstanding implementation of decisions made in earlier rounds by the end of 2002. Implementation-related problems cover a wide range of issues including S&D, SPS, and rules of origin, subsidies, and countervailing measures. Implementation issues are very important for developing countries because as Iddi Simba, Tanzania's trade minister, said before Doha, many developing countries would have preferred to solve the implementation issues remaining from the Uruguay Round agreement before advancing to the next round of multilateral negotiations.

Murasoli Maran, India's minister of commerce and industry, abstained from voting for the new round on behalf of other developing countries because of the failure of the rich countries to open their markets to developing countries in areas such as agriculture, textiles, labour, and apparel where they have a comparative advantage. Perhaps one of the most important decisions from Doha for the least-developed countries is the emphasis placed on the need to develop their competencies and capacities to enable them to participate most effectively as members of the WTO and to benefit from the global economy and global society.

This includes issues such as trade and the environment, transparency in government procurement, and adjustments to WTO rules, disciplines, obligations, and rights. In technical areas in which developing and least-developed countries were particularly weak and vulnerable, the conference agreed to postpone negotiations until after the fifth Ministerial Conference, when studies will have been done and capacities will have been developed. The conference also made provisions for periodic reporting to monitor progress made on issues important to developing countries.

Yet, Doha was no more than a promise to negotiate and assist developing countries. The real challenges are ahead for both rich and poor countries. The rich countries will need a lot of political support from their domestic constituencies in order to live up to the Doha commitments. For example, the

United States will have to negotiate countervailing duties and allow a wide range of imports from developing and least-developed countries. President George W. Bush will need fast-track negotiating authority from Congress, and the administration must campaign for a new domestic consensus in support of free trade. Europe must accept fundamental reforms to the European Common Agriculture Policy, which subsidizes European farmers and keeps agricultural products from developing countries out of European markets. Japan must also open its markets to both developing and developed countries.

The challenges for developing countries are also many. They must build the momentum and aspirations from Doha and make sure that their legitimate needs and concerns continue to be heard and receive high priority from America and other members of the international community. They must take advantage of the additional funding and support promised at Doha to develop their national competencies and capacities to participate more effectively as members of the WTO and to reform their economies for more gainful participation in the global economy.

They must continue to work together in groups or clusters that will advance their individual and collective interests. Finally, they must convince their domestic constituencies that globalization offers the best hope against poverty, joblessness, inequality, ignorance, and disease. Was Doha a tactical "feel-good" retreat, especially for the rich countries whose economies were on the verge of a global recession?

If so, then the ghosts of Seattle will continue to haunt members of the WTO as they begin to negotiate the new round. If, on the other hand, Doha was a strategic decision by the United States and other rich countries to show leadership and genuine support to the rest of the world, then the future of globalization looks promising. Only time will tell.

7

Globalization, Labour and Employment Practices

In this chapter the effects of globalization on labour and employment practices in developing countries and transition economies been discussed. To begin with a general survey of the global employment situation during the 1980s and 1990s before discussing major changes in employment practices in these countries owing to globalization and its drive for greater enterprise competitiveness. I also discuss the importance and challenges of human resource development for globalizing countries to become competitive through training, development, and a commitment to lifelong learning.

Then discuss the advantages and disadvantages of imposing extensive labour standards on developing countries and emerging economies, with a brief discussion of child labour and conclude the chapter with a discussion of the human and institutional competencies and capacities these countries need to develop to be able to manage labour and industrial relations and employment standards and practices for effective and equitable globalization. In general, while globalization has had positive effects on labour and employment practices, these vary across countries, sectors, industries, enterprises, and types of workers. Besides globalization and technological change, significant effects on labour and employment practices can be attributed to other factors such as growth-oriented macroeconomic policies, labour, employment, management practices, and industrial relations systems and practices.

THE GLOBAL EMPLOYMENT SITUATION

According to the ILO in Geneva, during the 1990s, the global employment situation was depressed-just as it had been during the 1980s. The ILO described a world characterized by high levels of unemployment, falling employment, rising poverty, and increasing social tension. It estimated that out of a world labour force of 3 billion people, 140 million, or 4.7 per cent, are fully unemployed. While this does not seem like a high rate of unemployment, another 25–30 per cent, or an estimated 900 million people, was underemployed.

Moreover, the East Asian crisis is estimated to have added another 10 million unemployed workers worldwide. The situation was particularly harsh, with high risk of exclusion from meaningful labour force participation, for many vulnerable groups including the unskilled and poorly educated, young people with no previous work experience, the long-term unemployed, older displaced workers, workers with disabilities, women, and ethnic and minority groups.

The report concluded with a call for action: "In sum, the employment situation in the world remains largely grim and the pressing need to find new ways to overcome barriers to employment poses a common and urgent challenge for countries around the globe." Is globalization to blame for the world's grim unemployment situation? Not entirely. It is true that global economic integration and increased travel have resulted in increased competitiveness at the national and enterprise levels, forcing producers to find ways to cut costs, improve efficiency, and raise productivity and profits.

To attract and retain foreign investments, countries and companies have had to pay much more attention to labour costs than they have in the past. Consequently, the globalizing countries experienced more frequent and severe labour adjustments during the 1980–2000 periods than during the previous twenty years.

In addition to globalization, two other factors explaining the world employment situation are technological change and national policy initiatives. Technological advances in information and computer technology, telecommunications including the Internet, biotechnology, transportation and logistics, and new forms of production, management, and work organization brought about significant changes in the nature and structure of the required labour force, especially in globalizing countries that are consistently open to new ideas and outside influences.

A combination of economic global integration and technological advances and the shift from protected import-substitution to competitive export-oriented industries brought about a drastic change in the demand for labour from a large number of cheap, unskilled workers to more educated, skilled, flexible, and trainable employees. In those countries where the economic structure shifted from predominantly agricultural or manufacturing to the service sector, there were sharp changes in the demand for more educated and skilled workers. In fact, one of the prerequisites for a country's ability to take full advantage of the benefits of globalization is the quality of basic education and workplace skills and capabilities in the general population.

Perhaps the most important factor for determining the level and quality of employment during the 1980–2000 periods was the national or regional macroeconomic policies and the vigor with which they were being implemented and sustained. Globalizing regions, developed and developing countries and transition economies experienced different levels of unemployment based on the particular labour, employment, and industrial relations systems, policies, and practices they pursued.

Those countries which, in addition to liberal macroeconomic reforms, pursued policies promoting flexible labour markets and employment practices, decentralized industrial relations systems, and judicious enforcement of labour standards focusing on "core human standards," fared much better in terms of employment creation and lower levels of unemployment. On the other hand, countries with rigid labour and employment laws, regulations, and policies experienced higher levels of unemployment because they were not able to attract and retain as many new jobs.

In Europe, the unemployment rate remained high (more than 10 per cent) and did not change much. In the United States, it was significantly lower and declined even more during the 1990s. Since both Europe and the United States are globalizing regions of the world, the most plausible explanation for the significant differences in unemployment rates is the differences in their respective labour and employment policies, regulations, and practices. In general, the United States pursues a much more flexible labour market and employment practices than Europe.

Within Asia and the Pacific, the differential effects of different national policies on the levels and changes of the unemployment rates for the years 1987 and 1996 (before the Asian crisis). Malaysia and Thailand recorded the lowest levels of unemployment in 1996. They also had the most flexible and decentralized labour markets, employment practices, and industrial relations systems. For Thailand and Malaysia, as well as other middle-income countries that achieved 5 per cent or more per capita growth between 1986 and 1994, wage negotiations are decentralized at the enterprise level.

None of them have national-level, regionwide, sectorwide, or industry-wide centralized bargaining or collective agreements for wages and other conditions of ser vice. While they have active unions, they are organized enterprise by enterprise. While trade union leaders complain that it is difficult to organize workers enterprise by enterprise, this process provides the necessary flexibility, especially for new enterprises, to negotiate affordable labour contracts.

Therefore, it creates attractive conditions for start-up small- and medium-size enterprises (SMEs), which are often the leading job-creating sector of a growing open economy. The globalizing countries enjoying low levels of unemployment provide a policy environment in support of flexibility in wage negotiation, in hiring and firing, and low rates of taxation. Countries experiencing high unemployment rates provide the opposite: rigid employment practices, centralized collective bargaining, and high rates of taxation.

The Czech Republic experienced significantly lower levels of unemployment during the 1990s than Bulgaria, Poland, or the Russian Federation. Likewise, in Africa, Mauritius recorded significantly lower levels of unemployment rates than Algeria and Egypt. In Europe, the same is true of the Netherlands as compared to Spain. In all these cases, the countries with the lowest unemployment rates pursued progrowth macroeconomic policies within the context of flexible labour markets. For example, Mauritius has a decentralized industrial relations system in which wages and other conditions of service are negotiated at the enterprise level.

On the other hand, Algeria, Egypt, and Spain-all high unemployment countries-have rigid employment practices, and employers have little or no flexibility in wage negotiations, firing and hiring of staff, and other changes in employment practices. The evidence strongly supports the argument that policy change and labour market flexibility explain the differences in unemployment rates across regions and countries of the world.

GLOBALIZATION AND EMPLOYMENT PRACTICES

Newly globalizing countries must undertake corresponding changes in their labour, employment, and industrial relations laws, regulations, systems, and practices. These changes must be effective at the macro (national), meso (industry, sector, region), and micro (enterprise) levels. The overall objective of these changes is to help the globalizing country move away from a rigid and regulatory regime to an increasingly flexible, open, facilitative, and participative labour and industrial relations system while at the same time providing appropriate protection for the workers.

Among other things, the new labour and industrial relations system must:

1. Encourage and support macroeconomic reforms and growth;
2. Promote the effective use of technology, labour market flexibility, and high productivity growth;
3. Foster the development of competitive export-oriented entrepreneurial private sector firms and discourage import-substitution, subsidy-dependent industries;
4. Reexamine and, where necessary, make changes to the roles, structures, and functions of trade unions, employer associations, workers, governments, and other key actors in the country's industrial relations system;
5. Establish effective collaborations and partnerships with government, employers, and workers' organizations to bring about and sustain required changes in the workplace in areas such as work organization, job design, skills development, technological changes, and employee participation, motivation, and commitment; and
6. D evelop appropriate policies and programs for dealing with the social consequences of globalization such as unemployment, deskilling, child labour, social justice, treatment of vulnerable groups, environmental protection, and so on.

For newly globalizing countries, the two most important newcomers to the industrial relations system are global corporations and entrepreneurial small- and medium-size indigenous private sector firms (SMEs). Global corporations bring in foreign capital, new technology, and management know-how. They create permanent jobs, pay better, tend to be more socially responsible if working within a high integrity governance system, and create business opportunities for the local SMEs.

They prefer an industrial relations system characterized by flexible labour markets; decentralized collective bargaining; low taxation; clear and fairly enforced laws, rules, and regulations; and a sizable pool of educated and trainable labour. Experience from the fastest-growing globalizing countries strongly suggests that SMEs are more competitive with a decentralized industrial relations system in which wages and conditions of service are negotiated collectively, or individually, at the enterprise level. This is particularly important for the growth of entrepreneurship and indigenous private sector development because it allows new enterprises to set affordable conditions of service.

A newly globalizing country must reexamine its industrial relations system as it relates to the trade union movement, its role, and organization, and relationships with government, employers, the work it represents, civil society, and the international community. For the most part, developing countries and transition economies have highly politicized trade unions organized nationally by industry, sector, or regions. They have tended to pursue employment policies designed to protect existing jobs and improve the working conditions of those already employed, rather than work for the development of an enabling environment for new job creation.

South Africa provides an excellent example. In 2000, the unemployment rate among blacks was almost 50 per cent. During the struggle for independence, the trade union movement worked very closely with the African National Congress and other anti-apartheid forces, and when independence came, union leaders gained new power and influence, which they used to push for improvements in wages and other conditions of employment. Consequently, wages for union workers in the formal sector in the major cities are three times the wages of nonunionized workers in the informal sectors in Soweto and other townships.

The unions lobbied the new government to pass the Wages Act and the New Industrial Relations Act so that these wage differentials are protected geographically and by sector. This has the unintended consequence of condemning the vast majority of black workers to the informal sector and makes it difficult for new enterprises to join the formal sector because the wages are more than they can afford. The new industrial relations system, designed to right past ills and to protect workers' rights to employment, appears to have the unfortunate effects of labour market rigidity and killing jobs for the unemployed majority.

CHANGES AT THE ENTERPRISE LEVEL

For newly globalizing economies, some of the most fundamental changes take place at the enterprise level, affecting production processes, human resource management, and overall enterprise management. Managers, employers, and owners of these enterprises seek to enhance competitiveness through attitudinal and behavioral changes; modern labour policies, legislation, and institutions; compensation and incentive systems linked to enterprise, group, and individual performance; a pool of skilled trainable and adaptable labour; flexible forms of work organization and management; and cross-cultural management and adaptation.

Behavioral and attitudinal changes are required on the part of management, workers, union representatives, and government officials from regulatory agencies. These changes must reflect a deliberate policy of getting away from conflictual modes of industrial relations and human resource management practices to more collaborative and participative practices. The managers must refrain from exercising restrictive and hierarchical close supervision and learn to manage using flexible, participative, consultative, and collaborative styles.

Workers need to have a positive and competitive attitude toward work and be well informed and involved in the decisions affecting their work, jobs, and lives. Both management and workers need ongoing feedback on how well they, their coworkers, and the whole enterprise are doing and what they need to do to maintain or enhance competitiveness. There must be closer coordination between industrial relations practices, including the terms and conditions of work as negotiated in the collective agreement and the personnel policies and human resource management practices within the enterprise.

In terms of modern labour policies, legislation, and institutions, the changes should be aimed at maintaining harmony in industrial relations and avoiding work stoppages (strikes or lockouts) by emphasizing conflict prevention rather than resolution and by being proactive in addressing enterprise-level labour and industrial relations problems, disputes, and grievances.

Collaborative approaches to industrial relations practices such as alternative dispute resolution methods and interest-based bargaining should be tried and, where appropriate, institutionalized. Perhaps one of the most profound changes is the pressures for increased enterprise efficiency and effectiveness and the corresponding demands by managers and entrepreneurs to link wage increases to clearly identified performance criteria, not only at the enterprise level but right down to the individual managers, supervisors, and employees.

This differs significantly from the old methods of wage determination based on seniority, which is what unions prefer, and job content as determined by job analysis and job evaluation, which is the traditionally favored approach by personnel administration. Enterprises interested in developing performance-based compensation systems should have in place management systems and practices that establish clear performance criteria and management, attract and retain competent staff by providing a component of compensation over and above regular pay, reward sound performance without significantly increasing labour costs, and maintain labour force flexibility so that the enterprise can quickly make labour adjustments in response to the economic/business cycle and its own poor performance.

Flexible forms of work organization and management are particularly common among competitive global corporations. These include job redesign, away from highly specialized individual jobs to broader, higher-value, and capabilities jobs requiring cross-training and multiskilling; flat and learning organizations with emphasis on cross-functional coordination and the application of lessons of experience related to superior performance to the work of individual managers and workers in other parts of the organization; and rationalization of enterprise operations.

Rationalization can take different forms, including identifying core functions-those which are related to the core mission and business objectives-outsourcing, downsizing, forming strategic alliances, and benchmarking. All these changes are designed to keep the enterprise competitive and, therefore, require a strategic approach to both industrial relations and human resource management. All this is aimed at improving enterprise productivity and global competitiveness.

SKILLS AND COMPETENCIES FOR GLOBAL COMPETITIVENESS

Globalization thrives on individual initiatives. In the old, partially closed systems of political economy, the emphasis was on the state, the party, the church, or monopolistic enterprises as the drivers of development and progress. Globalization is much more people-centered. Its success ultimately depends on many able and willing individuals taking risks and the initiative, learning, working hard, and persevering in order to create value, enjoy the fruits of their efforts, and contribute to the country's overall improvements in living standards.

Of course, institutions are still important, but without a critical mass of individuals with the commitment, motivation, skills, and competencies, no country can succeed in the global economy or global society. In this section, I highlight the importance for newly globalizing countries to develop and maintain-within their societies-quality education, skills, and competencies for global competitiveness. During the 1980s and 1990s, when more countries were responding to the challenges of globalization, it became clear that human capital development is a major engine of economic growth.

Differences in living standards both within and between countries could be explained in differences in the level and quality of education and workplace skills and competencies. Countries, cities, or parts thereof with a critical mass of educated and skilled people have the advantage of being able to understand and exploit new and emerging opportunities of globalization. They can adapt more quickly and efficiently to new ideas and technology, acquire new competitive skills, establish productive relationships with outsiders, and create new opportunities in response to the changing circumstances around them.

In this regard, successful globalization means that the country has the capacity to identify the right opportunities for the right people, with the right educational levels, skills, and competencies, producing the right goods and services, at the right time, place, and price for the world economy. How does a newly globalizing country develop the necessary skills and competencies for global competitiveness? While the particular strategies differ depending on a country's history, culture, demographics, and political economy, there are some common basic elements that can be applied to many globalizing developing countries and transition economies. Following are some of the key elements.

1. Basic education is necessary but not sufficient.

The population should be literate and numerate. It should be able to function not only in its local languages but also in at least one of the international languages. It should be computer literate as well. Yet, given the rapid and continuous pace of change in the demand for new skills, skill sets, and qualifications, the globalizing country must emphasize continuous training and a culture of lifelong learning for its population. For this reason, countries and donors focusing only on universal primary education without, at the same time, enhancing the population's competitive skills and competencies and providing opportunities for lifelong learning are not building long-term competitive capabilities. Low-quality primary education for the masses does not prepare a country for global competitiveness or build a learning society.

2. Successful globalizing countries need an effective system of portable skills.

The term portable skills are used here to refer to the transfer of skills from family and school to work and from work to work. In the first instance, the globalizing country must have an educational system with successful transition from school to work. This depends on three things: a solid, high-quality basic education; the development of sound analytical, cognitive, and behavioral skills and the ability to communicate ideas and solve problems individually and in groups; and close working relationships between the schools, their communities, and the prospective employers through activities that expose students to the practical realities of work. This can be done through apprenticeships, vocational training, coops, work–study arrangements, and staff exchanges between employers and training institutions.

The second reference to portable skills-from one work situation to others-is important because globalization involves a process of "destructive construction," which is destroying old industries or jobs and creating new ones. Therefore, the globalizing country's labour force should have the capacity to move from the jobs of declining industries to the emerging and growing sectors. This is determined by the workers' potential for learning and the quality of enterprise training and work experience they get. The more general and theoretical training-emphasizing principles and general applications-the workers receive, the better they become at transferring skills across jobs. Cross-training, multiskilling, and exposure to various jobs facilitate transfer. Narrow, highly specialized, job-specific training does not facilitate skills transfer across jobs, enterprises, or industries.

3. A globalizing country needs a general population and labour force with the education, training, and mind-set for flexibility in adapting to new technology and changing workplace demands and expectations.

Just as enterprises must be flexible in order to remain competitive, the labour force must also remain flexible in order to be employable. Workers with a higher education and a better level of skills and competencies tend to adjust better and more effectively to the changing workplace requirements. Young workers also tend to be more flexible than older workers. Yet, older workers have more work experience with valuable corporate memory. Therefore, to be successful, a globalizing country needs a mixture of young and experienced workers. There is also evidence to suggest that diversity at the workplace is associated with creativity and more effective group problem solving.

4. Newly globalizing countries need to review and modernize their educational and training institutional infrastructure to reflect changing labour market demands.

The new institutional infrastructure must be characterized by responsive and flexible partnerships. All the institutions involved in education and training must be responsive and flexible. Close working relationships, partnerships, or strategic alliances should be encouraged between and among academic schools and training institutions; between schools and employers, the trade unions, and the workers; and the government must play a leadership role in areas such as policy development, strategic funding, and facilitating the development of effective partnerships among the major stakeholders.

A case can be made for the development of a global (or regional) system of training for skills and competencies for the global economy. Before the recent wave of globalization started, most of the countries developed their educational and training policies and institutions independently of other countries. Citizens were educated and trained for the national labour market. Those who left were regarded as a brain drain or statistically insignificant loss. Although labour is still much less mobile than capital, highly educated people with portable skills and experiences are highly globally mobile. With increasing globalization, labour will become much more global as well.

The skills and competencies for global corporations and international organizations are also becoming more global in terms of the intrinsic requirements for effective job performance. Governments of globalizing countries also require public servants who are globally apt and experienced. As well, the third sector-NGOs, community organizations, traditional institutions, and so on-cannot provide effective leadership to civil society without acquiring the skills and competencies required to deal with others in the global society. Therefore, it makes sense for newly globalizing countries to get together and investigate the opportunities for the development of a global training, learning, and skills development system whereby local, national, and regional institutions will be linked together globally.

Global corporations and the world's leading education and training institutions can play an important role in providing resources and expertise for the development of the global learning and skills development system. Already, American and European education and training institutions are extending their services to the global market, but these are very limited and targeted only to those who can afford the exorbitant training costs. The proposed global training system should be more inclusive and affordable and be aimed at creating opportunities for citizens of marginalized globalizing countries to acquire globally competitive skills and competencies.

5. Most developing countries have a sizable and economically active informal sector.

   This sector creates business and employment opportunities for millions of people, especially those with less formal education, skills, and competencies needed in the formal sector. No discussion of education, training, and skills development is complete without paying serious attention to modernizing the informal sector and making it globally competitive. According to the ILO in Geneva, initiatives should be taken by globalizing developing countries to increase incomes, productivity, and working conditions for the informal sector.

These initiatives include upgrading traditional apprenticeship systems; increasing access to new technology through training and extension services; increasing operational linkages and developing strategic alliances between the informal sector and the emerging SMEs; increasing networking to arrange for cost-effective training and skills development for the informal sector; and rethinking the mix, packaging, and delivery of services to the informal sector including training, credit, extension services, technology transfer, infrastructure development, and government services. Newly globalizing developing countries need an efficient modernizing informal sector to serve the economy not only as an engine of growth but, equally important, as a cushion or insurance policy for the rest of the economy, especially during periods of economic crises.

6. Globalization creates and highlights the plight of vulnerable and marginalized groups who are unable to participate or take full advantage of the opportunities of globalization.

Although these groups can be found in every country, developing countries and transition economies have higher percentages of the excluded population. The typical vulnerable groups include the poorly educated and unskilled; young people with limited education and no previous work experience; displaced, often older, workers; women; people with disabilities; and ethnic and minority groups. Education, training, and skills development provide effective tools against exclusion. Newly globalizing developing countries and transition economies must develop policies and programs specifically targeted to their vulnerable groups.

Programs for education, training, and skills development for vulnerable groups have four basic objectives: integration into the labour force either as employees or self-employed persons; providing resources, opportunities, and skills for independent living; providing social and welfare services to enable workers to live with dignity; and respecting workers' human rights and protecting them from abuse and exploitation by other more powerful members of society.

In most globalizing countries, women provide the bulk of the increase in labour supply. By opening up education, training, and skills development opportunities and by providing supportive working conditions and a good environment, women can become more active participants in the global economy. By providing child care and other family services, flexible maternity leave, and enforcing antidiscrimination laws, women's employment opportunities, especially in the sectors in which they are underrepresented, can be greatly enhanced. In most newly globalizing developing countries, women need better access to education and training in mathematics, science, information and communication technologies, management, and entrepreneurship.

LABOUR STANDARDS

The ILO was created in 1919 primarily for the purpose of adopting and helping enforce standards to cope with the problems of labour conditions involving injustice, hardship, and privation. In 1944, the Declaration of Philadelphia was incorporated into the ILO's constitution, thus broadening its mandate to include more general, but related, social policy, human and civil rights, and general conditions of work. Therefore, labour standards have been around much longer than the current wave of globalization. Yet, with globalization, labour standards have become very controversial especially between the advanced countries, on one hand, and the developing countries and transition economies, on the other hand.

The controversy is directly related to international trade and competitiveness, with overtones for human and civil rights as well as social justice. The case for strict enforcement of labour standards is advanced by the ILO and supported by the WTO with strong backing from the industrialized countries. They argue that by not enforcing labour standards, emerging economies, developing countries, and transition economies are able to produce internationally tradable goods and services below cost and, therefore, gain unfair cost advantage over their competitors who pay to have the standards fully enforced. It is also argued that enforcement of standards protects vulnerable workers from abuse and exploitation from the powerful owners of capital and their agents.

The abuse and exploitation takes many forms, including low wages with no benefits; slavelike working conditions; endangering workers' health and safety; and depriving workers of their human and civil rights especially in terms of the right to support and belong to a union, the right to collective bargaining, and the right to refuse to work in unhealthy and unsafe environments. Exploitation can also be targeted to vulnerable and voiceless groups such as children, migrant workers, and the poor, uneducated, and unskilled job seekers. The history of industrialization is a history of abuse and exploitation of the weak by the powerful.

Therefore, governments and the international community have a duty and a responsibility to provide and enforce labour standards to protect workers from abuse and exploitation. Developing countries see it differently. While accepting the need to protect workers from abuse and exploitation from unscrupulous employers, they argue that the current labour standards go too far, cost too much, and are not related to their cultural, social, or economic realities.

In terms of international trade, the elaborate and costly labour standards take on the form of nontariff protectionism by the advanced countries. Emerging economies and developing countries are most competitive in labour-intensive industries such as agriculture, textiles, tourism, and other services. Labour standards have direct upward effects on labour costs and, therefore, raise the cost of production for these countries. By insisting on strict observation of labour standards and by threatening boycott if they do not observe them, advanced countries and the international organizations are undermining the developing countries' capacity to compete and participate in the global economy.

The debate about human and civil rights and social justice is much more complicated because it includes issues related to national political and governance ideology and systems, local cultural values and practices, national sovereignty, and international law. For example, over the years, different industrial relations systems and employment practices have evolved in different countries with varying degrees of effective protection of workers' rights. It is also necessary to consider labour standards in the broader context of society's economic realities and political and cultural development. Poor people are more likely to give up some of their political rights in order to improve their economy and personal standards of living.

As well, most traditional societies in developing countries do not have the same history of human and civil rights as practiced in the rich advanced societies. Therefore, it is reasonable to expect that as these economies grow and societies advance they will be less willing to continue giving up their political rights and, instead, insist on more strict enforcement of labour standards. In fact, this is already happening in many emerging markets and developing countries where the emergence of a critical mass of educated middle-class citizens has created conditions for the population to demand political reform and respect for human rights.

Since workers and trade unions are always part of this middle-class pressure group, there is a tendency for the reforms to focus on workers' rights and improved wages and working conditions. Are labour standards good or bad for developing countries? The answer is yes and no. They are good because they provide appropriate protection for the workers and attempt to ensure international standards of treatment. They are bad because they impose hardships on the developing countries. The international community should not impose minimum conditions of work or even institutional arrangements for collective bargaining on newly globalizing developing countries; this would cost a country an unreasonable amount of money and would produce few benefits to the population. Imposing standards on others is morally wrong and smacks of imperialism.

As well, there is no empirical evidence to support the view that these standards are significantly beneficial to the targeted groups, the total labour force, or the general population. Still, the international community has a role to play in protecting workers and their rights. Instead of developing and enforcing blanket uniform labour standards for all countries with widely different economic, political, social, and cultural realities, efforts should be directed to the development of core human standards.

These core human standards would cover a smaller range of items and limit itself to widely acceptable human standards such as protection against slavelike conditions, freedom of association and collective bargaining, protection from unhealthy and unsafe workplaces, and protection of vulnerable groups, such as children, from abuse and exploitation. These core human standards should be strictly enforced. However, they should not include "non-core" human standards such as minimum wages, conditions of work, the right to hire or fire, or the type of acceptable industrial relations system.

One of the problems with existing labour standards is that they are not adequately enforced by governments of most of the developing countries. This is partly because most of these governments lack the human capital and institutional capacity for effective enforcement and partly because they see them as an externally imposed obligation over which they have no local control, influence, or ownership.

GLOBALIZATION, WAGES, AND INCOME DISTRIBUTION

Globalization has been blamed for depressing wage levels and accentuating differences in income distribution among rich, developing, and least-developed countries. Differences in income, wealth, and opportunity have been escalating since the 1980s, and grew worse in the 1990s. According to the UNDP's Human Development Report 2000, in 1999 the combined wealth of the world's 200 richest people was U.S.$1 trillion, while the combined incomes of the 582 million people living in the forty-three least-developed countries was only U.S.$146 million.

Income distribution problems arise, in part, within income classes or between different skill and competence levels but not between economies, which grow more or less rapidly as a result of globalization. At the enterprise level, union wages are driven down by the openness of the world financial system. Capital mobility poses limits on trade unions' wage demands in light of high elasticity of demand for labour.

According to the Stoker–Samuelson theorem, increased globalization lowers the relative wages of unskilled labour in the advanced countries and raises the relative wages of unskilled labour in developing countries when the two groups of countries begin to trade together.

However, labour economists are not sure of the validity of this theorem or the conditions or contingencies under which it may or may not hold. What is clear is that besides globalization and trade, wages for unskilled labour are pulled down by technological change and the large supply of unskilled job seekers in most of the developing countries. It is predicted that most globalizing developing countries will continue to experience high unemployment and downward wage pressures for unskilled labour. A number of factors account for this: First, demographically, these countries have an almost unlimited supply of young, unskilled, inexperienced job seekers.

A typical developing country's population distribution is about 40 percent under fifteen years of age. In ten years' time, this young cohort will have left school and joined the already crowded ranks of the unemployed job seekers. In the short and immediate term, there is little policy makers can do to stem this flow. Second, the overall demand for unskilled labour is not growing. While the East Asian economies made their miracles based on cheap unskilled labour and while such opportunities still exist in the traditional labour-intensive industries such as construction, agriculture, and textiles, the new economy is increasingly dependent on skilled rather than unskilled labour.

Third, many of the newly globalizing developing countries have poor-quality education, especially in the rural areas where the majority of the population lives. For example, in East Africa, as the education systems expanded and grew fast to accommodate increasing numbers of students, the quality of education went down. This is particularly so in the government-supported public systems and the rural areas. A recent Canadian International Development Agency report on Uganda's education system confirms my impressions. It found that the results of a random national sample of third-grade students showed a significant decline in performance.

On the mathematics test, the number of students who achieved a satisfactory score declined from 48 per cent in 1996 to 31 per cent in 1999. In English, the scores declined from 92 per cent to 56 per cent. On the reading test, only 11 per cent of the sample achieved a satisfactory score in 1999. The results were even worse in rural areas, with Kampala (the major urban area in the country) outperforming all other regions. Therefore, with or without trade and globalization, poorly educated, unskilled workers-the majority of the labour force in many globalizing developing countries-will continue to be disadvantaged in the labour market.

CHILD LABOUR

Child labour is a multidimensional and often emotional problem blamed on globalization. It has taken on an international dimension, although its meaning and implications vary across regions, countries, and sectors and between urban and rural settings. Like many other socioeconomic problems, child labour is not entirely caused by the current wave of globalization. Stories of child labour and child abuse in the workplace date back to the early days of the Industrial Revolution, first in England, then in mainland Europe and North America. Globalization has made the problem worse and more visible, and therefore, newly globalizing developing countries must respond to the challenge by developing realistic policies, systems, institutional arrangements, programs, and enforcement mechanisms to protect their children from workplace abuses and exploitation.

According to the ILO, by the year 2000, there were some 250 million children 5–14 years old who were involved in economic activities in the developing countries. This is approximately 8.3 per cent of the total estimated global labour force of 3 billion people. Close to one-half of them-120 million-carry out these economic activities on a full-time basis, while the other half combines working with schooling. These figures do not include children who perform "noneconomic" activities such as domestic or family services on a full-time or part-time basis without pay. In terms of gender, approximately three-quarters of the child labour force are boys. On the other hand, more girls than boys perform the noneconomic unpaid domestic work.

The distribution of child labour varies by region, industry, occupation, and urban–rural setting. In absolute terms, Asia (excluding Japan) has the highest density of child labour with 61 per cent of the world total (about 152.5 million) as compared to 32 per cent (80 million) for Africa, 7 per cent (17.5 million) for Latin America, and a small number for other developing regions of the world. In relative terms, however, Africa has the highest child labour participation rate, with about two children out of five, or 41 per cent of the total number of children 5–14 years old, involved in paid economic activities.

Since the largest number of working children is in Asia and since Asia leads the developing world in globalization and trade, the link between child labour and globalization is easy to make. Yet, Africa, which is much less globalized, also has a serious and growing child labour problem. Child labour participation is directly related to underdevelopment. The less developed a country is, the greater the proportion of the child population who work. In most cases, these countries have a wide range of economic activities that require extra hands but no specific skills.

Accordingly, the least-developed countries have most of the child labour in basic industries such as agriculture, whereas the emerging markets have moved them to more "advanced" jobs in service and simple manufacturing. For example, in Cambodia, close to 90 per cent of child labour is in agriculture; but in the Philippines, an increasing number of children have moved from agriculture to wholesale and retail trade, restaurants, and hotels. Although statistics are always hard to validate for clandestine and sometimes illegal activities such as child labour, provides the best estimates from a number of developing countries.

By far, the largest number of working children, both boys and girls, are in agriculture, hunting, forestry, and fishing. This is because agriculture is labour intensive, requires no specific skills or previous working experience, takes place in rural areas where most of the children live, and is hard to regulate by labour inspectors often found in urban areas in the offices of the ministries of labour. Other sectors in which children are heavily employed are manufacturing, wholesale and retail trade, restaurants and hotels, transport and communications, and community, social, and personal services.

Contrary to popular belief, construction is not a heavy employer of child labour. This may be because of the heavy lifting required, increased mechanization and required skill levels, or simply better labour inspection on construction sites as compared to agricultural plantations. Likewise, mining and quarrying-despite their rural, isolated locations-do not employ large numbers of children. Children are more susceptible to injury or illness from work than adults; they are physically tender, mentally not fully mature, and are more likely to take undue risks at work. In the advanced countries, young drivers (16–21 years old) are involved in more driving accidents than other driver age groups. Similar factors are in play with children in the labour force in developing countries.

According to the statistics, the largest number of injuries occurs in agriculture and related industries. Other sectors of high injury rates for child labour include wholesale, retail, restaurant and hotels, manufacturing, construction, transport and communication, and community, social, and personal services. The injuries and illnesses vary in seriousness and include punctures; broken or complete loss of body parts; burns and skin disease; eye, hand, and hearing impairment; respiratory and gastrointestinal illness; fever; headaches; and other illnesses associated with exposure to excessive heat or harmful chemicals.

Both the distribution of injuries by sector and the type of injuries reported are similar to studies of occupational health and safety in the more advanced countries. For example, agriculture, construction, transport, and personal services continue to be the major sources of occupational accidents in industrial countries. Most of the injuries are to the back (due to lifting), fingers, hands, arms, legs, eyes, feet, and other exposed body parts. In an ideal world, there would be no child labour. In the real world, children have always been and perhaps will continue to be part of the labour force.

The international community, through the United Nations, bilateral donors, and NGOs, is working very hard to eradicate or at least reduce the incidence of child labour. In November 1999, the ILO celebrated the coming into force of the "Worst Forms of Child Labour Convention," which was adopted by the International Labour Conference in June 1999 and has since been ratified by more than forty countries. The convention came up with proposals to protect children against the worst forms of child labour. These proposals included research activities; development of international guidelines; capacity building and institutional development in labour ministries and employers' and workers' organizations; advocacy and awareness-raising campaigns; assistance in developing legal instruments to combat discrimination and stigmatization and offer social protection, training, and workers' educational programs; sensitization activities targeted at employers and their organizations; and care and support initiatives.

Since child labour cannot be completely eliminated, especially in the short run for the newly globalizing least-developed countries, one of the short-term protective measures should be improvements in health and safety targeted at the countries and industries with the largest participation of child labour. Most industrial accidents can be prevented through education and proper enforcement of basic safety rules and regulations: using proper safety devices (for example, clothes, boots, eyeglasses), using proper work procedures and supervision, following good housekeeping practices, complying with the law regarding reporting of accidents and injuries, avoiding carelessness or horseplay, and providing proper training and staffing.

Proper incentives at the enterprise, industry, and national levels can bring about required changes in behaviour. International campaigns such as labeling of goods that are not produced with child labour could also reduce abuse and exploitation. This has proven to be effective in international environmental campaigns such as "dolphin-friendly tuna." The trade union movement, as a business organization and champion of social justice, can play a leading role in eliminating or reducing child labour in developing countries and improving the health and safety of the workplace for all employees, both young and old.

CAPACITY DEVELOPMENT

In addition to reviewing the global employment situation as of the year 2000, this chapter has discussed the effects of globalization on employment practices, required skills and competencies for global competitiveness, labour standards, and child labour. It has emphasized the need for globalizing countries to maintain flexible and responsive labour and employment practices; a collaborative, decentralized, and facilitative industrial relations system; cost-effective and technologically adaptable enterprise management; and a regulatory system that provides effective protection of workers including protection of children from abuse and exploitation.

All this requires capacities and competencies. It requires human capital in the form of knowledge, skills, competencies and motivation, and institutional capacities within government, the trade union movement, the business sector, and civil society in general. Most of the newly globalizing developing countries and transition economies do not have the necessary capabilities and institutional capacities for the effective management of the required changes in labour and employment practices. For example, in the Asian countries with the worst cases of child labour, a major part of the problem is the inability or unwillingness by the authorities at the different levels of society to enforce existing laws, rules, and regulations for the protection of children against abuse and exploitation by employers.

As the ILO has stated in various field missions, the ministries of labour in most developing countries are often institutionally weak because they do not get the same priority as high-profile ministries such as finance and economic planning. The trade union movements tend to be politically active but professionally and organizationally weak, and most of the workers, especially in the informal sector and those employed by family and SMEs, are often unorganized. Even professional associations for trades and professionals are often small and organizationally weak. There are very few community-based organizations or NGOs specializing in labour and employment, especially in the context of globalization.

Very little empirical research has been done on the relationship between globalization, labour, and employment practices. Accordingly, policy makers are forced to make policy without local knowledge or to accept advice from outside. At the enterprise level, while global corporations have the resources and expertise to introduce and manage the required changes in labour and employment practices, the other parts of the business sector-the SMEs and the informal sector-have very limited capabilities and capacities to do so.

Even the global corporations often need to adapt their technology, products, services, and management knowhow to the changing local conditions. Therefore, it is quite clear that developing countries and transition economies need to develop and sustain a wide range of knowledge, skills, and competencies as well as institutional arrangements to be able to manage labour, employment, and industrial relations in accordance with the requirements for globalization.

The five key areas of required capacities and capabilities are policy management and coordination; reform of the country's industrial relations system; development of competitive knowledge, skills, and competencies; enterprise-level innovations; and effective protection of workers including all the vulnerable groups. If these institutions are unable or unwilling to perform the required functions, initiatives must be undertaken to address the performance gaps. For example, it is important for the newly globalizing country to formulate new policies regarding labour and employment practices. In this regard, the government must take the lead in consultation with other stakeholders in the private sector.

This requires political will and technical and administrative capabilities in the cabinet (executive), parliament (legislative), line ministries such as labour (technical and administrative), and local and international research institutes for knowledge and information. If any of these is lacking, then the government, in partnership with the international community and the local stakeholders, should take the necessary steps to address the identified capacity gaps.

When the government is so weak that it does not have the capacity to assess its own capacity requirements, the international community through bilateral donors and specialized U.N. agencies such as the ILO and the WTO should provide the necessary resources and expertise. The international labour movement can also play a developmental role by working closely with the weak, poor countries to strengthen their capacities for the management of labour and employment practices. Global corporations have extensive resources and expertise in this area, and they, too, should be involved in assisting these countries build the necessary knowledge, skills, competencies, and institutions.

For example, they are very good in the development of competitive knowledge, skills, and competencies as well as managing enterprise-level innovations and collective bargaining. Therefore, they can help these countries in their efforts to build the capacities they need in these areas as well as reforming their industrial relations system. International research institutions can also help the local research institutes to develop and retain the competencies they need to undertake labour and employment research needed for globalization. All this would need mobilization, coordination, and effective utilization.

Therefore, in terms of sequencing, it makes sense to begin by strengthening the human capabilities and institutional capacity of the ministry of labour, the workers' organizations, and civil society in general.

8

Occupying Places in the World Economy

When space feels thoroughly familiar to us, it has become place. Abstract knowledge about a place can be acquired in short order if one is diligent.... But the 'feel' of a place takes longer.... It is made up of experiences, mostly fleeting and undramatic. To capture what is distinct about the contemporary flight of social forces to the world economy, some have written of a more modest internationalism, others of grass-roots or demodernizing internationalism. In many works (including my own), Foucault's idea of 'resistance communities' guides the appraisal of what is being born of current movements.

Looking at concrete practices, this literature often offers great insights into transnational social movements and organizations. However, lacking a more general theory of global order and change, it frequently says little about their political importance, for now or for the future. To built on its findings, we need concepts that are both germane to contextualized practices (outside which only ghosts live) and can highlight the fundamentals of broader processes of order and change in the world economy. This is what 'modes of relation to the world economy' hope to do.

Here, we begin our investigation into contemporary modes of social relations to the world economy, by looking at social forces struggling against the ways and consequences of globalization. This work will inform a political argument, after we have looked at neoliberal ordering in the world economy.

This chapter is divided into two sections. The first presents a short historical review of oppositional politics in the world economy from the 1840s (when began the 'classical age' of left internationalism) to the Bretton Woods crisis (when global 'anti-systemic movements' began surfacing). In the second section, we take our first measure of contemporary happenings.

From classical Left internationalism to anti-systemic movements: abstract subjects out of place. Before the Bretton Woods crisis, the predominant challenge to world orders came not from social forces in movement in the world economy, but from internationalist and cosmopolitan programmes drawn on behalf of inferred, imagined or theorized planetary subjects. These were, then, to recall Marx, 'perfectly political' challenges, that spoke of 'Man's specied-life, as opposed to his material life' and appealed to 'an unreal universality'.

In the era of Pax Britannica, there were certainly attempts to organize what Marx called 'guerrilla battles' against capital and to get workers of different countries 'not only to feel but [to] act as brethren and comrades in the army of emancipation'. During the great European strike movement of 1866 to 1868, for instance, workers of different countries did come together for meaningful transnational campaigns, or in support of local strikes. Workers of different countries also met at universal exhibits where they 'chatted a while' (to borrow Victor Hugo's expression) and learned from one another.

At the 1851 Great Exhibition in London, for instance, 1,000 French workers met with their British counterparts to discuss ways to organize strikes, and to compare salaries and work hours. Lessons learned in London had a significant influence on the development of French societes de resistance and on the fight for workers' rights in France: In 1863 French workers gained the right to form co-operatives and in 1864, the right to form associations for the purpose of negotiating collective agreements.

Born out of the support of English and French workers for Polish autonomy, the International Working Men's Association (1864-1876) did call for 'the immediate combination' of the still-disconnected working-class movements of European countries, and it did attempt to organize circumstantial and purposeful struggles: 'One of the best means of demonstrating the beneficent influence of international combination is the assistance rendered by the IWMA in the daily occurring trades' disputes.' This strategy of active resistance led the IWMA, for instance, to fight concrete fights: for the regulation of the international supply of labour ('to counteract the intrigues of capitalists always ready, in cases of strikes and lockouts, to misuse the foreign workman as a tool against the native workman'), the extension of the ten-hour days, and the defence of national autonomy.

It also brought the First International to give its 'complete and emphatic allegiance' to the Geneva International Peace Congress, and Marx to write that, at the moment of Lincoln's re-election as President of the United States pledging to abolish slavery, 'the star-spangled banner carried the destiny of the working class'. But strategic presence on the terrain of the world economy remained an exceptional event. For all their differences, the many internationals that met in the classical age of Left internationalism (the Democratic Friends of All Nations, the Fraternal Democrats, the First and the Second internationals and so on) were all occasional gatherings of out-of-place subjects.

In political terms, they were akin to cosmopolitan salons, distinct in their intent from philosophical gatherings of the previous century, but not in their relationship to the world economy. So it was with the international women's movement. In the nineteenth century, the movement was concerned principally with putting forth an alternative cosmopolitanism based on the universalization of what were assumed to be innately female values. The International Council for Women, for instance, was founded (in 1889) on the basis that 'the cause of women is the cause of religion and morality all the world over', and proposed to represent, as founding member Lady Aberdeen put it, the 'mothers of the world'.

It was on behalf of this abstract subject that it lobbied for a higher moral order. In the same period, the International Women Suffrage Alliance (1904) fought for equal citizenship rights for women on the bases both of the need for equity and the moral contribution of women to the cause of justice the world over. More immediate concerns, closer to the material experience of women, were of course also part of the early phase of women's internationalism. The Congrès International de la Condition et des Droits des Femmes that met at the Paris world fair, for example, demanded that women's domestic work be regulated, and that fair wages be paid by the state.

Women also fought for international conventions on the regulation of night work and childbirth (adopted respectively in 1906 in Bern and in 1919 at the first session of the Conference Internationale du Travail). In both cases, however, struggles were not waged by a global movement of women fighting concrete, situated struggles, but by nationally grounded institutions arguing for an abstract political subject on whose behalf was drawn a Universalist agenda (concerned in this case with the protection of women's motherly duties and the preservation of women's reproductive labour). For the women's movement as for workers, the world economy was not a field of practice.

Until the First World War, global gay politics was also rooted in salons where would-be representatives of an imagined global subject gathered. In that period, the Cercle Hermaphroditos (1895) and the Scientific Humanitarian Committee (1897-1942) organized largely scientific campaigns and petitions that addressed themselves to doctors and other 'prominent figures' that had roles to play in constructing, and treating, homosexuality. That 6,000 'prominent figures' signed a petition of the Scientific Humanitarian Committee against Paragraph 175 of the 1871 Second Reich's Penal Code (which criminalized homosexual acts), 'of whom half were doctors', was, of course, crucially important, but it did not indicate a global social movement in the making.

In the inter-war period, cosmopolitan institutions fighting programmatic battles on behalf of imagined global subjects easily over-determined attempts to organize concrete, situated struggles on the terrain of the world economy. Again, global politics was severed from contextualized experiences, and ghostly proxies were invented on whose behalf struggles were waged.

A key development here was the split between rival internationals that began at the Zimmerwald Peace Conference of 1915, when pacifists and social democrats wishing to end the First World War clashed with Spartakists and others who wanted to radicalize it. This split was institutionalized with the creation of the Third International (1919) and fully consumed by the thesis adopted at the 6th Congress, that turned, as Julius Braunthal put it, 'the Communist International into an organ of the Soviet state'.

From then on, there was little room to manoeuvre for global movements, campaigns or actions not allied with one of many competing internationals: the Socialist Workers International (1923-1940), the Second International (1889-1914, 1945-), the Second-anda-Half (1921), the Third (1919-1943) or the Fourth (1938-). The tragic history of anti-fascist brigades during the Spanish civil war ('the most impressive example of internationalist practice according to Michael Lowy) illustrates well the over-determining of transnational praxis in this period.

Started as somewhat fragmented, 'primitive, unprepared and leaderless' units of anarcho-syndicalist, communist and Trotskyist workers, the brigades became stakes in fractional struggles between the Comintern and Trotskyists, and, as Franco's phallanges were winning the war, the control of internationalist brigades became more important than the defeat of the fascists. Similarly, many efforts to assemble a global labour movement that would represent all workers and organize effective campaigns were recuperated and distorted by cosmopolitan chicaneries. In the inter-war period, the Amsterdam International and the Red Trade Union International, for instance, competed, according to Zinoviev, to, 'win them workers over to our side ... and bring them under our control'. Again, Left internationalism was severed from experience.

After the Second World War, state-centred modes of regulation prevailed throughout the world economy (Keynesianism and Fordism in the centre, state socialism in the East, 'peripheral Fordism', 'bloody Taylorism' and 'over-developed statism' elsewhere), and the national level remained the privileged place for social forces to meet. Occupying the terrain of the world economy were, again, imagined subjects easily bent out of shape by cosmopolitan agendas.

To take but one example: in countries at the centre of the world economy, the women's movement was principally defined by issues and institutions close to the heart of the Keynesian state, and sometimes sponsored by the state itself. In the USA, for instance, the National Organization of Women (1966) was created by the Kennedy Commission on the Status of Women. In England, the state was the privileged terrain of socialist feminists. In Canada, the National Action Committee on the Status of Women was, and is still, a state-funded and state-bound group. In socialist countries as well, state agencies structured the women's movement.

On the terrain of the world economy, women were represented by ghostly institutions that hosted occasional gatherings and drew cosmopolitan blueprints, but did not organize a meaningful political movement. As late as 1984, Robin Morgan's Sisterhood is Global, intended as a survey of 'women as a world political force', found little that was transnational about the women's movement and presented, instead, a collage in sixty-nine chapters concerned with nationally centred movements.

In addition, the cold war and related peripheral conflicts (e.g. in Algeria, Korea, Indo-China, Egypt, Yemen) turned - as Emma Goldman had said of the First World War - 'the whole world into a collection of national peniten-tiaries', and they submitted the global movement of social forces to the discipline of competing cosmopolitan blueprints. The world of labour, for instance, was colonized by the World Federation of Trade Unions (WFTU) and the International Confederation of Free Trade Unions (ICFTU), both cold war creatures. Again, the global movement of social forces was distorted out of shape and participants were impressed into global regiments.

Some global movements, of course, did have a measure of relative autonomy from inter-state relations, but only in exceptional circumstances, and only for a while. Most notable in this respect were the student movement, the anti-apartheid movement and the anti-nuclear movements. Like the anti-slavery movement - that began with Quakers in Pennsylvania in the 1680s, two centuries before internationalism had installed itself as an organizing strategy - it was a focused, circumscribed struggle.

Thus it was that, between Pax Britannica and the crisis of Pax Americana, in a period when transnational capital was moving beyond an 'international' understanding of its activities towards a 'world' perspective, Left internationalism installed ghosts on the terrain of the world economy.

CONTEMPORARY HAPPENINGS: CONCRETE FIGHTS OVER LOCATIONS

In the past twenty years or so many of the dynamics that had kept social movements grounded to the national level have lost their structuring power. First, the East-West axis has ceased to be a conditioning framework, and room to manoeuvre has opened up for transnational movements that do not explain themselves in terms of grand plans for the ordering or the reordering of the world. Arguably for the first time since the end of the Napoleonic wars, the structuring of state-to-state relations does not now wholly over-determine social and political relations in the world economy.

The crisis of Fordism in countries at the core of the world economy and the accelerating transnational segmentation of production has also had a considerable impact on social movements in the world economy. Starting in the mid-1970s, the accelerating globalization of production and finance precipitated a crisis of state-centred modes of regulation everywhere in the world economy that both reduced the political benefits of state-centredness for social movements and made it more urgent for them to build what Baldemar Velasquez, president of the US Farm Labour Organizing Committee, called 'organizing' rather than 'political' alliances with counterparts elsewhere in the world economy.

More generally, the acceleration of globalization and what Alberto Melucci called the 'planetarization of human experience' has precipitated a veritable flight of social forces to the world economy. Although a hastily assembled and disorderly movement, involving a bewildering variety of groups and social forces often coalescing in short-lived alliances that left few traces, enduring programmes or convenient synthesis, this flight can generally be said to be made up of (1) campaign-centred movements that are both, (2) linked to one another increasingly by transnational institutions, and (3) grounded by, and constitutive of, a sense of place. Through them, the world economy is becoming a field of practice.

CAMPAIGN-CENTRED MOVEMENTS

In the world of labour, a many-fronted struggle is being waged against neoliberal restructuring of the world economy. A first front is made up of local strikes projected transnationally. A well-known but revealing story comes from local 5668 of the United Steelworkers of America's (USWA), which organized a model transnational campaign on behalf of 1,700 locked out workers of the Ravenswood Aluminum Corporation's (RAC) metal-smelting facility in Ravenswood, West Virginia. In 1991, the Kaiser Aluminum and Chemical Corporation (KACC) was purchased by RAC, a company formed for that purpose by Charles Bradley of Stanwich Partners Inc, a group of international investors headed by global commodities trader March Rich.

At that time, Rich had been living for several years in Zug, Switzerland, where he had sought refuge from prosecution by the US Department of Justice on '65 counts of tax fraud and racketeering'. Within months of the sale, jobs and wages were cut, the pension plan was altered, working cadences were increased and workplace safety became a central concern of workers. Union activity increased and a walkout appeared imminent when workers were summarily locked out by RAC.

In the following eighteen months, USWA's local 5668 organized a transnational campaign with help from the Industrial Union Department of the AFL-CIO, the International Metalworkers' Federation, the International Union of Food and Allied Workers' Association (IUF), the International Federation of Chemical and Energy Workers' Union (ICEF) and the International Confederation of Free Trade Unions (ICFTU).

For the most part, the campaign focused on anti-Rich activities. It involved lobbying Jamaican politicians (up to, and including, Prime Minister Michael Manley), Swiss and Dutch Bankers (financial backers of Rich), developing contacts with a Czechoslovakian metalworkers' union (that led to President Vaclav Havel personally intervening to prevent the purchase of a Czechoslovakian aluminium company by a Rich-controlled group), and organizing an international campaign, in collaboration with the IUF and the ICEF, to protest the acquisition of the 'Athenee Palace' Hotel in Bucharest by a group also controlled by Rich. All in all, the Steelworkers organized sustained anti-Rich activities in twenty-eight countries on five continents.

Another significant transnational labour campaign was organized by Bridgestone Firestone (BS/FS) workers in the USA, 'one of the longest and toughest disputes in recent US industrial history'. During the 1994 round of negotiations, Bridgestone - BS/FS's parent company - demanded several crucial concessions from the union, including wage and benefits reductions, mandatory twelve-hour-shifts, the abolition of seniority rights, the gutting of safety protection, the elimination of labour-management co-operation schemes, a reduction of holidays and, significantly, greater freedom to outsource. On 12 July 1994 a strike began that involved 4,200 workers at five BS/FS plants.

In January 1995, 2,300 striking workers were discharged and 'permanently' replaced by non-unionized workers - the largest such replacement in US history. On 22 May, the United Rubber Workers (URW) changed strategy and strikers offered to return to work under BS/FS's conditions. Some workers did go back to work, but the company forced more than 1,000 men and women on to a waiting list, in violation of the back-to-work agreement.

On 1 July 1995, URW merged with the United Steelworkers of America (USWA), which launched its biggest corporate campaign ever. The scope of the campaign was truly extraordinary: 3.6 million handbills, nearly a million 'Don't Buy Bridgestone/ Firestone' stickers and bumper stickers, 250,000 campaign buttons, 115,000 black flags (on which more later) and 15,000 'Don't Buy' T-shirts were distributed, and 63,000 yard signs were displayed.

Thousands of separate campaign events were organized that involved over 60,000 USWA participants and volunteers, and 1,100 separate USWA locals were actively involved. The campaign reached eighty-six countries including sixteen that were visited personally by replaced Bridgestone/Firestone workers. Forty-three delegations of foreign workers visited the USA to lend support.

The first results from the campaign were felt in the autumn of 1996, when BS/FS started recalling illegally 'replaced' workers who were still without work. In early December an agreement was reached between USWA and Bridgestone that included wage increases (40 cents per hour on basic pay), signing bonuses ($750 for all employees), gains on holidays, increased pension provisions and, most importantly, an extension of the 'pattern bargaining' system. On 12 and 18 December, BS/FS workers voted by a three-to-one margin to approve the new contract.

As well as specific strikes, a host of work and safety issues have also kindled significant transnational labour campaigns: work conditions in export zones, living wages for apparel workers, redundancy firings, increased work cadences, systematic overwork and so on. On the last subject, a significant campaign was mounted in Asia against karoshi - death by overwork.

Where the push for regional integration has been the strongest, transnational campaigns have also become regional affairs. In the Americas, for instance, projects for regional or hemispheric integration have been at the forefront of the political agenda for a decade. In this context, a veritable saturnalia of transnational strikes, social movements and 'crossborder coalitions' has been organized that has involved 'agro-industrial workers, rubber tappers, papermakers, milk producers, building and wood workers, steelworkers, automobile workers, metalworkers, professionals, government workers and bank workers' as well as women's groups, indigenous organizations and environmental groups.

Most remarkable have been campaigns waged by the Amalgamated Clothing and Textile Workers' Union (ACTWU), the International Ladies Garment Workers' Union (ILGWU), the Teamsters and the United Auto Workers (UAW) on behalf of Lunafil workers in Amatitlán, Guatemala; the UAW's campaign in support of Ford workers in Cuautitlán, Mexico, following the murder of labour activist Cleto Nigmo in January 1990; and the cross-border campaign organized by the AFL-CIO, the International Longshoremen's Union, the United Farm Workers (UFW) and the International Union of Electrical Workers, on behalf of Mexico's independent bus drivers' union (that became a cause celèbre when film-maker Oliver Stone began supporting it.

At the time of writing, the Federation of Textile Union Workers (FTUW), the US Guatemala Labour Education Project (US/GLEP) and the Campaign for Labour Right were still involved in a significant hemisphere-wide campaign against the Phillips-Van Heusen Company (PVH) that began in December 1998, when PVH locked out workers at the Camisas Modernas factory, less than a year after they had won a six-year battle for union recognition (to become the only export factory workers in Guatemala to be both unionized and represented by a collective agreement.

Resonant symbols of global integration, corporate brand names have also served as starting points of numerous transnational campaigns. In the past decade alone, General Electric, Guess, Mitsubishi, Monsanto, Nestle, Nike, Reebok, Suzuki and GAP have been targeted by significant transnational campaigns, especially in East Asia and in the USA. (In the USA, 'the ZAP the GAP' campaign is credited with bringing back streaking). In the San Francisco Bay Area - a nodal point of transnational activism - Global Exchange, Sweatshop Watch, UNITE (the Union of Needletrades, Industrial and Textile Employees) and the Asian Law Caucus have campaigned against Tommy Hilfiger and sixteen other clothing manufacturers on behalf of workers in Saipan, in the Pacific Northern Marianas Islands. They organized a public awareness campaign, called for a boycott and filed a lawsuit ('the first legal attempt to hold US retailers accountable for the abuse of workers by subcontractors').

Transnational labour campaigns have also concerned themselves with prominent labour activists. After the oil strike of 1994, for instance, the UAW, The International Federation of Chemical, Energy, Mine and General Workers' Unions (ICEM) and the AFL-CIO's Solidarity Center (SC) involved themselves in important campaigns for the release of imprisoned Nigerian labour leaders from Nupeng and Pengassan, the two principal unions of oil and gas workers. In January 1996, they secured the release of four leaders of oil workers, detained without trial since the summer of 1994: Wariebi K. Agamene (Nupeng president), A. Aidelomon and Mr Eleregha, (Pengassan branch chairmen) and F. Addo (Pengassan's third vicechairman).

Another key imprisoned union leader was freed later in 1996. Still about Nigeria, an important transnational campaign for the release of Ogoni activist Ken Saro-Wiwa ended with his hanging on 10 November 1995. Recently, the global women's movement has also been an increasingly campaign-centred affair, concerned for the most part with concrete and situated struggles: abortion rights, teleworking, excision and female sexual mutilation, household consumption, wages for housework, the rights of immigrant workers, control over reproductive technologies, homeworking and the putting-out system in the garment industry, and gender exploitation in export-processing zones.

This last struggle has involved principally groups in the Americas (Mujer Obrera, Mujer a Mujer, the Coalition for Justice in the Maquilladora, the Maquila Solidarity Network, the Support Committee for Maquilladora Workers, the Centro de Orientacion de la Mujer Obrera, Despacho Obrero) and in Southeast Asia (the Philippine Workers' Assistance Center, the Asian Pacific Workers' Solidarity Links). In Europe and South Asia there have been significant women's campaigns against sexual tourism and to defend the rights and freedom of sex workers.

In Southeast Asia, the Asian Women Workers' Center has organized a modest campaign to bridge the gap between Japan's extensive daycare system (established in the 1960s) and daycare arrangements elsewhere (Nitta 1995). In Muslim countries, the International Solidarity Network of Women Living Under Muslim Laws (WLUML) documents cases and issues action calls on behalf of three feminists arrested and jailed without trials, kept incommunicado for seven months in Algeria for having discussed ... the project of law known as 'Family Code', which was highly unfavorable to women '... an Indian Sunni woman who filed a petition in the Supreme Court arguing that the Muslim minority law applied to her in her divorce denied her the rights otherwise guaranteed by the Constitution of India to all citizens ...' '... a woman in Abu Dhabi, charged with adultery and sentenced to be stoned to death'.

Although by and large still nationally bound and structured by cosmopolitan agencies - the International Gay and Lesbian Association (ILGA, 1978) and the International Gay and Lesbian Human Rights Commission (1991) - that lobby on behalf of an absentee subject, global gay and lesbian politics has also shown signs of moving towards more punctual, campaign-centred actions at the global level, organized by more radical organizations such as Lesbian Avengers, Act-UP, Radical Faeries and Queer Nation, that favour direct contact between activists.

The AIDS crisis, of course, has focused political energies, and made organizing more urgent, as have the imprisonment and torture of gays and lesbians (LaViolette and Withworth 1994), and the rise of 'family-values' politics in the USA. On this last subject, US-based organizations (Lesbian Avengers, Act-UP, the Radical Faeries and Queer Nation) have acted globally in a strategic manner quite in contrast with the abstract, policy-minded ways of the ILGA.

> We have declared war on heterosexism and homophobia. This of course means the [heterosexuals], but also the mainstream, nicey-nicey, assimilationist, '[w]e're just like you nice straight folks except for who we sleep with' Gay and Lesbian bowel movement. This movement needs to be flushed, and we are the tidy bowel Queers! We will target many with our random, unpredictable, terrorist attack who are deserving punishment. Hateful breeders who bash us and assimilationist scum that water down our angry voices and channel our effort into a system that oppresses us are both cause to pull out the ammu[nition] and come out shootin'.

Frequent subjects of realpolitik reckoning - about who stood or fought with whom, did what when, won or lost which battle or what was won or lost in it - transnational campaigns are also significant in terms of the relation they establish to the world economy. This is something we will discuss below, when we consider emerging modes of relation to the world economy.

TRANSNATIONAL INSTITUTIONS AND HORIZONTAL LINKAGES

In a note to Paul Lafargue written in answer to anarchist concerns, Marx referred to the International Working Men's Association as 'a link ... not a center of power'. However fair Marx may have been in his assessment of the First International, he certainly did not foretell future developments: without exception, internationalist agencies born in the century that followed the demise of the IWMA in 1876 did attempt to install themselves as centres of power.

In the past two decades, however, established centres of power have either been supplanted as locus of global political organizing, or they have been re-centred to play a more modest role in support of transnational campaigns. The last internationals (the second and the fourth) have become debating societies, trailing the transnational movement of social forces rather than initiating it. In the world of labour, what remains of the WFTU acts as a lobby, playing a negligible role in the global movement of social forces?

For its part, the International Confederation of Free Trade Unions (ICFTU) - once a star chamber of cold war cosmopolitanism - has reinvented itself to support transnational campaigns organized by affliated federations, unions or even locals. While still a centre of business unionism, the ICFTU has become more of a link, in an effort to catch up with transnational campaigning. This has encouraged national federations that had hitherto pursue a more independent path to international solidarity (Quebec's Confederation des syndicats nationaux, for instance) to join, or rejoin, it.

Alongside re-engineered and recentred institutions now also exists a group of relatively new research institutes, think-tanks, TSMOs and information clearing-houses that document, assist and inform transnational campaigns. Facilities listed, of course, vary enormously in terms of resources and membership, and in their relationship with governing agencies. For instance, the consumer politics of the Women's Environmental Network (WEN, which has organized consumer campaigns for organic chocolate, cotton nappies and sanitary towels) contrasts sharply with PARC's 'People's Plan for the 21st century' (PP21), Mujer Obrera's work to assist displaced workers in the Maquilladora of El Paso (López 1991), or with the ICCSASW's efforts to organize solidarity campaigns among sugar workers of the world.

What institutions do share is a rootedness in concrete, situated, struggles. Many were born directly of transnational campaigns and have remained intimately connected to concrete struggles. The US/Guatemala Labour Education Project (US/

GLEP), for instance, was born in the Lunafil campaign and has played an important role in organizing other labour protests in Guatemala, most notably for workers at Petrosteel, Confecciones Transcontinentales and Phillips-Van Heusen.

In similar fashion, the Cuautitlán campaign led to the creation of MEXUSCAN, the North American Ford Workers' Solidarity Network, that later played a key role in co-ordinating activities from other labour groups involved in cross-border solidarity movements: the Canadian Auto Workers (CAW), the UAW, Labour Notes, the Coalition for Justice in the Maquilladora (CJM), Alianza Civica and so on.

Likewise, the 1992 'Strategic Organizing Alliance' (SOA) between the United Electrical, Radio and Machine Workers of America (UE) in the USA and the Mexican Frente Autentico de Trabajadores - a model of the genre - led to the creation of the North American Worker-toWorker Network (NAWWN), a gathering of over 700 local unions and activists. Besides organizing other transnational campaigns, the NAWWN has also formed a core of 'committed activists [capable of organizing] rapid-response solidarity action to support workers and organizers who are victims of firing, threats, violence'.

These activists later played a key role in the transnational campaign to reinstate workers fired during a union organizing drive at General Electric's Armadora Plant in Ciudad Juarez in November 1993. In this campaign, the UE/FAT alliance obtained 'the first secret ballot election in Mexican labour history'. In environmental politics, Greenpeace's campaign against the 1989 Basel 'Convention on the Control of Transboundary Movements in Hazardous Wastes' gave birth to the International Toxic Waste Action Network, now in its tenth year.

In the same manner, the Asia Pacific Workers Solidarity Links (APWSL), the International Labour Research Center (ILRC) or Southerners for Economic Justice, for instance, are all rooted in labour organizing, and all have explicit mandates to support ongoing struggles. Also in Asia, the Asian Women

Workers' Center (AWWC) has worked to document the transnational experiences of women of the region, emphasizing what is personal in the transnational, following what Le Corbusier would have dismissed as a donkey's path to the world economy. In the early 1990s, for instance, the AWWC documented and compared three murder cases involving Thai women pressed into prostitution in Japan, who had stabbed bar owners to death.

In the same period, the AWWC launched an information and documentation campaign on behalf of nine women who had filed suit against Hitachi, claiming gender discrimination in wages, job posting and job training. With the Hitachi 9, the AWWC took on 'the twincareer track system' now replacing wage discrimination as the principal form of gender discipline in Japanese transnational corporations. In taking these paths, the AWWC did not rise above lived contexts, or reset placed experiences, but rather worked horizontally to link hitherto unconnected cases.

Similarly, PARC is not a centre of power but rather acts as a 'switchboard for Asia's people's movements'. PAN also gathers information and links union workers and NGOs in countries where Japanese transnational corporations are active. The Asian Migrant Center and the Asian Migrants Forum both work to document and link transnational experiences, as do the Center for Transnational Labour Studies, the Transnational Institute and the Asia Monitor Resources Center.

In a similar manner, the Korea Labour Society Institute (KLSI) works on call from trade union federations and national centres to document labour/management relations, labour policies and labour problems. Having gathered the necessary information, the KLSI then distributes it to labour activists through its Professional Research Center, where labour activists from abroad also gather. In the same spirit, the ICCSASW informs sugar workers of living and working conditions, strikes and wage settlements elsewhere, interpellating them not as part of a generic whole (the would-be united 'Sugar Workers of the World'), but as workers brought together by their involvement in the sugar industries, and differently contextualized, through a variety of factors: home country dependence on export crops, working conditions in other industries and so on.

In the world of labour, International Trade Secretariats (ITS), World Industry Councils (WIC) and World Corporation Councils (WCC) have put themselves increasingly in the service of transnational labour campaigns. ITSs in particular (and among them most notably the International Metalworkers' Federation, the International Federation of Chemical, Energy and General Workers' Union, the International Textile Garment and Leather Workers' Federation and the International Union of Food and Allied Workers' Associations) have played a key role in support of transnational campaigns, and they have served as key links between locally rooted strikes and struggles.

During the Ravenswood campaign, for instance, the International Metalworkers' Federation (IMF) worked alongside the AFL-CIO's Industrial Union Department to provide key research facilities that allowed for the transnationalization of the campaign. In addition, the International Union of Food and Allied Workers' Associations (IUF) and the ICFTU 'organized [an anti-Rich] rally of some 20,000 trade unionists in Romania' that was a key moment in the struggle. Created in the mid-1960s as co-ordinating bodies for national unions, and long enfettered in international politics, World Corporation Councils have lately grown to play a key role in organizing transnational labour campaigns.

In the women's movement, the Women's International Information and Communication Service, has 'connected more than 10,000 women's groups in 130 countries' working 'against economic development policies that marginalize and exploit women workers'.

In the same spirit, the International Feminist Network (1976) has worked 'to facilitate the mobilization of the women's liberation movements on an international scale when needed', the 'Feminist International Networks of Resistance to

Reproductive Technologies and Genetic Engineering' has worked 'to stimulate and link worldwide feminist research on, analysis of, and resistance to the use, abuse, and control of women in reproductive and genetic research and technologies', and the 'Women and Global Corporations Project' of the American Friends Service Committee links 'workers, activists and researchers worldwide who are promoting legislation to stop TNC practices that are reducing jobs and wages for women workers in the North and exploiting women's cheap labour in the South'.

In the struggle against sexual slavery, Human Rights Watch's 'Women's Rights Projects' has completed a key work of documentation. Recently, Web-based institutions have also served as clearing-houses for placed information, and have linked between placed experiences. In the world or labour, for instance, the Campaign for Labour Rights is the principal site-based information centre. Sweatshop Watch and the Corporate Watch Web Site Online are both 'watchdog websites' designed to provide activists (as well as academics and journalists) with up-to-date information and analysis on specific transnational corporations.

In the women's movement, notable links include: 'Virtual Sisterhood', an electronic support network committed to encouraging exchange of information and strategies between women's movements; Modemmujer, an electronic link founded by five Mexican NGOs, and the 'Directory of Information' of the Women's Environmental Network, which provides 'instant accurate information on consumer product' to link women of different countries. Against the MIA, such groups as the People's Global Action Against Free Trade (PGA), Global Trade Watch, The Third World International Network Forum on Globalisation and the Polaris Institute (Canada) used Wed-dased resources to link movements around the world, and the world's largest, searchable, anti-globalization archive was assembled.

As well as documenting specific struggles and linking them with one another, transnational institutions have also been involved in what I have called elsewhere 'solidarity tourism'. Since the beginning of the 1990s, for instance, Global Exchange has offered 'Reality Tours' that 'allow people to go past what they read in the media and travel beyond hotels and beaches'.

Destinations offered in 2000 included Cuba ('Explore the many faces of Cuba.... Learn about our island neighbor and the warmth of the Cuban people while experiencing their dramatic history and culture reflected in their daily lives'); Haiti/Dominican Republic ('Explore the depths of Haiti's rich history and culture.... Learn about Haiti's long struggle for democracy and see how Haiti offers the openminded visitor an opportunity to understand vibrancy and hope in the midst of challenge); India ('Learn how Gandhian solutions are still being applied'), Mexico (¡Bienvenidos!.... Visit ... Chiapas and learn more about the history and culture of indigenous communities. Speak with representatives of a variety of local organizations and gain a better understanding of popular movements and modern day social struggles in Mexico').

In the world of labour, solidarity tours have become frequent events. In the Americas, the UE/FAT alliance is an important broker of worker-to-worker exchanges. In a typical visit, a rank-and-file delegation of UE women visited Mexico in August 1996 and toured plants, meeting with workers and leaders of the union and co-operative sectors to discuss problems facing women workers.

In 1997, FAT representatives made three trips to the USA; in exchange, three groups of UE workers travelled to Mexico, 'becoming familiar with the work of the FAT ... in the interior and in Ciudad Juarez. During their stay, they toured plants where workers are represented by FAT-affliated unions, participated in organizing sessions, meetings of the Mexican Action Network Against Free Trade, a FAT national meeting, and other activities. Between 23 July and 1 August 1999 CISPES (Committee In Solidarity with the People of El Salvador) sent 'labour rights' delegates/clients (costing US $1,300) on a one-week tour of El Salvador to help strengthen the international labour movement and build cross-border solidarity. In a spirit reminiscent of The Times, enjoinder to visit pickets of dockworkers, 'curious' solidarity tourists were encouraged to meet organizers of the Salvadoran labour movement.... Witness the harsh effects of neoliberal policy.... Hear testimony from workers.... See how workers are fighting for their right.... Discuss youth organizing with FMLN juventud.... Visit FMLN-governed municipalities.... Help build cross-border solidarity.

In the same spirit, the Canadian Auto Workers' 'Southeast Asian Campaign Tour Against Globalization' (24 February to 10 March 1999) took thirteen Canadian women workers and organizers to five Southeast Asian countries (Indonesia, Thailand, Malaysia, The Philippines, Singapore) to 'share their experiences and views on the recent Economic Crisis and Globalisation... how they have affected their lives and what they are doing to cope as well as resist'.

Four days of leadership training workshop in Malaysia, hosted by the Women Development Collective, were followed by tours of Manila and Zamboanga, a free trade zone where the tour joined in a picket. The 'Tour Against Globalization' then went on to Korea, 'to share with the movement there and exchange our experiences [and] to forge genuine international solidarity'. On 8 March the tour arrived in Seoul, and met with representatives of the women's committee from KWWAU, the Korean Confederation of Trade Unions.

In East Asia, the APWSL's co-organized - with the Hotel Employees and Restaurant Employees' Union (HERE) - the first Japanese-American solidarity tour, in support of striking workers at the Japanese-owned 'New Otani' hotel in the Little Tokyo district in Los Angeles. In the same period, the APWSL was organizing 'alternative tours' of export zones in New Zealand, to study the effect of deregulation. In like spirit, the AWWC organized 'grass-roots exchanges' between women workers and activists; and the GAATW 'Comparative Workshop' with invited representatives from Cambodia, Vietnam and Laos.

Ways for transnational institutions to gather money solidarity tours are also means through which local struggles are transnationalized and enduring links established. As I have documented elsewhere, solidarity visits were key to the building of cross-border solidarity movements during anti-NAFTA campaigning in the Americas. Similarly, SHF's 'mining exchange project' opened up channels of communication between mineworkers in Canada, South America and Southern Africa that have had a structuring impact on transnational campaigns.

During the BS/FS campaigns, replaced workers went to Izmit and Istanbul in Turkey, and to Tokyo, where they met with ICEM affliates and, as if to emphasize that global politics, like all politics, is local politics, with Revd Jesse Jackson, who was in Tokyo to meet high-ranking Bridgestone offcials. Demonstrations in Argentina and Brazil during an 'International Day of Action and Outrage', for instance, were organized by replaced workers touring South American Bridgestone plants. During the Camisas struggle, the AFL-CIO, UNITE and the US/GLEP organized tours where workers' representatives met with university students, investors, union members and religious groups.

Although often negligible in terms of realpolitik influence, solidarity tours are significant in that they highlight well the position of transnational institutions vis-à-vis the global movement of social forces. This too we must keep in mind when we consider emerging modes of relation to the world economy.

TRANSNATIONAL CAMPAIGNS AS PLACED EVENTS

In marked contrast to neoliberal governance - that begins and ends outside all political and social contexts - transnational campaigns are rooted in both concrete and situated struggles, and they are constitutive of a broader, more political sense of place. The Ravenswood campaign, for instance, was rooted in 'a powerful sense of place' growing out of long-standing ties between workers and the community (the average striking worker had twenty-four years' experience at the plant). Strengthened by community support, local pickets endured long enough for the transnational campaign to be effective.

In turn, the transnational campaign strengthened community resolve and broadened the local social basis of the strike. In the end, the connection between the local strike and the transnational campaign strengthened both, and the Ravenswood struggle became more than the sum of its parts. That is why Ravenswood strikers won their struggle. In the BS/FS campaign, the first sites of struggle were BS/FS plants themselves, where pickets were held daily until 22 May 1995, when the URW made its unconditional offer to return to work.

Once removed from BS/FS plants was 'Camp Justice', a tent city set up in front of the BS/FS headquarters in Nashville, Tennessee, following the ICEM/USWA/AFL-CIO 'World Conference on Bridgestone/Firestone'. There, replaced workers and their supporters gathered for events that Benjamin Tillet and London dockers would have easily recognized. On 12 July 1996 (the second anniversary of the strike and an 'International Day of Action and Outrage' against BS/FS), a rally was held at 'Camp Justice' which was attended by more than 600 USWA members and community supporters:

they heard fiery speeches by USWA Secretary-Treasurer, Leo Gerard and John Sellers, Executive Vice-President of the USWA-RPIC who has led negotiations with the company. Afterwards the crowd gathered around a circle of miniature black-flags. On each was written the name of one of the 400 workers who were illegally fired and have not yet been called back to their jobs.... The crowd then marched the short distance from Camp Justice to the BS/FS headquarters, led by Leo Gerard and three local religious ministers.... Previous marches had stopped in the roadway facing the building. This one took a different route ... the angry workers invaded the building's parking lot and swept to the front door where they were met by security guards and police.... After the chanting crowd withdrew, the ministers were admitted to present a petition and a scroll citing the names of all the replaced workers. They later reported that ... management had received their message but appeared unaffected by their requests.... With that message the crowd returned to Camp Justice to continue the fight.

For the duration of the campaign, 'Camp Justice' was occupied twenty-four hours a day, seven days a week, by replaced workers and their supporters. 'We're going to sit in their face one day longer than it takes to win this battle, and get a fair contract' said Ron Holder, of USWA Local 1055, representing workers at the Bridgestone plant in LaVergne, Tennessee.

Indy car races were also sites of note during the BS/FS struggle. Taking advantage of Bridgestone's efforts to publicize its products and build a base of American customers, 1,000 replaced workers carried black 'Bridgestone/ Firestone Flags' to the Indy 500 on Memorial Day weekend in May 1996. On the weekend of 29-30 June 1996, 500 members of USWA locals from throughout Ohio converged on Cleveland to demonstrate at the Cleveland Medic Drug Grand Prix and promote the 'Don't Buy' campaign. Again, workers displayed black flags, distributed leaflets and gave away miniature black flags. In Toronto (12-14 July 1996), 500 USWA members converged on the Molson Indy, again carrying black flags.

Still further removed from BS/FS plants were 'cyberpickets' (invented then), and real-life processions that took place in Europe and South America, especially during 'International Days of Outrage': on 10 July 1996, 2,000 Bridgestone workers in Argentina stopped production and held a two-hourlong General Assembly in front of their plant. On 12 July Brazil Bridgestone workers in São Paulo stopped work for one hour at shift changes at 5:30 a.m. 7:30 a.m. and 1:30 p.m.

Three days later, several thousand rallied outside the Pirelli tire plant (where workers are also ICEM members). The following day, a procession of several thousand workers (also ICEM members) gathered outside the Goodyear tyre plant. In Tokyo, where BS/FS's world headquarters are situated,

Zenroyo organized a 'Solidarity group to support BS/FS Workers in Dispute'.

Brand-name campaigns have also drawn from community-based alliances between labour organizations and others, and have also been constitutive of community. The PVH campaign, for instance, brought together grass-roots and religious groups, human rights advocates, AFL-CIO workers and UNITES members, students and CISPES and STITCH activists in a wide variety of sites hitherto barren in terms of politics. At the Valley West Mall in West Des Moines, Iowa, PVH campaigners distributed several hundred leaflets and marched in procession, carrying signs that read: 'Support Workers in Guatemala' and 'Van Heusen Shirts Made in Sweatshops'.

In Salt Lake City, eight activists 'spent a few hours spreading the word about how PVH fired all 500 unionized workers at its Guatemala factory when they came to work expecting to receive their Christmas bonuses'. During the second week of June 1999 alone, the PVH campaign brought local activists together in Canoga Park, Long Beach, San Francisco, Trumbull, Washington DC, Chicago, Boston, Detroit, Minneapolis, St Louis, Buffalo, New York, Portland, Philadelphia, Pittsburgh, and elsewhere in the USA. To further local mobilization, US/GLEP and CLR distributed leaflets and 'Activist Packets'.

The GAP campaign that began on 18 June 1999 (the 'International Day of Action Against Economic Globalization') has also been rooted in places and constitutive of it. In San Francisco, it has been an important factor of mobilization (Global Reach and Global Exchange report almost weekly leafleting activities). On 1 May 1999, during a rally to 'Stop Saipan Sweatshops' and 'Celebrate International Workers' Day', a large crowd of protesters gathered outside GAP's flagship store at Powell and Market Street, holding signs, banners and handing out leaflets. A quartet sang 'The Sweatshop Hokey Pokey' and the protest culminated with the 'pieing' of an eighteen-foot effgy of GAP Chairman Donald Fisher, 'whose face was splattered with a whipped cream pie by a lovely stilt walker'.

After the pieing, a procession left for the GAP store on Duboce and Market. There, a sea of people stopped traffc on Market Street and cheered while Donald Fisher, Gap Sweatshop CEO, again got a pie right in the kisser! Redwood forest activists, protesting the Fisher family's clear cutting of the last old growth redwoods in Mendecino County, led the chant 'Mr. Fisher - you've got a store, what do you need the redwoods for?'

Six weeks later, a GAP crowd again gathered at the Justin Herman Plaza for a 'street takeover' of the financial district. In a similar manner, the Nike campaign has brought activists together and charged new places with politics, singing songs as social as the dockworkers':

Just Don't do it

Just Don't

Justice, Do it, Nike

The Swooshtika

Just Boycott It

(Klein 2000a, 366)

Particularly interesting here have been efforts to charge nodal points in Nike's marketing scheme with political significance (basketball and golf tournaments), sporting goods and shoe stores, university campuses). To further mobilization there, CLR compiled a list of universities that have contracted purchase agreements with Nike, and it assembled a network of speakers 'to come to your campus to talk about the campaign to win justice for Nike's production workers'.

Brand-name campaigns have also encouraged national gatherings of social forces. In Japan, for instance, APWSL's 'New Otani' and 'Don't Buy Reebok' campaigns were both privileged occasions for the strengthening and broadening of coalitions between hitherto dispersed social movements. Support pickets were organized, political action committees set up and organizations linked. In the case of the 'New Otani' dispute, the hub of activity was HERE's Local 11, where was headquartered the 'New Otani Workers' Support Committee'. There, rank-and-file members from Osaka Zenrokyo, the Union Network (an independent union group), members of the Hanaoka Support Committee, RINK (Right of Immigrants Kansai Network), and a variety of citizens groups met and worked together, on a terrain that was, at once, local, national and transnational.

Still in Japan, APWSL's campaign for the rights of migrant workers spawned a 'National Network in Solidarity with Migrant Workers' (1997) that brought together representatives of documented and undocumented migrant workers in Japan, union representatives (from Zenrokyo, the National Union of General Workers, Tokyo South, the Foreign Laborers' Union, the All-United Workers' Union) as well as various citizens' groups (the Japan Association for the Study of Chinese Forced Labour, the Hanaoka Victim Support Group).

At its June 1999 meeting, the Network gathered more than 500 Japanese activists, as well as foreign workers from a dozen countries (McLaughlin 1999). In the same spirit, the AMRC and the Committee to Support Kader Workers organized a transnational campaign on behalf of the families of 189 victims of the May 1993 fire at the Kader Toy factory (in the export-processing zone of Buddhamonthorn in Thailand) which received much external support (in Hong Kong, for instance). Significantly, the Kader campaign brought together all major unions and social movements in Thailand in an unprecedented coalition that remained united until a compensation agreement was signed.

In the summers of 1988 and 1989, the PP21 campaign brought together more than 120,000 Japanese and foreign activists in nineteen different regional gatherings. Importantly, each gathering had a different theme, linked with the ambient community. The Sapporo meeting, for instance, focused on deindustrialization and the crisis of dairy farming, salient local issues.

Transnational campaigns against the politics of global regulatory institutions have also spawned placed events.

Launched in February 1998, the loosely gathered 'People's Global Action Against Free Trade and the World Trade Organisation' (PGA), for instance, has inspired innumerable local events. The first WTO ministerial conference in Geneva (May 1998) occasioned PGA-style 'global street parties' on all five continents. In Geneva (not a habitual location for street parties) a 'beautiful gypsy circus' of 200 tractors and bicycles was met with 1,000 police offcers, customs offcials and army volunteers.

In New York, 10,000 people gathered at the United Nations - the largest such gathering since the Reagan-Gorbachov Summit (1984). Again, the protest brought together social forces with little in common besides their opposition to the ways of the WTO. The people came with the banners of all kinds of struggles against some aspect of globalization: local unions fighting privatizations or austerity, groups of solidarity with the south, squatters, plus many personal banners, musicians, and the caravan tractors towing a huge sound system. Everyone there agreed: stupendous, unbelievable demo.

In front, holding the PGA banner (with a four meters high banner from India behind them) were some members of the international Convenor's Committee and some other representatives of peoples' movements that participated in the First PGA conference. In Hyderabad (the symbolic heart of peasant struggle in India), the 'Joint Action Forum of Indian People against the WTO and Anti-People Policies' (JAFIP) organized a procession that gathered tens of thousands of peasants, agricultural labourers and industrial workers. In Tel Aviv there was a street party: 'over 500 people walked and danced from Dizengoff Square to the beach, while a van with DJ was driving in front doing the music.... The party ended in a pleasant sunset rave.' In Leuven (Belgium), a 'Reclaim the Streets' party took place. In Prague, 3,000 people joined the street party.

'They blocked the city's main road with thirty drums, a puppet show, fire performances, four sound systems and twenty DJs.' In Lyon, the PGA street party attracted 200 people, and 'lots of crazy anti-corporate costumes and signs, a few dogs and bikes, several drums and whistles, and even a float'. In Seville, the 'Network of Struggles against Neoliberalism' distributed a manifesto 'For Humanity, against the Dictatorship of Money'. In Brasilia, an anti-WTO march brought together 50,000 people. In Brisbane, 'a small but effervescent crowd partied 'til dark and then went home'.

In Montreal, Operation SalAMI held a street party outside the Montreal Stock Exchange, and a Teach-In Citoyen on 'The Globalization of Injustice: Resistance and Alternatives'. Echoing the PGA's call for non-violent civil disobedience, sit-ins and blockades were organized. 'Today' said SalAMI's Philippe Duhamel, Montreal has done its part for the globalization of resistance. We're proud of what we've done. 'The promoters of the globalization of injustice cannot say that their programme of huge profits, the destruction of social programs and the impoverishment of ordinary people has any longer a consensus in Quebec.

In the United States and Mexico, border communities have been both the starting point for a wide variety of transnational campaigns (that have for the most part focused on working conditions in Maquilladora industries) and have been transformed by transnational campaigning. As Elaine Burns suggested, this is perhaps explained by the central role played by women's groups in cross-border activism (e.g. la Mujer Obrera in El Paso, Fuerza Unidas in San Antonio, the Support Committee for Maquilladora Workers in San Diego/Tijuana, the Coalition for Justice in the Maquilladora in San Antonio Texas).

Shaped by concerns about the relationships between work and community, transnational campaigns have been built as community projects, and they have reinforced a local sense of place. In the Americas, the hemisphere-wide struggle against neoliberal integration has not only transcended national locality; it has also been constitutive of it. The effect has been felt especially in Canada and in Mexico. By virtue of their proximity to the USA, these two countries are at the centre of the movement for continental integration into the Americas; by their national political mythology as well as by the self-interest of social groups most urgently interpellated by regionalism, they are rebuffed by it.

In a word, social movements, especially in Canada and Mexico, are at once driven by the emerging regional context to forge inter- and transnational strategic links of the sorts discussed above, as they are pushed inward and encouraged to broaden the social basis of opposition to integration. This latter effort has brought such networks as the Red Mexicana de Acción Frente Libre Comercio (RMLAC) and the Action Canada Network (ACN), that were the principal driving forces behind the creation of inter- and transnational coalitions of social movements in the Americas, to the forefront of national-centred struggles to broaden the democratic process.

In Canada, the ACN positioned itself as handmaiden to 'coalition politics', and the national case against integration adopted a broader, and somewhat idealized, notion of 'community sovereignty', defined by the Canadian Center for Policy Alternatives as 'our ability as a nation to determine our own destiny', as a necessary barrier to transnational neoliberalism. What Tony Clarke called a 'new nationalism' spoke of 'Canadian workers ... reclaim[ing] the sovereignty of the[ir] country, ' of the refusal to 'give up on Canada, [and] abandon the rich legacy of rights and benefits... our fore-bearers fought so hard to give us' and of 'holding the country together'.

It prompted such initiatives as the Council of Canadians' 'Citizens' Agenda', the Commission populaire itinerante of Solidarite populaire Quebec, and the 'People's Agenda', launched by the Canadian Labour Congress in December 1991 after two years of consultation with other groups opposed to the North American Free Trade Agreement. If, as Alain Touraine put it, political struggles are struggles over historicity - that is to say, struggles over 'the set of cultural, cognitive, economic, and ethical models by means of which a collectivity sets up relations with its environment' - Canadian opposition to integration in the Americas looked to have been as much about constructing a national collectivity as it has been about assembling inter- and transnational coalitions of social movements.

In Mexico as well, there has been an intimate connection between the growth of regional and hemispheric coalitions and networks of social movements and the transformation of national political relationships. Indeed, campaigns against NAFTA, the Enterprise for the Americas Initiative and, more broadly, against the Maquilladorization of Central America, have served as anchoring points of sorts for democratization, alongside other crucial episodes such as the 1988 and 1991 elections, the 1994 devaluation of the peso, the Chiapas uprising and subsequent peace process.

In such landmark episodes in the development of grass-roots democratic politics in Mexico as the Referendum de la Libertad (Liberty referendum, 24 September to 23 October 1995), the Consulta Ciudadana (the citizen's consultation, 26 February 1995) and the Primera Jordana Nacional de Con-dena a la Política Económica del Gobierno (the first day of condemnation of the economic policy of the government: 8 September 1996), the RMLAC played a central co-ordinating role, alongside other newly formed social groups and networks of social movements: the Pacto de Grupos Ecologistas, La Convergencia de Organismos Civiles por la Democracia, El Foro de Apoyo Mutuo, Ganando Espacio, Mujeres Punto, Entre Mujeres, the Red Nacional de Organismos Civiles de Derechos Humanos.

Even in the USA, where coalition politics has not been stimulated by nationalist sentiments energizing popular coalitions in Canada and Mexico, the struggle against regional and hemispheric integration has also spawned unprecedented coalitions of unions, environmental and women's groups. In MERCOSUR countries as well, schemes for hemispheric and regional integration have created a context which appears favourable to the widening and broadening of links between different segments of national social movements.

In Chile, most obviously, this broadening has brought the Red Chile Para una Iniciativa de los Pueblos (RECHIP) to the forefront of a broad coalition of social movements - of unions, women, peasants and human rights groups - which has argued for a Carta de Derechos Económico, Sociales, Culturales y Ambientales y de Derechos Ciudadanas. To a lesser extent, Paraguayan social forces have also broadened links in response to MERCOSUR. These fragments suggest that transnational campaigns are situated events which begin and end in contexts.

Borrowing Jane Jacob's terminology, they may be thought of as 'hop-and-skip' events that force 'working relationships [on to] people ... who enlarge their local public life beyond the neighborhoods of streets and specific organizations or institutions and form relationships with people whose roots and background are in entirely different constituencies'. When such campaigns unite people of distinct backgrounds and preoccupations into a working relationship, neighbourhoods become successful, that is to say capable of self-government 'in its broadest sense, meaning both the informal and formal selfmanagement of society'. This too is something we must keep in mind as we try to theorize the movement of social forces in the world economy.

For score sheets: Ravenswood and BS/FS workers won, partisans of Ken Saro-Wiwa and opponents of NAFTA did not, and the campaigns for the rights of Saipan, Nike and Reebok workers, for abortion rights, wages for housework, against excision, sexual tourism and gender exploitation continue. More broadly, these campaigns offer us glimpses of a new political subject creating itself in the world economy, and, perhaps, of a new mode of relation to the world economy.

In marked contrast to grand absentee subjects (e.g. the proletariat, global sisterhood, global civil society, humanity) this is not a syncretic, totalizing (and easily recuperable) subject, but a conjunctural subject, 'present in the now' as Walter Benjamin wrote of surrealists. Neither just 'here' in the local or parochial sense of the term, nor simply 'out there' in the world economy, this subject is both 'deterritorialized' and 'reterritorialized' - to borrow Michael P. Smith's expressions for the dual belonging of transnational migrants.

Already, times and places exist where this new subject

may be seen. The curious may want to visit Nike towns during 'Nike Days of Action', or when visits from sales representatives give CLR activists occasion to talk about its global campaign; GAP stores in San Francisco during an 'International Day of Action Against Economic Globalization'; Bangkok brothels being picketed by GAATW activists; and Maquilladora communities in El Paso and San Antonio (probably the most enduring meeting points between placed struggles and the global context).

Bibliography

Anker, R. and C. Hein, 'Why Third World Urban Employers Usually Prefer Men', *International Labour Review*, Vol. 124, No. I, Geneva, 1985.

Beech, C., *Women and Women into Information Technology*, a report by the British Computer Society, 1990.

Byrne, E., *Women in Science and Technology: The Institutional Ecology Approach*, Interim Research Report, Department of Education, University of Queensland, 1988.

Chew. S.B. and R. Chew, 'Information Technology as a Strategy Human Resource Development', in E.C.Y. Kuo, C.M. Loh and K.S. Raman, *Information Technology in Singapore Society: Trends, Policies and Applications*, Singapore University Press, 1990.

Davidson, M.J. and C.L. Cooper (eds), *Women and Information Technology*, Psychology and Productivity at Work Series, London, John Wiley and Sons, 1987.

Deakin, R., *Women and Computing: The Golden Opportunity*, London, Macmillan Press, 1984.

Eriksson, I.V., B.A. Kitchenham and K.G. Tijdens (eds), *Women, Work and Computerization: Understanding and Overcoming Bias in Work and Education*, Amsterdam, North Holland, 1991.

Faruqui, A.M., M.H.A. Hassan and G. Sandri (eds), *The Role of Women in the Development of Science and Technology in the Third World*, proceedings of the conference organized by CIDA and the Third World Academy of Sciences, Trieste, Italy, October, 1988.

Harrison, P. (1983), *The Third World Tomorrow*, NY, Pilgrim Press and Harmondsworth, Penguin

Irvine, J., 'Women into Information Technology', *Information Technology and Public Policy*, Vol. 8, No. 3, Summer, 1990.

Kluzer, S., *Computer Diffusion in Black Africa: A Preliminary Assessment*, unpublished paper, SPRU, University of Sussex, Brighton, UK, 1988.

Lim, G.K., 'Women's Participation in the Computer Industry in Singapore', in Ken Tijdens *et al.* (eds), *Women, Work and Computing: Forming New Alliances*, Amsterdam, North Holland, 1989.

Lovegrove, G. and B. Segal (eds), *Women into Computing: Selected Papers*, 1988-1990, London, Springer, 1991.

Mitter, S., 'Computer Aided Manufacturing and Women's Employment: a Global Critique of Post Fordism', in I.V. Eriksson, B.A. Kitchenham and K.G. Tijdens (eds). *Women, Work and Computerisation: Understanding and Overcoming Bias in Work and Education*, Amsterdam, North Holland, 1991.

Mumford, E., *Where are Tomorrow's Top Women Executives?*, Manchester Business School Review, Vol. 4, No. 3, 1980.

Ng, C. (ed.), *Technology and Gender: Women's Work in Asia*, Women's Studies Unit, UPM and Malaysian Social Science Association, 1987.

Ng, C. and J. Othman, 'Information Technology, Gender and Employment in Malaysia', in S.C. Bhatnagar and M. Odedra (eds) *Social Implications of Computers in Developing Countries*, New Delhi, Tata-McGraw Hill, 1992.

Odedra, M., *Information Technology Transfer to Developing Countries: Case Studies from Kenya, Zambia and Zimbabwe*, unpublished Ph.D. thesis, London School of Economics, 1990a.

Odedra, M., 'Poor Management leads to Gross Underutilization', *Computer in Africa*, Vol. 4, No. 5, July, 1990b.

Parikh, I., *Women in Management: an Annotated Bibliography with Emphasis on Commonwealth Sources,* London, Commonwealth Secretariat, 1987.

Stamp, P., *Technology, Gender and Power in Africa,* Ottawa, international Development Research Centre, 1989.

Subramaniam, P.R., *The Future for Women in Information Technology,* M. Sc. dissertation, London School of Economics, 1991.

Tijdens, K., M. Jennings, I. Wagner and M. Weggelaar (eds), *Women Work and Computing: Forming New Alliances,* Amsterdam, North Holland, 1989.

Virgo, P., 'The Case for Women into Information Technology Campaign', *Information Technology and Public Policy,* Vol. 6, No. 3, Summer, 1988.

World Bank, *Sub-Saharan Africa: From Crisis to Sustainable Growth,* Washington DC, World Bank, 1989.

Wright, B.D. (ed.), *Women, Work and Technology: Transformations,* Chicago, University of Michigan Press, 1987.

Index